370.71

Inviting

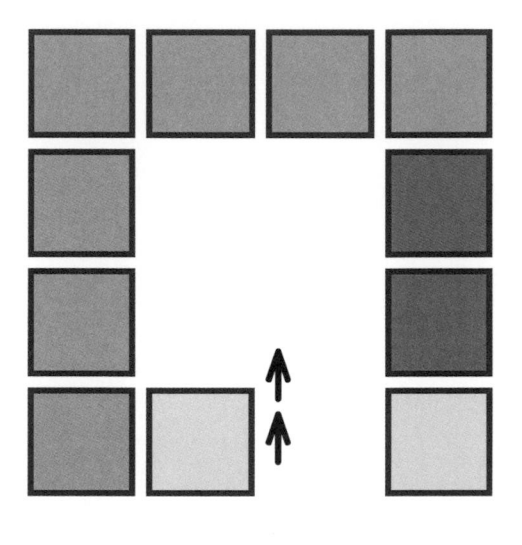

Learning

An exhibition of risk
and enrichment
in adult education practice

Inviting

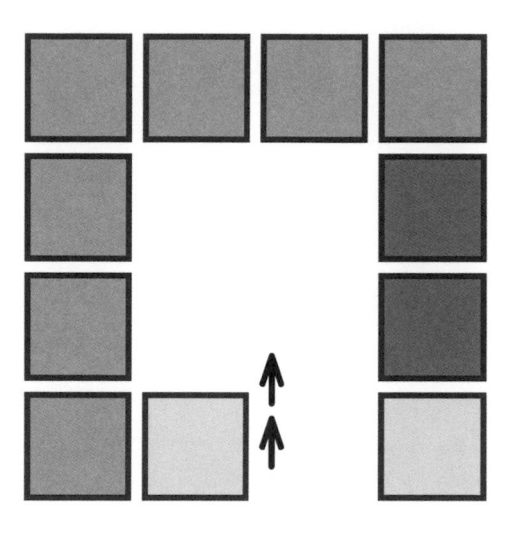

Learning

An exhibition of risk
and enrichment
in adult education practice

Peter Willis

NIACE

THE NATIONAL ORGANISATION
FOR ADULT LEARNING

For Eileen

Published by the National Institute of Adult Continuing Education
(England and Wales)
21 De Montfort Street, Leicester, LE1 7GE
Company registration no. 2603322
Charity registration no. 1002775
The NIACE website can be found at www.niace.org.uk

First published 2002
© NIACE

CATALOGUING IN PUBLICATION DATA
A CIP record for this title is available from the British Library
ISBN 1 86201 129 X

Typeset by Q3 Bookwork, Loughborough
Cover design by Hobo
Printed in Great Britain by Antony Rowe

Contents

Acknowledgements

The completion of this extensive project has been made possible through the assistance and support of family, friends and colleagues. The enterprise had elements of a quest made over time in the company of my family and academic mentors, enriched at various crisis points by significant meetings with inspirational and supportive colleagues and friends.

I would like to thank firstly members of the groups with whom I have travelled; Eileen, my wife and best friend, and our three children, Frances, Monica and Tom. I also wish to thank particularly, academic mentors Dave Boud and Michael Crotty, and my long-term friend and co-worker Angela Morrison.

In the course of this study, I have met and been inspired by writers and thinkers whose wisdom and grace helped me find a way through impasses of educational theory, research method, presentation, writing style and the like. I would like to thank and pay tribute to Mechtild Hart, from de Paul University in Chicago; Nod Miller, then from Manchester University and now at the University of East London; Ted Thomas and Brian Graham from Nottingham University; Noreen Garman from the University of Pittsburgh; Max van Manen from the University of Alberta, Edmonton; Maxine Greene from Columbia University, New York; Mike Welton from Mount St. Vincent University in Halifax; Mike Newman, Sue Knights, Jane Sampson and Alec Nelson from UTS in Sydney; and poets and mentors Jeff Guess and Jeremy Nelson.

This litany of appreciation needs to mention the strong support from the University of South Australia. Towards the end of this project I received a special Cathie scholarship which gave me six months' study leave to finish writing. Such infrastructural support indicates considerable support from colleagues. I wish to thank Kym Adey, Dean of the Faculty of Education; Bill Lucas, Head of School; Robert Crotty, in charge of research in the faculty; and Roger Harris from the Centre for Research in Education Equity and Work. I would also like to thank colleagues Michelle Simons, Tom Stehlik, Marie Crotty, Doug Boughton, Basil Moore, Bob Smith, Judy Gill, Sue Shore and Alan Reid for encouragement and conversations.

As a student enrolled at the University of Technology of Sydney and visiting there regularly, I spent time with friends and colleagues on many visits. I would like to thank Mike Newman, Sue Knights, Jane Sampson, Mark Tennant, Griff Foley, Rick Flowers, John McIntyre and Roger Morris for their kindness and, from the cavaliers among them, a robust belief in the romance of adult education, even in the thickets of economic rationalism.

I would particularly like to thank undergraduate and especially post-graduate students pursuing research under my supervision. The classroom discussions and one-to-one dialogues have been of great assistance in the clarification of ideas and approaches used in this study. Thanks are due especially to Fiona Underwood, Vicky Sanders, Marie Smith, Carol Schultz and Michelle Hogan.

I also want to mention friends whose support was invaluable: Ted Kennedy, Chris Fox, Ted Mulvihill, Lisa Ehrich, Peter Newall, David Rampling, Sandi Fischer, David Hope, Judith Condon, John Said, Anna Sinn, Alec Nelson, John McIntyre, Mary Thompson, John Knight and John Duley.

At the end of the project there was the challenge of rendering the research into a book. I would like to thank Mary Davis, Maria Argitis and Tess Raggio for their valuable help with typing and corrections; Wally Dobkins and Kate Krieg for work on the graphics used in the thesis text; Angela Morrison, Bob Smith, Roger Harris, Paul Gunning, Margaret Bowden and Rosie Antenucci for special proofing; and Document Services at the University of South Australia for printing and binding.

Abstract

This study attempts to present adult education practice as a lived experience using an expressive research method drawn from the work of Reason (1981, 1988), Eisner (1991, 1993) and Garman (1996). Expressive research seeks to develop imaginal textual forms for its work of 'portrayal' rather than 'explanation'.

The thesis is configured as an accompanied, walk-through exhibition introduced and concluded by a brief prologue and epilogue. It begins with an *Entrance Foyer* which introduces the expressive approach. This is followed by the *Main Gallery* which explores seven episodes of the author's adult education practice. Each episode is presented as an 'installation' made up of six 'panels' containing some background of each episode, a significant anecdote of practice from that episode, a poetised reflection of the experience and then two linked panels which attempt to 'intuit' and 'distil' the experience using direct metaphorical and imagistic language

The Main Gallery is followed by the *Gallery of Method*, which expounds and explains the expressive method used and its foundations in what are called 'empathetic' and 'intuiting' forms of phenomenology. The exhibition concludes with the *Exit Foyer*. It builds a collage of the images developed in the Main Gallery and then looks at their significance for practice.

Some of the images of the experience and their implications were:

- respectful mobilising for learning and the requirement of respect;
- monitoring and serving the learning group and the need to be 'safeguarding';
- mentoring and the need to engage, challenge and nurture;
- listening, hearing and responding and the need to attend and be present;
- rendering things to be learned, learnable and the requirement of didactic clarity;
- making friendly spaces and silences for learning and the need to let go, to relinquish control;
- cranking the learning flywheel and allowing time for healing and the need for patience, care and commitment;
- being transparent to inspire and assess and the need for vision, consistency and clarity.

One overarching theme of the adult education experience which gives the thesis its name is its invitational character. Practising adult education in the form pursued here is shown to be like accepting the risks and enrichments of inviting friends and would-be friends to a banquet, hoping they will fit in and benefit from its offerings but knowing that what happens cannot be wholly predicted or controlled.

It is argued that this element and others along a similar vein supplement instrumental notions of adult education which concentrate exclusively on its objectives and outcomes while omitting its risky, interpersonal and invitational character. It is also suggested that careful and detailed portrayal of the experience of adult education practice, as is attempted here, can provide a solid ground for more critical inquiries which seek to uncover interests embedded in its discourses and the assumptions upon which it is based.

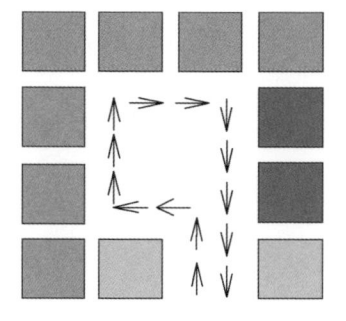

INVITING LEARNING

I'm inviting you, I'm inviting you.

Midnight Cowboy

my poems
have not eaten poems –
they devour
exciting happenings,
feed on rough weather,
and dig their food
out of earth and men.
I'm on my way
with dust in my shoes
free of mythology:
send books back to their shelves,
I'm going down into the streets.

(Pablo Neruda 1970, p. 287)

Becoming aware of the ways in which particular novels (or poems, or plays, or short stories) defamiliarised my experience, I came to see that the taking of odd or unaccustomed perspectives can indeed make a person 'see' as never before.

(Maxine Greene 1991, p. 110)

Once it's wound up and the weight of that big flywheel is turning fast enough, there's no stopping it. But you've got to learn to crank it up to speed at the beginning with the big handle. It takes a lot of strength and perseverance to start it turning slowly and to wind it up faster and faster until it almost pulls away from you. Then, when you flick the compression lever, the spinning wheel will take up the load and pull the engine into life. Even with dirty fuel and faulty lines the momentum will take it over those flat spots and keep it going.

(Fr. McKelson 1966)

Reflective teachers never stop asking themselves what the nature of teaching really is.

(Max van Manen 1994, p. 140)

PROLOGUE

In the course of two decades of adult education practice, many experiences I encountered were challenging, disquieting and often exhilarating. When, after more than a decade in the field, I took up academic study of adult education, there seemed few texts that carried its colour, risk and adventure. An exception seemed to be the writings of Mike Newman, an Australian who had spent many years as an adult educator in London. One of his earlier books, *The Poor Cousin* (1979), was a source of delight since its text carried more than a hint of the risks and challenges and enchantment I had encountered. There were similar feelings in reading texts from Jane Thompson (1980) and Malcolm Knowles (1980), and latterly Nod Miller (1993) and Jane Vella (1994). As a researcher and academic teacher, I sought to find a writing and research style that would carry something of the immediacy and vividness of these texts while at the same time contributing solid scholarship to the academy as they seemed to have done.

There seemed to be few 'tales from the front', especially in Australia. The romance and challenges of adult learning, expounded for example in the collection of writings by Boud and Griffin (1987), seemed to bring the lived reality of learning to life. What seemed to be needed were tales in a similar vein on the experience of facilitating that learning.

Was there a way to catch the excitement and risk of the experience of adult education practice? Was it possible to follow the writing/reporting tradition of notable adult educators like the philosopher Socrates (through Plato); St Paul the Apostle; Hildegard of Bingen, medieval abbess, writer and educator; and social activists and educators like Dorothy Day, Peter Maurin and Miles Horton?

Several commercially available films from America, Canada and England have taken as their theme the engagement of a teacher with young adults in their last years of college, or young army recruits, for example *Stand and Deliver, The Dead Poets' Society* and *Army Intelligence*. These present versions of varying quality and vividness of the experience of teaching young adults within and outside the classroom. They gain their dramatic interest by exploring the risky, interactive, intense elements of the teaching experience that are recognised as common elements in teaching, even if not highlighted in much technical educational writing.

When adult education practice, understood in the broad meanings it has in this thesis, is pursued in community groups and workplaces around issues like ecology, human rights and the liberation struggles of various groups, there are many dramatic presentations and films. These tend to tell the story of the courageous and visionary actions of women and men who, more often than not, without a classroom or textbooks, use the cultural actions of discussion, meeting, action planning, implementation and review, and writing and publishing newspapers to raise and change human awareness, knowledge and skills.

This thesis seeks to be a text with some of the immediacy and holistic appeal of such films and stories. It seeks to pursue research that will somehow display and make real the lived experience of adult education practice. As will be elaborated later, its main voice is thus 'expressive' rather than 'explanatory', although the explanatory voice is heard in its support, particularly in the Gallery of Method.

The vehicle for portrayal

According to Garman (1996), there has been a tendency to confine research texts in education to explanatory projects and to use psychometric or objectivist scientific report genres. As she says, referring to work by Eisner and Peshkin (1990), '[to] conduct experiments and surveys was scientific: to do otherwise was to be soft, wrong, or muddle-headed' (Garman 1996, p. 14).

In such psychometric studies, the outcomes of an inquiry into education are spelt out in ways not dissimilar to those used to report on research in physics or earth sciences. A hypothesis is outlined expanding or testing existing theory, and experiments are designed and carried out to test the hypothesis. A third party tests the methods for validity and reliability by duplication, and the results are written up in a report of the experimental sequence carried out, observations and measurements made, and conclusions drawn. The findings are then presented, beginning with the hypothesis and the proposed method, the experiments carried out and the data collated and analysed. The findings of the research, and their contribution to the grand theories that the project set out to test or extend, form the final part of such reports.

A report of this kind seemed quite unsuitable to carry ideas, feelings, intuitions, flashes of passion and fears that would need to be represented in the account this project was seeking to produce. A different research inquiry and presentation genre was needed to construct a vivid portrayal of the lived experience of adult educational practice. The challenges of such a project would be considerable. In addition, it would need an appropriate vehicle to carry its ideas and findings and to convey the flavour and style of expressive modes of thinking in the actual research writing. The expressive approach would also need careful academic defence for its validity.

Fortunately the concerns of this project were not unique. A number of researchers in education, health and social services had been working with forms of expressive qualitative research that had similar agendas. Peter Reason (1988, p. 79), for example, wrote of developing research approaches that would express more 'the liveliness, the involvement and even the passion' of the experiences being researched. The researchers in Reason's account began to use stories of their lives and inquiries. Stories are also used in this study, along with other representations, to generate 'installations' in an 'exhibition'. This approach, which is elaborated in the Gallery of Method, is based on a traditional, epistemological distinction between two modes of knowing: one called 'explanatory' or 'analytic', the other 'expressive' or 'narrative' (cf. Reason 1988; Bruner 1985; Eisner 1990, 1991, 1993; Barone and Eisner 1997). Elliot Eisner and his colleague Tom Barone have elaborated this expressive approach in their work on applying what they have called 'artistic' rather than 'scientific' approaches to research (Barone 1997, p. 75).

Expressive knowledge is generated by the researcher adopting a receptive rather than a proactive stance, allowing an element of the world – in this case adult education practice – to present itself for contemplation, then attempting to construct a text which accounts for that experience in its wholeness. Heron (1996, p. 45) suggests a distinction between 'linear, rational, Apollonian inquiry and Dionysian approaches which are more imaginal, expressive, spiral, diffuse, impromptu'.

The researcher's tool for this project is not the surgeon's analytical scalpel but the poetic pen or artist's brush, called upon to produce focused, expressive work. Its quality is to be judged not by the more positivist canons of validity and reliability, but by its degree of verisimilitude and integrity (cf. Garman 1996, p. 18). In my view, a touch of detachment to ward off narcissism and self-indulgence is also required.

It was the metaphor of the artist's brush that inspired the idea of using the metaphor of an exhibition that could serve to predispose readers to expect expressive writing and to judge the project in such a light. The idea still had the challenge of creating spaces for the different elements of the thesis: the introduction and conclusion of the project, the implementation of the expressive method chosen, its explanation and the rationale for its use. This was catered for by creating four galleries in the planned exhibition and imagining the reader as a visitor traversing each one in turn.

At the end, after the exhibition has been traversed, a brief epilogue refers back to this prologue and closes the thesis.

Reading the exhibition

The main exposition of the thesis is thus configured as an accompanied 'walkthrough' exhibition that is presented in two galleries with an Entrance and Exit Foyer before and after. There is a brief Orientation before the two Galleries and Foyers to suggest the 'mood' of the section about to be visited and to 'position' the reader/visitor as she or he visits each stage of the exhibition. Thus a mood of 'preparation' is created in the Entrance Foyer; one of 'engagement' in the Main Gallery; 'dialogue' in the Method Gallery; and 'reflection' in the Exit Foyer.

In summary, after this Prologue, they enter the Entrance Foyer immediately in front of them and are welcomed by the author turned curator. There, in the first chapter of the thesis, they will be introduced to the agenda of the thesis/exhibition, its method and its layout. They will then accompany the curator into the Main Gallery along a walkway that conducts them, in turn, to each of its seven installations (which are the chapters in that section). On completing their visits to these installations, visitors emerge from the Main Gallery and are invited by their guide to call into the two chapters of the Gallery of Method for some epistemological and methodological explorations. They then head to the final chapter, located in the Exit Foyer, for a glass of champagne and some final reflections from the curator. While the Main Gallery has a whole orienting chapter preceding it, visitors are provided with only brief notes of orientation at the respective beginnings of the Entrance Foyer, the Gallery of Method and the Exit Foyer.

At the completion of the exhibition, the thesis then provides a brief Epilogue to balance this Prologue where it looks back to the completed project and comments on its overall achievements and limitations.

Before moving to the exhibition chapters, the Prologue's last task is to introduce the graphic map chosen to represent the exhibition and to locate the readers at its various stages. It is thus both a symbolic representation and a kind of street map.

The graphic map

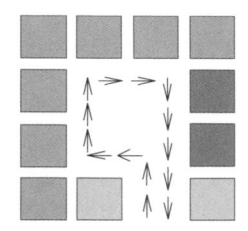

This graphic figure represents the exhibition as a whole. It has eleven small squares to represent the chapters of the thesis, arranged in an open square with a line of arrows representing the visitors' path. The exhibition begins with the Entrance Foyer, with its single introductory chapter represented by a lightly shaded square. Seven mid-shade squares follow in sequence, representing the seven chapters that are the installations of the Main Gallery. The two chapters of the Gallery of Method, which follow, are represented by heavily shaded squares. The final chapter, which constitutes the Exit Foyer, is represented by the second lightly shaded square.

The Prologue thus introduces the exhibition with this general orientation. As has been pointed out above, this will be referred back to briefly in the Epilogue at the very end of the thesis.

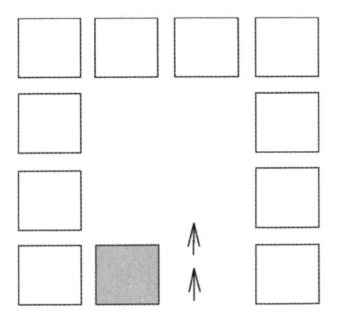

PART I
THE ENTRANCE FOYER

Orientation

Readers at this point, having been alerted in the Prologue to the exhibition metaphor being used in this thesis, are imagined to have entered the exhibition building and to have congregated in the Entrance Foyer to meet the author/ curator. The visitors, as is to be expected of newcomers to an exhibition with some idiosyncratic quirks, are presumed to be somewhat adventurous, with a good-humoured and compliant attitude to the expected cues of the author/ curator.

These cues are aimed at providing a brief map of the exhibition with its galleries and installations, and of the general theories underpinning each gallery's approach. His final cue, embarked upon with some trepidation, is to suggest an appropriate stance visitors might adopt to gain the greatest advantage in each gallery. This has been adopted, in effect, to maximise the impact of the approach used, which, as will be argued in the Gallery of Method, is one of the method's direct validators. It is also intended to pre-empt dissatisfaction or irritation from readers who, approaching the text as a thesis, might expect it to have had, as many do, a more analytic and explanatory approach.

Now it is time to meet our curator and guide for this exhibition.

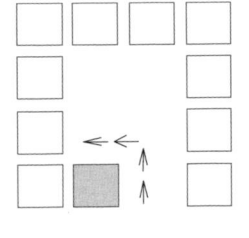

Chapter 1

The visitor's guide

Introduction

This exhibition/thesis aims to portray adult education practice by presenting and reflecting on seven episodes of the author's adult education practice, with different styles and learners, which occurred over more than two decades in various locations throughout Australia. It is directed to past, current and would-be adult education practitioners and other interested citizens, with the aim of portraying a real 'lived' face of adult education with its fears, failures, delights and rewards.

The exhibition itself is presented in an expressive pedagogic form in which attempts are made, through the installations in the Main Gallery and the ancillary interpretative processes before and after, to engage, instruct, illumine and challenge the reader/gallery visitor. The rationale for this approach is explored at length in the Gallery of Method, located in Part III of the thesis.

The expressive approach used in the installations of the Main Gallery invites the reader/visitor to stand before each one in turn and allow it to 'speak', to present itself, without too much analysis or debate. The expressive approach, as will be pointed out in the Gallery of Method, has a long tradition, but although it is currently enjoying something of a resurgence in some human science research, it does not sit easily with other contemporary and more wide-spread analytic and explanatory thinking.

The research processes are thus aimed at facilitating engagement with the lived experiences of adult education practice so they become named and, to some extent, communicable. The focus on lived experience is to help the inquiry avoid 'a priorism' and reductionism and come to adult education prac-tice as an experience – contextualised, subjective, messy and ambiguous. Other outcomes and infrastructural explorations particularly concerned with the genesis and validity of this expressive approach and the method that evolved in the study are significant but ancillary to that aim.

While the exhibition is built on episodes from real-life practice, it is not to be understood as a series of memoirs – reminiscences of exciting times in adult education, although they often were – but of course there may well be occasional elements of reminiscence in the projected texts from time to time. Nor is it an analysis of the causes behind certain events of adult education practice or an attempt to explain events and outcomes by locating them in categories linked to one or other predicting theory. The aim is to construct an expressive, interpretative portrayal built on general phenomenological theory: a portrayal of the lived experience of adult education practice.

Before the readers/visitors move to the Main Gallery, the following brief notes are provided as an introduction. The first note introduces the author/curator/researcher and provides a brief profile of his personalist approach to adult education. There are then some introductory ideas about how adult education is understood in the study, followed finally by some guidelines on the interrelated panels of each installation: how they fit together and what they are supposed to convey.

Situating the researcher

My work in adult education began in the late 1960s when, as a newly ordained Catholic priest, I worked with a group of young volunteers to set up and manage a 'coffee lounge with folk singing' as a kind of 'drop in' centre for youth in inner-city Melbourne. In that context my adult education practice was as a team leader/staff developer. I then spent more than a decade pursuing forms of Aboriginal adult education practice, firstly as religious teacher, then community development worker with Miriwung people at Kununurra in the Kimberley region of Western Australia. I spent a further 6 years at Alice Springs at the Institute for Aboriginal Development (IAD), an adult learning centre mainly for Aboriginal people and some non-Aboriginal people who worked with them. During that time, I was involved in classroom teaching with Aboriginal people preparing for employment or further study, and cultural awareness workshops mainly for non-Aboriginal people working in human services with Aboriginal clients. Finally, I also provided learning opportunities for Aboriginal trainees at IAD. I then continued adult education practice with adult students in my present post as university lecturer in adult education in Adelaide.

My adult education practice, which began in religious adult education, has tended to focus on the interpersonal engagement and subsequent dynamics between aspiring educator and would-be learner. Religious adult education practice, as I understood it, was invitational rather than prescriptive. It was epitomised in Jesus' teaching style – teaching and challenging his disciples. He invited them to join him and built a respectful friendship with them while safeguarding their freedom. It is significant that the word 'disciple' means 'those seeking to be taught'.

This invitational learning facilitation which I espoused was linked (largely unconsciously, but on reflection quite strongly) to notions of grace in

Catholic theology. It was about attempting to exert influence without coercion by presenting various forms of learning as 'desirable' to people with whom a relationship of mutual respect and care had been established. And the desirability would be due to their capacity to provide skills and knowledge, to dismantle negative ideas and attitudes, to generate wisdom and to enrich and delight.

Subsequent movements from religious education to community development, cultural awareness, professional development and university teaching seem to have been variations on the original enterprise. My work has tended to foreground 'teaching people' rather than 'teaching something to people'. Such emphasis led me to explore whether such person-centred education, since it appeared to be different from didactic instructor-centred education, warranted being called a different species of the genus adult education. I explored whether such education, which had the transformation of the learner as its goal, should be differentiated from conventional adult education concerned with so-called 'transferring skills and knowledge'.

I was to discover that this tentative distinction did not, in fact, exist in practice: that all educational exchanges had elements of interpersonal engagement, exchanges and transformations which at the same time involved, or could involve, some kind of transfer or taking up of skills, knowledge and attitudes. What my practice highlighted were elements that were present to a greater or lesser extent (but not to the same extent) in most adult educational activities, and not necessarily with the acknowledgment and awareness that they were indeed present.

Adult education practice

In this study, adult education is taken in its broader contemporary meaning of any act that engages adults in dialogue and attempts to facilitate their learning while respecting their freedom and autonomy. This usage is similar to that espoused by Cranton (1992, p. 3) when she referred to adult education as 'any set of activities or experiences engaged in by adults which lead to changes in thinking, values or behaviour'. There is a proviso that, in the usage of this thesis, adult education refers to the acts of a learning facilitator working with adult learners or potential learners. It does not include self-education.

Squires (1993, p. 105), in his comprehensive survey of the meanings and practices of adult education, writes that:

> The scope of the adult curriculum is so wide that it tests the limits of education itself, by turning into politics, therapy, entertainment or work ... One is forced to the conclusion that education for adults is inherently diverse, and that there are few if any common elements in all the different kinds of teaching and learning that exist.

In earlier days this claim would have been somewhat contested since adult education, at least in places influenced by British educational practice like Australia, had a meaning restricted to liberal, non-credit, organised courses offered by university extension and providers like the Workers Education Association. This is no longer the case.

An alternate and complementary way to somehow delineate adult education practice is to follow the approach adopted by philosopher Max Charlesworth when he was attempting to carve out a meaning for the word 'religion', a term as slippery as, and in even more common use than, 'adult education'. He used Wittgenstein's suggestion (1953, *sec.*, 66–7) that certain clusters of human experiences which are easily named as one thing have enough commonality to admit a 'family resemblance'. Allowing us to refer to them by the same word. In this sense adult education, like Charlesworth's religion, is a 'family resemblance' concept:

> Wittgenstein uses the concept of a 'game' as an example to make the point that there is nothing common to all the activities we call 'games'. Instead there is 'a complicated network of similarities overlapping and criss-crossing: sometimes overall similarities, sometimes similarities of detail'. Since 'the various similarities between the members of a family: build, features, colour of eyes, gait, temperament etc., etc., overlap and criss-cross in the same way', Wittgenstein calls 'game' a family resemblance concept.
>
> (Charlesworth 1997, p. 2)

Adult education similarly can be called a 'family resemblance' concept in that it has a range of meanings – to instruct, to inform, to train, to inspire, to mobilise – which are considered to have enough commonalities to justify its continued use. There remains a difficulty in the use of such fuzzy terms to which Squires alludes when he mentions that some of the educational activities under the contemporary broad umbrella of 'adult education' are also called other names like 'professional development', 'training' or even 'proselytising'.

A significant element in this study is that the educational activities under consideration are directed at people understood to be, and treated as, adults. Again analytical definitions of 'adult' also suffer in the quest for precision. In this context, the thesis uses Cranton's reference to adult as a person who has left school and has taken on the roles and responsibilities of adult life, and is so regarded. A significant point here is that the 'adult' in adult education is partly a kind of expectation that educators often build into their learning generative processes and through which they look for, and expect, co-responsiblity for the desired learning outcomes from those being educated.

Contexts and roles

Squires, (1993, p. 106) distinguishes three social contexts, or collectivities, in which learning can be generated among their adult members: associations, communities and movements. In the first context, *associations*, groups of people freely come together to pursue a common interest or purpose. The second context, *community*, tends to refer to existing groups of people whose learning needs may relate to their coherence, collaboration and 'community spirit'. He points out that adult educators often seek to raise community spirit by taking a catalytic or facilitative role, working to prompt group members to critique and change their orientation to the group and its goals. *Movements*, Squires' third form of collectivity, suggests people progressing in a particular direction that is more intense and places more demands on members. He points out that the educator's role tends to be more directive: a functional role contributing expertise to the common cause.

Squires completes this survey by referring to another form of collectivity, the *working group*, where people with various forms of expertise have to learn, not their own craft, which it is presumed they know, but ways of working together to produce an integrated artefact of their collaboration.

All these forms of adult education practice are included in the broad meaning of the term used in this study. As will become apparent, most of the activities and contexts mentioned by Squires are realised in the episodes of practice represented in the Main Gallery.

In many of the contexts mentioned above, the adult educator's role has many faces. As Squires (1993, p. 103) writes:

> ... the teacher may not be a 'proper teacher'; she may be called a facilitator, a group leader, or resource person, or animator – anything but a teacher ... there may be no textbooks ... there may be no 'teaching' but rather 'discussion' and 'talk' and 'interaction'.

In many ways, expertise in the broad range of adult education practices requires skills and dispositions that are more oblique and opportunistic than those required in the more commonly recognised didactic adult learning facilitation. The educator involved in these kinds of learning facilitation may rarely, if ever, be referred to as a teacher, although the role is concerned with learning facilitation. Nor would the learning facilitative activity be named as adult education. It would be referred to with words like 'development work', 'union education', 'issues discussion', 'values clarification', 'working for justice' and 'preparing for non-violence'. Adult education practice in this kind of environment reflects the multiplex facilitative agenda in these non-formal contexts. The facilitator/educator's task is often to build a learning agenda onto group members' engagement in community projects, while at the same time safeguarding their initial commitment to the project itself. The educational agenda is partly embedded in the enterprise and there is a presumption that people joining the project agree implicitly to the necessary learning linked to it. The educator's task is to make the learning agenda apparent and to arrange facilitative experiences for this learning. In many cases the facilitative experience includes demonstrating and celebrating learning that has actually taken place incidentally, without participants being very conscious that they were actually learning.

Another dimension of learning facilitation is *generating enabling dispositions* in potential learners in an ethical and respectful way, almost like setting up something antecedent to learning that leads to learning and without which learning will not happen.

There is nothing 'cooled out' or necessarily rational and studied about many of these processes. They are hot, passionate and full of energy and drive. While this makes for high commitment, it also makes for prejudice and intolerance, and for disparity in learning outcomes where those who are better resourced get on better. Squires (1993, p. 101) goes on to point out that education is not the same as indoctrination:

> Indoctrination can be seen as a process applicable to any kind of content which lacks or rejects certain of the characteristics which are associated with the word 'education': the making explicit of assumptions and values, the exposure to conflicting ideas and arguments, the tolerance of doubt and indecision, the encouragement of rationality rather than belief, and the limiting of pressure on students to conform.

He is of course aware, as he goes on to show, that much education fails to satisfy these conditions. He also notes that the ideals he lists which are linked to the liberal tradition are quite problematic for some, and that his high-minded ideals of detachment and intellectuality can be seen as impeding action.

Learning facilitation stance

Adult education practice can be examined in terms of the emphasis the educator places on a subject-centred or didactic approach that focuses on the learning to be facilitated, and a learner-centred or personalist approach that focuses on developing the dispositions and skills of the learner in relation to the learning to be pursued.

One of the personalist stances of interest here, since it represents a key element in the espoused theory of adult education I have pursued, is the invitational approach. This refers to an approach that seeks to engage the learner in friendly, interpersonal exchanges that respect the learner while encouraging him or her to take up a proposed learning agenda, because in this way he or she will be enriched. This invitational stance tends to place the adult educator 'on the line'. It is essentially an engaged rather than detached approach: warm rather than cool, holistic rather than purely logical or rational.

The following attempts to portray the contradictory and risky nature of invitation in poetic form.

Invitation

I risk inviting;
I want you here.
And when you come
I feel enriched, believe
you feel the same.

If you refuse,
that says
I have no worth to you,

And if, when you agree to come,
you don't show,
your absence makes a wound
and I fall lower
than before I invited.

No-one invites for fun;
if you say 'drop in if you like'
that is not a real inviting;
there's no risk, a bob each way
against rejection.

Inviting is for keeps
a friend, a lover in pursuit:
no half measures.
It's black or white,
not blurred or lukewarm.

And guests know the rules
to dress up, cradle
the eggshell of friendship
at your place;

And trust that
while you stand
unarmed and welcoming
your guests will not turn;
refuse to dance the party's tune;
humiliate and bring you down
and turn your grapes of bounty
into ash.

The poem carries the notion of the person making the invitation, putting him or herself at risk and of wanting to condense or push what might have been an acquaintanceship to a more solid friendship: something intimate and challenging where responses cannot be postponed or not acted upon. The poem also carries the sense of heightened tension: that to invite a person is to risk rejection on the first part when the invitation is returned, or a full-scale shaming as when a guest attacks the 'unarmed' host or seeks to shame or betray him or her.

These metaphoric explorations have interesting resonances with forms of adult education practice, as will appear in the exploration of adult education sequences of practice that follows.

Adult education sequences

A related way to approach adult education practice for this expressive study, particularly when it is used in the contemporary, all-embracing definition with its boundary difficulties, is to list learning facilitative activities which recur in various adult education practices to a greater or lesser extent. These are drawn in the first instance from a reflective revisiting and analysis of my own practice. It is during the carrying out of these activities, which in many cases overlap and recur even in one episode of practice, that adult education practice is experienced as a phenomenon. The following represents a list of activities that are loosely grouped in a kind of longitudinal sequence. Not all such activities can be distinctly identified in every educational project. In some cases, one activity may seem to contain several activities nested within it but occurring to a greater or lesser extent in practice. These activities are briefly described below.

Validate teacher and learners	The adult educator introduces him or herself to potential learners
Orientate towards learning	The adult educator invites potential learners to adopt a learning stance
Teacher sets out agenda	The adult educator sets out the learning to be gained from the facilitative processes
Set up a learning project	The adult educator seeks to engage with potential learners, greeting and setting out the things to be explored and learned
Forming the learning group	The adult educator calls the learners together to form a group
Teaching/learning actions	The adult educator opens the topic
Monitor processes	The adult educator checks the learners' responses, seeking to find out how the learning facilitative processes are being received and acted upon
Instruct	The adult educator expounds the knowledge to be gained
Teach skills	The adult educator demonstrates skills to be gained
Invitation to learn, to take knowledge in	The adult educator invites questions and comments
Reflection on topics discussed	The adult educator checks the value placed upon the learning being pursued by the potential learners
Grounding learning in reality	The adult educator invites learners to integrate their new learning into their real life
Settling into new knowledge	The adult educator makes spaces in the learning facilitative processes for learners to adjust to their new learning and their commitment to related unlearning

| Appraise learning | The adult educator assesses the participants' learning |
| Evaluate the program | The adult educator participates in evaluating the learning facilitative processes used in the project |

The significant point here is that adult education practice, in so far as it is initiated by the adult educator, is made up of variations to a sequence of the learning facilitator's and learners' proactive and reactive activities that can be separated at least notionally, if not really, in episodes of adult education practice. Not all such activities occur in every adult education episode. In many cases they can be deduced from the activities of the adult educator and the learners, and from a deduction of what needs to happen for educational exchanges to take place. When the study looks at the phenomenon of adult education practice as experienced in each episode of practice, the experiences are linked in some way to learning facilitative activities initiated by the facilitator and responded to by the learners. These activities then develop an interactive life of their own which is experienced as the phenomenon of adult education practice.

Since this thesis is concerned with the exploration of the phenomenon of adult education practice – what presents itself to the adult educator as a lived experience – activities originating from the adult educator alone cannot be said to constitute the phenomenon of adult education practice in different episodes. The actual 'lived' experience consists of the educator's experience of putting out learning facilitative initiatives – experiencing the learners' responses and then the educator's subsequent responses to these reactions. The phenomenon under question is the experience of this multiplex chain reaction as it presents itself to the adult educator.

The inclusion of the table of activities serves to indicate the kinds of things learning facilitators do in the course of their adult education practice. It can be read as a component of the Backgrounding panel in each of the installations discussed in this thesis, since the learning facilitative processes will be concrete examples of the implementation of some or all of these activities.

Having completed this brief visitation of adult education practice, the following section introduces the Main Gallery and its installations.

Introducing the Main Gallery

Overview

Immediately in front of this Entrance Foyer is the Main Gallery. Its entry is imagined to be framed with an archway with the words *Inviting Learning* written in bold around it. It is composed of seven installations standing some distance from each other, joined by an access path that provides a clear road for the visitors to visit the installations in turn and so get an idea of the exhibition as a whole. Each installation consists of six panels set in a semicircle, imagined to be in front of a large, landscape photograph of the physical environment of the adult education episode in question. Visitors/readers follow the access path and enter on the left side of each semicircle. They read each panel in turn, following the installation pathway that finally leads out of one semicircle and on to the next.

Installations in the Main Gallery

The readers/visitors enter the exhibition and follow the path from installation to installation accompanied by the researcher turned curator of the exhibition. As the group stops before each installation, they see six panels. First they read about the social and personal context of each episode in the Backgrounding panel. Next comes the Sketching panel, presenting a story of a significant event from each episode. The third is the Poetised reflection panel – a poetised revisiting of these experiences (which are more soliloquies using some poetic features than they are finished poems). This allows some space for the author's feelings and reactions to be revealed. The fourth and fifth panels use a classical phenomenological approach, as will be explained at length in the Gallery of Method. In the first text, the author/curator attempts to 'intuit' the phenomenon of adult education practice revealed in the episode: to 'bracket out' conclusions and analytical developments that might have occurred during the backgrounding, sketching and poetising just completed but retaining the 'presence' of the experience. He attempts to contemplate the adult education experience itself, seeking to allow it to declare itself and somehow be caught and presented in text. In the following panel he 'distils' elements of the phenomenon emerging in the related intuiting texts just completed. Recurrent elements from each installation will be juxtaposed later to form a collage at the conclusion of the exhibition. His last word is contained in the sixth panel, Comment, which provides a space for possible significances emerging from the various panels of the installation.

The following provides a brief elaboration of all six panels: Backgrounding, Sketching, Poetised reflection, Intuiting, Distilling and Comment.

Backgrounding

Backgrounding provides an account of the circumstances; the dramatic stage on which the adult education events generating the particular experiences occurred. Its task is to set the scene; to locate the event within the social context of the adult educator's experience. Backgrounding attempts to provide a detailed account of the context and circumstances of the teaching/learning episodes under consideration. It thus has an ancillary function to locate and frame the sketching anecdote and the poetising reflection. Its task is to ground the expressive texts in a particular time, space and social world, and to relieve the story teller and poetic reflector from the tasks of telling the reader where things took place, what the place was like, who was there and what was going on. These tasks are often necessary in view of the plot or ideas.

The backgrounding text is structured around the following general areas: the location and circumstances of the adult education practice; the educator's culture and concerns; the learners and their culture and concerns; the sponsor of the adult education programme; the learning facilitative processes in their location; and any significant issues exerting an influence on the teaching/ learning exchange.

There is an autobiographical flavour in the backgrounding text. The curator identifies the narrator as himself, and each installation is introduced as being located in subsequent periods of his life as an adult educator. Because the focus is on the phenomenon of adult education practice and not on the curator/ narrator, the text prefers a more objectifying mode, placing actions and events rather than the person of the actor in the foreground. Thus, where possible, the text will tend to say 'a meeting was held', in preference to 'I attended a meeting'.

Sketching: stories of significant moments of practice

Within the project being pursued here, 'sketching' refers to an anecdote of a significant event in each of the seven episodes of adult education practice chosen for the thesis.

The sketching genre is chosen for this task to reach out and engage – to 'seduce' – the reader. It is able to carry dramatic quality. The memory of the significant event is converted to a re-collected text, constructed as a story with its situation, actors and plot. It is designed to engage members of the audience, who, in their turn and in their own way, are 'taken in' to the experience. The dramatic quality of the sketch is significant here. Where the backgrounding genre provides a stage setting which locates the event and frames it, the sketch – a story on its own, or in one case interwoven with the following poetising voice – becomes the play on the stage, representing the event and the experience and something of its significance.

Sketching as pursued here is a kind of narrative which is somewhat similar and somewhat different to phenomenological anecdote as described by van Manen (1990, p. 115) and discussed extensively in the Gallery of Method. In so far as it has the character of a story that vividly brings out the structure of the lived experience, it has characteristics of van Manen's 'phenomenological anecdote'. On the other hand, since it maintains more detailed physical links with actual events following the backgrounding process through which it is located in real place and time, it is less purely phenomenological and somewhat more interpretative.

Poetised reflection

This third panel gives the writer a free rein to ask himself in what way an episode of practice in that particular time spoke to him. This genre gives him room to move, to express feelings and ideas surrounding, and generated by, the phenomenon. By comparison with the subsequent, more classical phenomeno-logical texts on the intuiting and distilling panels, the poetised reflections are open to a more subjectivising subjective voice and as such belong more in the empathetic, interpretative camp of phenomenology discussed at length in the Gallery of Method below. The poetised reflection allows the author to represent his experience of the episode of practice – to include his feelings, fears, joys in his presentation of the phenomenon, and to tell at least a little of his reactions to, and interpretations of, the experience. In this poetised soliloquy, all these can be named and celebrated if that is what the episode has invoked in him.

The following two panels, Intuiting and Distilling, foreground the phenomenon itself. They attempt to look past the subjectivity necessarily contained in responses to it that are interwoven in the Backgrounding, Sketching and Poetised reflection panels. Here the exhibition, through the panels, attempts to move from the contextualised and dramatised accounts of the experience which contain subjective and objective elements, to 'the phenomenon itself' – that which presents itself in the experience. We are after the 'that' which presents itself – the 'whatness' of it – rather than the reactions of the subject experiencing the phenomenon which of course is somehow also a part of the experience. The panels thus attempt to focus on the phenomenon of adult education practice itself with a more objectivising subjectivity, a term explored at length in the Gallery of Method.

Intuiting

In the Intuiting panel, the researcher, having been brought back to the phenomenon in the process of developing the various processes listed above, now attempts to 'bracket' any interpretative conclusions contained in them and to enter a process through which an attempt is made to let the phenomenon itself 'speak', and to somehow represent this revelation in text. Two strategies have been developed to facilitate this contemplation.

Exploring the phenomenon along four dimensions

The first strategy follows Merleau Ponty (1962) and prompts the researcher to contemplate the phenomenon as it is experienced along four existential dimensions of human living: space, bodiliness, time and interrelatedness. Van Manen, commenting on Merleau-Ponty's approach (1990, p. 103), writes that 'spatiality, corporeality, temporality and relationality are productive categories for the process of phenomenological question posing, reflection and writing'.

Naming the experience

The second strategy draws on the work of Crotty (1996b), who developed a matrix of questions to be posed to facilitate phenomenological contemplation. Having reminded his readers to focus on 'the phenomenon (what you are experiencing) and not on yourself (the one experiencing)', he then suggests the researcher attempt to complete 'sentence stems' like the following:

> What comes to light when I attend to practising adult education in
> this context is … Practising adult education in this context is like … I
> picture practising adult education in this context as … Practising
> adult education can be described as … What shows up when I think
> of practising adult education in this context is … (p. 272).

(The words 'adult education' have been inserted in the space left for the phenomenon being explored.) The kind of sentence stems one does not complete are: 'When I contemplate practising adult education in this context, I feel like … When I think about practising adult education in this context, I find myself …'

The researcher thus builds a new text in which the phenomenon itself is directly intuited and named from several angles. Readers who have been looking at the previous exhibition panels need to go into this intuitive portrayal, allowing the event made present in the previous panels to present itself but trying not to attend to any theorizing ideas that might have sprung to mind while visiting the earlier panels. The text in this set may appear less finished and literary, and more inchoate, as the contemplator, holding gaze on the phenomenon, tries to generate a text that is first and foremost faithful to the experience, before attempting to be interesting or entertaining to readers.

Distillation

The distillation text is an attempt to summarise the meanings of the lived experience as illumined in the intuiting texts. It is an attempt to identify 'emerging themes' that seem to be a central part of the experience.

In demonstrating his approach to phenomenological writing, van Manen gives an example taken from his research into children's experience of being left in the care of others by their parents (1990, p. 86). In his research, he collected anecdotes from various people concerning their childhood experience of this phenomenon. He explores these experiences initially under the heading 'situations'. He then begins the laborious task of what he calls 'seeking meaning', in which he builds a thematic account of the structure of this childhood experience.

In the text being constructed here, 'distilling' represents what 'unearthing something thematic' does in van Manen's text. As he writes, '[w]e try to unearth something "telling", something "meaningful", something "thematic" in the various experiential accounts – we work at mining meaning from them' (1990, p. 86).

Whereas there is provision for a summary of the experiences of a range of contributors in the account of van Manen's research, in the Distillation panel of this project there is provision for a clustering of phrases, culled from writings from the Intuiting panel, that are used as different ways of intuiting the phenomenon.

Comment

The set concludes with the sixth panel that is designated for the curator, this time as a reflective practitioner locating and owning the experiences portrayed in the installation. This final section is deliberately open-ended. It provides a space for brief comment on learning emerging from the experience, on the research experience itself. It also comments on the significance of elements of these experiences for adult education practice.

Summary

Each installation provides four complementary expressive processes over five panels, with a final one for comments. Each has a complementary expressive agenda. Backgrounding grounds the experience of adult education practice in real time and place and people. It also provides brief pointers to some of the interests and social forces impinging on the adult education pursued in that time and place. Sketching brings adult education practice to life by providing a story of a significant moment in a dramatised fashion so that the reader is transformed through the narrative's dramatic movement and resolution. In the movement of the story, readers 'become present' to the dynamics of adult education practice in that episode and engage in its challenges and experiences. Poetised reflection brings the author centre stage and provides a medium for his witness to his own experience of the phenomenon as it impinged on him, his feelings, his ideas and his reactions. The poetised reflection is intended to generate an 'empathetic stance in the reader', who is invited to identify with the author as he portrays some of his feelings and reactions while engaged in this adult education episode. The Intuition and Distillation panels revisit the episode of adult education practice as an objectivised, subjective phenomenon. The focus is most strongly on the 'whatness' of the experience as it presents itself to the contemplating eye. The intuiting and distilling texts are designed to generate 'insight' into adult education practice as a lived experience. The Comment panel provides 'space for reactions' to the previous panels in the installations about things being learned, elements of practice made visible, or about broader issues to do with research and adult education practice.

The ruminative spiral

One of the ongoing difficulties of using intuiting expressive text, employed particularly in the intuiting and distilling panels, is its 'ruminative reverie' quality, in which the experience is visited and revisited, language is used and reused and images are laid and overlaid in the quest for so-called imagistic density and verisimilitude. There is some similarity with the use of recurrent themes in music where the same musical phrase is played and replayed in different ways and by different instruments. The overlaying of images in the text is intended to have a repetitive (but hopefully not stultifying) effect, to slow the reading eye and to feed the contemplative stance. The eye traverses the text allowing its various and similar metaphors and images to present them-selves and provide slightly differently tuned pictures of practice. In such a slow move, the recurring themes become inescapable and hopefully begin to deepen their imagistic grip on the viewer; to burn themselves into the viewer's eye so that the dimensions of the lived experience are not just cognitively understood but intuitively received. As will be pointed out in the Gallery of Method, there will always be an element of risk in such prolonged and slow movement of image and its attempt to hold back the human desire to 'get on'; to analyse and generalise and link the categorised phenomenon to great research narratives. The curator needs, as far as possible, to move through each installation as a whole so that the more racy 'present making' panels can carry the viewer into a kind of 'whole' experience.

Without further ado, let us enter the Main Gallery.

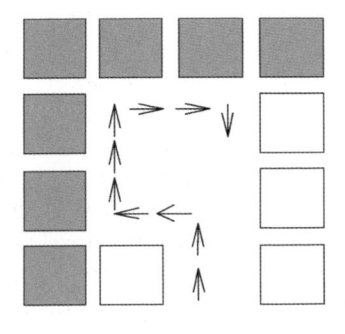

PART II
THE MAIN GALLERY:
INVITING LEARNING

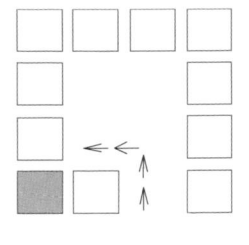

Chapter 2

Reality at the Outpost Inn

This opening installation is set in inner-city Melbourne in 1966. It is the earliest episode of my adult education practice. Like much community adult education it is pursued within a human service project, only one agenda of which is linked explicitly to learning. Versions of this kind of adult education practice are commonly encountered in social and community projects. One of the other features of this kind of work pursued in the early days of professional life is the extent to which pursuing adult education practice is a major learning challenge for the educator as much as for the people in receipt of the education.

The experience of adult education practice is revealed as a personal living-out of youthful and pious needs, wants and fears, where a huge amount of energy and focus is spent on working to achieve a kind of predisposing rapport which would facilitate the educational agenda.

PANEL I: Backgrounding: the Outpost Inn

Location

The location referred to in this installation is the Outpost Inn, a coffee lounge in inner-city Melbourne with provision for folk singing on the weekend nights, which a group of young adult Catholics and myself, their chaplain, began in 1966. The adult education practice under consideration here is the staff development exercises pursued through informal weekly meetings that were carried out for about six months. I was then transferred to the Kimberley region of Western Australia. The Outpost Inn, directed by a changing group of Catholic young people, continued for nearly a decade.

The adult educator: personal interests and culture

In 1966, as a newly ordained priest of the Pallottine Fathers, a Roman Catholic religious congregation largely concerned with adult religious education, I was placed at the central training house in Melbourne and given a range of experiences for the first year as a kind of internship.

Apart from the directly religious influences of the Bible and the Pallottine order, Dorothy Day, an activist, pacifist, Catholic lay woman who had founded the Catholic Worker movement in America (cf. Day 1952; Miller 1973), exercised a profound influence. Her vision promoted a movement of radical Christian life, emphasising hospitality and care for poor people by sharing food and clothing and shelter in a humanistic and cultured environment while taking political action to redress unjust social systems. The Outpost Inn project was to be similar to centres developed by Dorothy Day in the Catholic Worker Movement in America.

The vision of quality – linking music to food and welcome which was the ideology of the Outpost Inn – was linked to incarnational theology expressed in the principle of 'quality' and 'reality'. The Catholic theology of the incarnation – of God becoming a human person and ennobling human life – was a strong influence. Teilhard de Chardin's ideas on the incarnation and its links with the whole of creation, and the work of Christians to build up the world as so-called co-creators were central themes (cf. de Chardin 1966).

There was a strong appreciation and celebration of everyday life and the avoidance of what was called too much transcendentalism – ignoring the human dimensions of earthly life in favour of a kind of other-worldly pietism. This grounded concern had considerable echoes in the anti-Vietnam war movement and the interest in bringing religion from heaven to earth.

The aim of the project was not to recruit people to join the Catholic church but to generate a holistic commitment to working for a new creation in culture and society. It was not a highly developed or articulated approach but it formed one of the major values driving the staff development processes.

The learners and their learning arena

About eight women and three men regularly attended management sessions and helped staff the coffee lounge. Of these, about four women and two men formed a core group who took major responsibility. The others were less regular and more likely to attend when asked to provide a particular service. The leadership among the young people was exerted informally by a woman in her thirties who had been the leader of the Legion of Mary group from which most of the core group came.

The dining and kitchen areas of the Outpost Inn formed the environments for the adult learning exchanges promoted there. I was the chaplain and the leader of the group and its teacher. I was also the person who counselled individual members of the team and said Mass with the team on occasion. The day-to-day management of the coffee lounge was carried out by a paid, experienced manager who was sympathetic to the ideas of the project.

The religious dimension, even expressed in secular terms as the pursuit of 'quality' and 'reality', was very strong.

Adult education practice, principles and methods

As was pointed out above, the adult education activities associated with youth work at the Outpost Inn were linked to weekly meetings of its management committee. It followed an informal agenda through which the participants engaged with each other around Christian themes, reported on and assessed their Christian action, and planned future work. The main activity around which this programme was based was running a coffee lounge concerned with promoting social inclusivity and good folk music. The activities for personal and social change were linked to planning, refurbishing the coffee lounge, recruiting volunteers and then running the food and singing programme each night. The meetings talked about, interpreted and critiqued the adventures of the project in the light of the vision of a new world of quality, reality and inclusivity. The initial narratives were full of the adventures of redecorating and setting up the coffee lounge – picking up second-hand materials with a borrowed and unreliable truck, singing in the stairwell between breaks, buying and putting down new floor coverings, going to a bankruptcy sale and picking up industrial stoves. After the redecoration was completed, narratives tended to concern the day-to-day events of the programme – cooking disasters when the coffee machine exploded, harassment from drunks trying to disrupt the programme, singers failing to turn up, people refusing to be quiet during the singing. These activities were done in the context of creating an institution that would promote the vision of quality and reality in music, in food and in inclusive social relations.

Thus these weekly staff meetings formed a loosely structured educational site for the articulation and development of ideas and issues, clarification of skills required and their level of expertise, and ways for participants to gain the skills needed.

The major principles that inspired adult educational practice at the Outpost Inn were influenced by the theological considerations mentioned above, together with a focus on the autonomy of each participant and the importance of supporting and being supported by the community of workers. Adult education principles in this project tended to highlight the autonomy of the learner and the importance of respecting each person's way of managing their learning, while at the same time focusing on encouraging all the individuals in the group to feel committed to, and accountable for, the project. The adult education processes attempted an invitational rather than authoritarian style, while attempting to meet learning needs emerging from the group's commitment to the project.

The overall educational strategy was to encourage the working group which had staffed this coffee lounge to reflect on their practice so that the coffee lounge and its activities would be a form of Christian witness to their ideals of quality, reality and inclusiveness.

The group also supported participants in their own learning projects associated with requirements of the coffee lounge and its activities. A number of the core group learned a lot about redecorating – painting, floor coverings, etc. They also learned the skills of coffee-making and table service in the coffee lounge. The teaching and learning resources were built into the project itself.

There was never express mention of assessment as such. Formal reporting was never required by the superiors of the order, nor was assessment ever formally mentioned. In fact there was a high degree of continuous assessment through the public performance of the team members and their support for each other in pursuing the Outpost Inn ideals.

Issues

A major issue was the different expectations of the staff. Some wanted a more defined and ordered form of practice. One of the core group – a major contributor to the coffee lounge – wanted to have things spelt out and laid out for all to see and understand. Others were happy with the *laissez faire* style with which it had begun.

Another issue was the nature of the relationship that developed between different team members. There were two enthusiastic and committed young women who were paid employees and formed a core group with me. Our habitual and familial relationship tended to be in marked contrast to the less personally intense and more task-oriented relationships of other part-time co-workers in the coffee lounge. As an educator increasingly enmeshed in the affections and relationships of the group, I was also feeling a need to develop ways to pursue the educational agenda increasingly from *within* the group, rather than clerically removed as the chaplain.

Another more educational issue was the lack of any kind of developed philosophy. A need was emerging to move from the spontaneity and intuitive approaches that go with the beginning of an enterprise, to a consolidation period that would be a more reflective and thought-out approach to the ideas and ideals of the project.

An issue that was emerging was the need for a process of evaluation so that we could decide to what extent the project was emerging as we wanted, to what extent it was meeting the dreams and how it could be improved.

This completes the Backgrounding text. The next section is a sketch of a significant moment of the lived experience of the adult education practice in this project.

PANEL II: Sketching: the broken mug

In the kitchen at the priests' house in Kew, Henry, George and I have been hammering out ideas about the significance of the incarnation of Jesus and his entry into the world. As Catholic priests interested in finding new ways to pursue ministry, we discuss creativity and religion, and how one seems to feed the other. Henry is a photographer with his own studio and is in demand by religious sculptors to photograph their work. I am an amateur folk singer. I see myself as a troubadour of God, a singing priest. Later that day I ride my motorbike into Melbourne to the Outpost Inn, our recently reopened, renamed and refurbished coffee lounge in a beautiful tree-lined Melbourne street. I park the motorbike in an alley at the back and enter by the rear door, along a short corridor and open the swing door into the brightly lit kitchen contrasted with the dim, intimate light of the coffee lounge itself.

It is 4 p.m. The management group, four women and two men, has gathered in the kitchen in preparation for an informal, on-the-run management meeting. We have become very close in the struggles of the preceding months while we renovated this previously run-down coffee lounge and renamed it the 'Outpost Inn' – an outpost of the kingdom of God incarnate in the world through Christian life and work. It has been going for about a month with coffee and light meals. On the weekends folk singers perform and the patrons are required as a policy of the place to be quiet during the singing. Most nights it is full. People who come for coffee are often engaged by the enthusiastic team members talking about the meaning of the Outpost Inn project and its agenda to transform the world by pursuing quality and reality in work, cultural activity and social relations.

The team repairs to a quiet corner of the coffee lounge. We pray together and I welcome everyone and speak about how pleased we have all been with the functioning of the whole plan. I remind them of our vision to create a mini community in the city manifesting concern with quality and reality of material and spiritual life. I commend Jane's kindness to a man blinded in the Vietnam war who had come to the coffee lounge. Emily, the leader, herself crippled by polio, commends Sheila and Margaret who had stayed so late to clean up after the last customers went home. They comment on the word 'customer', thinking that patrons of the Outpost Inn are seen as so much more than that. Roland, the day manager, laughs and points out that the additional kindness and welcome the team seeks to offer has been built on good, basic, customer service – clean plates, hot coffee, quick and accurate processing of orders – which he commends. He is listened to with pleasure. Roland came from a coffee lounge that was to be demolished and was looking for a part-time position. He had brought a grounded approach to the nuts and bolts of ordering materials, controlling stock and dealing with the bureaucratic requirements of running a coffee lounge in the city. He is a good team member and is supportive of the general vision while representing a voice of practical common sense.

Jane holds up yet another broken mug from our dwindling store of designer pottery mugs specially commissioned from a potter friend according to our ideology of reality and quality. She complains that those that are not broken are stolen. Raymond recommends purchasing stronger crockery from a catering supplier. Sheila questions how she can maintain the vision of quality and reality – real coffee, real service, real music and real acceptance – if we are constrained to use plastic-looking crockery. Roland smiles. He points out that some catering items are quite tasteful. I propose we all visit the suppliers to see if we can discover suitable items, and we make a time for this to be done. There is a pause as the group looks at the broken cup, the square base tapering to a circle at the lip. The comfortable handle, the squat grounded shape, the mysterious muddy blues, greens and browns swirling in the glaze. Is it so soon that the romantic idealism has to move over to allow room for rationality?

I ask if there are any things to be discussed. Margaret reminds the group that she has raised a matter before without any result. She is concerned that the vision of the Outpost Inn and its practices are not clearly articulated and written down. She points out that it is not clear for the volunteers who come to help for one or two nights a week just what it all means and what people should be doing.

There is a pause. The other three women in the team feel no need for formalisation. They are friends who share the one house and two of them are sisters. They had been members of a city branch of the Legion of Mary, a Catholic lay group interested in social action that had originally taken on the Outpost Inn project. They had accepted the project's ideals as I had sketched them and had elaborated them in endless conversations prior to and during the renovations, when they were active painters and cleaners with me. Margaret had come later. She was also recruited from a different Catholic group. She is well liked, efficient and reliable. The group turns to me. I acknowledge Margaret's need but point out that the ideas around the project are still evolving. I can also see that Dorothy Day's ideal of autonomous responsibility, which is one of our ideals, seeks to avoid formalisation so that if something was to be enunciated it would be at the level of ideals and visions rather than from a book of rules. I wonder if such a publication would satisfy Margaret's need for predictability and order. The three are happy with things as they are – with the excitement and ferment of it. Margaret shrugs but in later weeks she will become increasingly unhappy and leave. I feel a closeness with the other three. The experience of building has been quite difficult and exciting. We gutted the whole structure and rebuilt with materials donated from a wrecker, loaded and carted by these women and additional male volunteers in an unreliable borrowed truck. We have miles of companionship under our belt and are easy together. I am aware that such camaraderie could not be generated in less dramatic circumstances. I spend additional time with Margaret and the other volunteers but there is always something of 'us and them' between the founders and the late arrivals.

The meeting closes with a prayer. Jane takes the broken mug back to the kitchen. Roland goes home. The others move on to the coffee lounge and kitchen cleaning in preparation for the evening

PANEL III: Poetised reflection

Outpost Inn

Is there more than coffee and guitars
in this dark café? You talk of quality,
you with your white priest collar,
black suit and leather overcoat for the motor-bike.
What do you know at twenty-five,

barely out of college,
you're but a jump ahead of these kids
who sit around the table
and talk of the 'place' and the 'vision'
and you their teacher.

You never told them anything;
just praised some singers
who worked out quality in their song
and practised and practised,
changed and distilled,
until the real song emerged;
and that you were determined
to call silence
and give the singers space.

You, the priest gave all this
to your little flock.
And not just music on your mind,
you wanted the music's truth
(you called it reality)
in the coffee and the food;
and how the workers brought it
to the people sitting at the tables.
No lectures in the teaching –
the warmth or distance of your approval
spoke more loudly; the learners' actions
drew your praise or silence.

You were their priest teacher
placed on high and still to learn
how you were to them and they to you.

Like when you named
the plastic and self-indulgent world
contrasted to the coffee lounge's quality
and the search for real;
and yet you did not see
between the teacher and the taught
camouflaged in sacrament and grace,
questions left unanswered, confidence undisturbed.

And you sang too, tutored by the singers
and played guitar, enchanted
by the singing's intimate magic
and listeners rapt and adoring.
You sang religious songs
of justice, grace and chivalry.
In the darkened stairwell, they echoed

wrapped around the girls and boys
as they sat on different stairs.

You went from priest to troubadour
and back; said Mass with them;
brought to them the God
of your monastic years
welcomed in the smoky, friendly gloom.

The learning of your teaching
was not much of this hidden God.
Yours was seen and worshipped in the greeting
held out to strangers and
food and coffee laced with song.

You were with them in a mad religious dance.
Were you their leader, father, troubadour?
And what were they to you?
They gave you admiration, audience,
devoted, undemanding love;
they made you live another way.

When you were called away,
to other work,
the unexpected joy you'd found
became an unexpected dark.
You knew the end of freedom
to dance and dream and let the dream
be turned to action, changed
and stopped and changed again
with no criterion but your own.

Your teaching was a dance of youth,
outside of time and flesh and space,
when the music and the place were right.
It was never so easy
nor yet so quickly gone.

PANEL IV: Intuiting the phenomenon

As explained in Chapter 1, the intuiting looks at four dimensions and then at
naming the experience.

The experience in body, space, time and social relations

As I think back to the adult education experience as *bodily*, my senses are
charged with intense signals. There is the smell of freshly ground coffee that
permeates every corner of the coffee lounge, the sound of plates and knives and
forks clattering and the sound of laughter – the experience of adult education

practice was carried out in the joy of youth. The sight of shiny eyes, flashing teeth, young, strong, supple bodies sitting, moving, dashing into the kitchen. The sight of youth is framed in the intimate dimness of the coffee lounge's public space – the huge beams and indirect light glowing behind them. This muted sight is contrasted with the bright white light of the kitchen and the array of stacked dishes and coffee cups. Touch in this experience is positive and negative. Positive is the particular feel of the wooden tables and benches with no backrest – of leaning forward over the table. Negative is the sense of space between me and the lay people – avoidance of touch and maintenance of 'priestly' distance. My body leaning forward at the planning meetings, concerned to be present to all in the group, sleepy from long hours after dark, nervously jangled in permanent excitement and caffeine. My body seems permanently sensed with excitement and opportunity and exhilaration even in fatigue.

As a *spatial* experience, adult education practice in the Outpost Inn was cramped, confined, pushed together and distant at the same time.

The members of the group distant from me by a small margin are intimately connected to each other. Crowded round a coffee lounge table with me at one end, elbow to elbow at the washing-up sink and food preparation. Crushed into my car being driven home after closing the coffee lounge.

Practising adult education meant being almost physically connected. People registered engagement and compliance by their physical closeness to me and to one another.

As a *temporal* experience adult education practice was endless – the knowledge and enthusiasm exchange was built into all the processes of the project. There was no time when the educational exchanges were not folded into the interactions of the project. Time was always 'high time'. It was so exciting, so rewarding, such a BUZZ. It was time experienced as golden time, while the time at the monastery was experienced as mundane and somehow lifeless, even in the close exchanges with colleagues in the project.

As a *social* experience, I experienced adult education practice as being given status and potency – as being treated as attractive and interesting – especially in reaction to the approval and friendship of the women in the group. My words and ideas were experienced as having potency and carriage. I experienced adult education practice as giving my priest fatherhood huge influence and responsibility above my years. This fatherhood of nurturance and encouragement was complemented by the sonship and daughterhood, compliance, respect and heedfulness of the group.

Naming the experience

'Being with' co-workers

Adult education practice is like being with co-workers, learning as you go. It seems to be a kind of loving exchange in several themes. One is the theme of personal affection and affirmation; another is the theme of engagement in, and care for, the pursuance of the project; and the third is the theme of growth, development, learning in and with the project, nurturing the affection between participants and resolving/managing conflict. Adult education practice in the Outpost Inn can also be depicted as a prolonged last supper – a sacred time pursued around a convivial meal time, shaping and protecting the affection one for another – an experience of loving delight in discovering fellow visionaries and activists.

Educator on the make

Practising adult education manifests itself as an educator 'on the make' – the educator, as a person behind a teacher's masks, reaching out to learners seeking fulfilment and satisfaction in expression, connection, resonance, even a kind of discharge, a downloading of discovery, insight, joy. The phenomenon of adult education practice also appears as a kind of theatrical soliloquy for the teacher – a constructed street theatre presentation where the learners become unwitting, press-ganged extras in the teacher's script for displays and apologias of some of his or her joys, fears, lusts, desires, prejudices and vanities.

Siren singing for learning

Adult education practice presents as a form of enchantment in which the educator presents, portrays, sings the lovable, attractive, enchanting faces of the project. It can also be described as expounding ideology and seeing it grounded in applied action and questions returned from its application.

Dance of hope and possibility being made present

Adult education practice at the Outpost Inn feels like a glorious enterprise full of hope and possibility. It feels young and early and successful. It is like leading a dance, making up steps to follow. When I gaze at this experience of adult education practice I see young people dancing with a priest; I see a priest dancing with each participant; I see each participant self measured and group measured in the exchanges of the project.

Participants being drawn out and their learning energy focused

Adult education practice presents itself to me as inviting and directing people to draw on and focus their learning energy. It is like people's enthusiasm being shared and people being encouraged. It is the experience of 'reciprocal resonance' where one enthusiasm and mission caught the other and the other's reciprocation generated further affirmation and confidence in the educator. It is about damping the fire – not to put it out and not make it flame any higher to avoid burn-out.

Scripting learning processes

Practising adult education appears as *scripting a play*, requiring engagement and compliance of its participants.

A kind of uncle navigator act

Adult education practice in the Outpost Inn looks to me like a kind of uncle navigator act. The uncle metaphor highlighting the mentoring, familial experience in the exchanges between the educator and the learners; the navigator pointing up and encouraging engagement among the learners while keeping the ideals and commitment to the project on track.

Being remedial and catalytic, removing barriers

My experience of adult education practice is largely of it being remedial and catalytic. As an experience, adult education practice is like removing barriers. It is like standing back and allowing the learning energy of the group to build up and flood, as if participants are encouraged to learn by the very act of being involved in the project in an intense and buoyant and open way.

Sailing a boat in the dark

Practising adult education seems like sailing a boat in the dark, feeling one's way by hints and sensations and reactions but with little clear direction. It is like trying to find a way to articulate ideals held by the group in an undeveloped way: to preside over the group's increase of interest and energy and to look for and attempt to convert signs of disengagement; to meet and resolve difficulties in their early stages.

Getting up to speed

What is uncovered when I focus on adult education practice in the Outpost Inn is a kind of getting up to a certain speed of commitment, engagement and success, at which time the participants can be/are brought to a sense of potentiality – learning, reflecting, elaboration of ideals, growth in confidence and aspiration to develop; to become transformed, enriched.

Bandaging and healing

Finally, practising adult education at the Outpost Inn was like running a medical aid post in a battle – giving solace to the soldiers while they rested, had their wounds bandaged – encouraging them to plan their best response to the requirements of the ongoing project.

PANEL V: Distilling the phenomenon

This Panel lists distilled elements of the phenomenon.

- 'Being with' co-workers
- Educator on the make
- Siren singing for learning
- Dance of hope and possibility being made present
- Participants being drawn out and their learning energy focused
- Being remedial and catalytic, removing barriers
- Sailing a boat in the dark
- Bandaging and healing

PANEL VI: Comment

This installation gives a vivid portrayal of the 'heady wine' of the early days of an episode of what can be called 'resonative' adult education. 'Resonative' refers to the engagement of learners responding to an invitation to a shared project as being like the way the shaped wooden body of a guitar will resonate to the plucked strings and in the ensuing resonance create something large and beautiful and not achievable by one without the other. The learning group comes together around a shared vision and particularly in its early stages, becomes a self-driven learning engine of transformation. In this case adult education is a catalytic process for predisposed learners.

This portrayal of adult education practice points out the aspect of curriculum in incidental and informal learning. In many ways, learning and doing are not separated. In this project, making coffee, serving customers and maintaining decorum while singers were performing were activities for which the skills were largely learned by doing. There was also collaborative learning on how to ground the ideas and visions of the Outpost Inn in day-to-day practice – being 'real' in food, music and service. This kind of learning was a mixture of what Squires (1993, p. 101) calls 'movement teaching' and 'group learning'.

In Rogerian style, most of the educative 'input' was largely about removing barriers and facilitating the translation of already strongly held ideas to action.

Another significant point is that the adult educator was having such a great time seeing his ideals and visions gobbled up by his collaborators in a heady mixture of group excitement and unfocused reciprocal affection between himself and the group. He was also enjoying almost everything being done 'by the seat of the pants'. His withdrawal at such an early stage of the project left unattended huge amounts of the kind of learning that was beginning to be required about things like conflict resolution, forward planning and internal discipline.

This concludes the first installation. Our short travel to the second installation in this exhibition area represents a significant move from inner-city Melbourne to Kununurra in the Eastern Kimberleys at the northern tip of Western Australia.

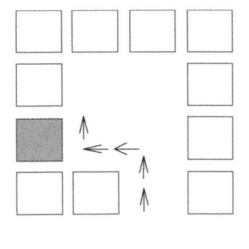

Chapter 3

Ringplace teaching at the Kununurra Mass

The events in this episode took place in 1970 at a specially built 'Mass shelter' beside the Kununurra Aboriginal reserve in Kununurra, a small town at the northern end of Western Australia near the Northern Territory border. The Aboriginal reserve was a piece of land at the outskirts of the town with a few small huts and a toilet block that was allocated for Aboriginal people. A special Aboriginal Mass was said each Saturday morning.

PANEL I: Backgrounding

Historical context

The introduction in 1967 of the referendum that gave all Aboriginal people citizenship also meant the end of the feudal life on cattle stations where they had been living in large numbers, with basic food provided in return for work but virtually no wages. Aborigines living on the Kununurra Aboriginal reserve had moved from their homes on cattle stations that had been located in many instances on their traditional homelands. In those early days, few people had social services and life on the Kununurra reserve was one of poverty, with considerable disturbance from alcohol-related violence.

I was parish priest, operating from a small parish centre in Kununurra which served the local region as well as the town. There was a convent school that served many of the Aboriginal children from the Aboriginal reserve. This was staffed by two religious sisters who had a strong influence on the Aboriginal people through the children. I knew most of the Aboriginal people even before their arrival at Kununurra since I had visited them in their previous lives on cattle stations. In addition, during their time on the cattle stations, many Aboriginal people sent their children to Catholic residential mission schools at

Beagle Bay and Lombadina. They relied on the priest to link them with their children.

Developing and maintaining the Christian missionary work I pursued in and around Kununurra had two related clusters of activities. The first was friendship and connectedness with the Aboriginal people. To this end I visited the people frequently in their camps at the Aboriginal reserve and also gave them rides and informal welfare assistance. In addition, I showed strong interest in their ceremonial life, and attempted to get to know their culture and customs. I accepted invitations to Aboriginal public ceremonies and later was invited to secret men's ceremonies. Several times I helped the Aboriginal elders move their sacred totemic boards from one place to another using the parish Toyota.

The second cluster was the actual engagement in religious adult education practices, which I pursued during a specially designed Aboriginal-oriented Mass celebrated at a purpose-built Mass place.

Attitude and culture of educator

My missionary practice in those early days was largely an attempt to follow the expected behaviour, so I tended to model myself on the practice of the senior priest in the region who was my self-appointed mentor. The major principle that inspired my practice in these early days of my missionary work was to obey the command of Christ to preach the gospel. But I wanted to do this in a respectful and egalitarian way, respecting the Aboriginal people's culture and their post-colonial status of strangers in their own land. In this regard, I followed one senior missionary who was a gifted linguist and who emphasised the importance of knowing the culture of the Aborigines and their language. He was aware of their beliefs, their ceremonies and their cycles.

Another influence on my practice, which I would now tend to call a magical notion, was to let the power of the church's ceremonies, especially the Mass, influence the people directly. This so-called 'sacramental' approach shaped my early practice. In those early days I said Mass in all kinds of places, believing this was an approach with which the Aborigines seemed comfortable and within which I could attempt more teaching.

The learners: Aboriginal settlers at Kununurra

In the late 1960s and early 1970s many Aboriginal people living on Kimberley and Northern Territory cattle stations left or were dismissed from cattle work under the influence of the pressure of cash wages, falling cattle prices and the use of helicopters to muster cattle. They left or were driven away from their homes on these stations to live in reservations and fringe camps around town-ships in the Kimberleys and Northern Territory.

Around Kununurra, the Aboriginal people who came in from the stations in the region were mainly Miriwung-speaking from the East Kimberleys, who had strong links with their traditional culture and spoke 'cattle station English' as their third or fourth language.

I had met most of these people in the course of my pastoral duties as the local parish priest when I visited the isolated cattle stations that had been their homes. Two Aboriginal members of the reserve community at Kununurra mention my link with the reserve mob in their recorded recollections (cf. Shaw 1981, 1983).

Aboriginal religious life was integrated with their everyday world. The people had beliefs in totemic ancestors and followed laws 'from the Dreaming' concerning marriage, kinship obligations, rights to land, etc. There were ceremonies for levels of initiation as well as more generic celebratory rituals the people gained from other groups. There were also rituals of inquest after the death of one of the people. I suggested in an earlier publication (Willis 1987, p. 12) that Christianity was at least in some way identified with the ceremonies the people took on from other groups. The language of buying and selling was often used to describe this exchange.

Sponsorship

I was parish priest of a Catholic mission parish under the authority of the Catholic Bishop. I was also influenced by being a member of the Pallottine religious group in the Church. The 'official' mission ideology, such as it was, was more or less a straight 'replacement' ideology that was echoed in the assimilation policy of the Australian government. In this view, just as Aboriginal people under their newly promulgated citizenship could now leave behind them their traditional ways and take on the benefits and customs of white Australia, so they could also take on Christianity which would replace all Aboriginal beliefs and values with a kind of white Australian, suburban Christianity. This view was one which I did not espouse but I suspect I was considerably influenced by it, particularly the effects of its deeper assumptions about white Australian sovereignty and the place of Aboriginal people in it.

Processes

Introductory processes

As a proselytising missionary, the method I used to generate introduction to my longer-term evangelising strategy was non-judgemental and resourceful friendliness. I approached the Aboriginal people in a friendly way. I knew them well from long acquaintance with them when they lived on the remote cattle stations I visited regularly. When they came to town, they were exiles from their traditional homelands on which they had been able to remain when their land had been occupied by the white settlers and redesignated as cattle stations. I offered them access to some of the resources I had, particularly transport and some advocacy with officials and police in the management of their penurious and precarious life in Kununurra. I often gave Aboriginal people rides in the parish Toyota.

Learning facilitative processes

One of my major evangelical strategies was to indigenise the liturgy, at least to some extent. I created a liturgy that was closer to Aboriginal style. I said Mass

sitting on the ground like they did for much of the time during their own ceremonies. I made up simple songs they could accompany with clapsticks and
didgeridoo. I played guitar. I also used a kind of modified pidgin English which
was my version of Aboriginal station English. I used that particularly in
sermons. At that stage I did not use Aboriginal people for any of the church
teaching. The Mass was a little more collaborative. The didgeridoo accompani-
ment and clap sticks were played by Aboriginal church members.

The assessment of the Aboriginal acceptance of my attempts to change
them was largely done by Aboriginal self-report and their wish to enter the
church. On the whole, Aboriginal people did not report that they had changed
so much, but they did report that they had become affiliated with the Catholic
mob and its priest.

Evaluation

The proselytising action was never formally evaluated. The Bishop used to call
for informal reports on the activities that the missionaries were carrying out
and would get some kind of feedback from the people he spoke to. My
missionary work was sometimes questioned by the Bishop but there was never
really any formal evaluation. However, I was conscious of many of the contradictions inherent in trying to preach the gospel to people who were oppressed,
who spoke another language and who had such a radically different culture. I
was at pains to try to improve my practice by attempting to modify my activity
to increase communication and feedback. There was never anything done
formally.

Issues

One of the major issues I encountered in practice was lack of communication
between myself and the Aboriginal people. This was due to the language difference and the obscurity of concepts and categories linked to that language,
particularly things to do with Roman Catholic theology, ceremonial and
church law. There were massive translation problems to get these into a
communicable format. My attempts to communicate via cattle station English
were always inhibited by the very basic vocabulary it used.

The other issue was the inequitable relationship that existed between me,
as a white coloniser, and the dispossessed and oppressed Aboriginal people. In
my early days my interaction with the people of Kununurra was such that I was
perceived as their protector and patron. It was not an equitable relationship
between us.

Another issue was that the changes I was suggesting were not just a change
of belief but also a change of affiliation. I was suggesting, in effect, that when
these people accepted Christianity and were baptised, they would be affiliated
to the Catholic Church and to some extent separated from other groups.

Another issue was the disparity in the equity promoted through the Christian ideology of equality and love, and the inequity (particularly Catholic
clericalism) and devaliding of many Aboriginal customs, not because they
were anti-Christian, but because they were not western. I also saw an issue in

the fact that the Aborigines would never be able to have any corporate exist-ence within the Church's structure other than the most basic recipient of its services. They would never have any kind of leadership role in the Church because of its clericalised structure. These circumstances became an issue for me when I promoted membership of the church to Aborigines, on the ground that I knew that for them to join was to enter a group that seriously devalued many of their cultural practices and values.

Another issue in this particular proselytising period of my life was my own ambiguity. While I saw my work at this stage to promote Christianity on behalf of the Catholic Church and to invite Aboriginal people to become members, I had serious misgivings about attempting to persuade them to uproot and take on a new identity and new affiliation. In my early days of ministry this was, in effect, the institutional position. The missionaries were expected to preach and convert. The early concept of conversion meant that the Aborigines should stop their own cultural practices and carry out Roman Catholic religious practices. In my later period I became much more at home with a different form of ministry in community development. But in those early days when I was effec-tively an evangeliser, it was an issue for me that I didn't have a total commitment to converting Aborigines to take up what I saw as suburban white Catholicism.

These brief backgrounding notes lead to a story of adult education prac-tice in this period. It concerns the day when Pearly, a devout member of the Miriwung Catholic group who had spent many years in the leprosarium at Derby before returning to her people who had moved from cattle stations to Kununurra, announced that she had made up a new 'Djaanba' song for Mass.

PANEL II: Sketching: a new song for church

At 7 a.m. I park the parish Toyota utility, with its steel cabinet and canopy, under a tree close to the 'Mass ringplace' beside the Aboriginal settlement on the edge of the Kununurra township. The sun is already heating the open spaces but there are long morning shadows from the boab and eucalyptus trees and from the hills surrounding the Aboriginal reserve.

I sound the Toyota horn to let the people know Mass is about to start, and prepare the site. The 'Mass ringplace' is a circular clearing about 8 metres in diameter, surrounded by a ridge about half a metre high at the perimeter, like a small, low profile amphitheatre 'in the round' with a flat central section. It is roofed by a conical pergola of radiated beams and cross pieces meeting at the centre and suspended at their ends by five heavy posts set immediately outside the perimeter ridge at regular intervals around its circumference. The frame of the roof is covered with chicken wine awaiting thatching with spinifex to make a sun shade. At present the open frame creates shadow patterns on the ground.

I brush away fallen leaves on the floor of the circle and put down a mat about 2 metres square. I sit cross-legged and in front of me, also on the mat, I place the white cloth of the corporal – a linen mini table-cloth for the chalice and gold plate. I turn over the front cover of a large flip chart and attach it by a short thread to its rear cover. When I stand it up beside me on the easel made from its front and rear covers, its top is level with my head as I sit beside it. It has elegant stylised pictures representing significant events in the life of Christ – birth, last supper, crucifixion, resurrection and pentecost. I unpack the guitar and place it in its case behind me within easy reach. Beside it I place the didgeridoo and clapsticks for the song men to use in the Mass.

Two sisters from the school convent arrive in their station wagon and drive slowly around the settlement road. They park near the Mass place and walk over to the huts, visiting and inviting the people. They greet the children who they know from school. The children ask for a ride to the river for a swim: 'After Mass, Sister, after Mass', they chorus. The sisters think that can be arranged. The children roar and chortle and skip in front of them as they move along the road.

I blow the Toyota horn one more time. About 60 people are on the move, leaving their camps and swags, moving with their relatives, children and dogs to the Mass place.

The Mass ringplace had to be built outside the boundary of the Aboriginal settlement to respect the settlement's non-sectarian character and avoid objections from missionaries of other denominations. Competing missionaries are a source of interest. Their visits and their various services – music, films, etc. – are noticeable features of settlement life. The Aboriginal people are almost always courteous to the various missionaries and often get a ride into town with them or to the river at the conclusion of their services.

The people greet me and arrange themselves in family groups on the peripheral ridge around the classroom. I sit on the southern side. Two of the older men pick up the didgeridoo and clap sticks.

'Father, we got a song for you about that Holy Spirit', Pearl calls out. She walks awkwardly with white sandshoes to protect her toes, damaged from leprosy. She arrives with brothers-in-law and uncles and her child reunited with her since she came home from the leprosarium. Pearl has made a *Djaanba* song about the Holy Spirit coming down on the people. *Djaanba* is one of the local ceremonial clusters in the Miriwung Gadjerong repertoire. As I understand our Aboriginal English exchange, she has taken one of the *Djaanba* songs and put Christian words to it about the Holy Spirit. I am delighted that she, a devoted church member who spent many years with the nuns at the Leprosarium in Derby a thousand miles away, has been able to link and translate the Christian practices which she had used for many years in Derby into the language and idiom of one of the local ceremonial cycles. I am also excited since it is the first time this has happened and it is unsolicited. I suggest that we use this song several times during the Mass: after the reading and sermon; to introduce the communion service; and then during communion time. She is pleased and withdraws to speak to the song men.

Before Mass we rehearse the new *Djaanba* song. The text is short and there is some difficulty in translating the Miriwung into English. I am not completely sure what the words of the song actually mean.

The music is clap sticks without didgeridoo. Many of the adults recognise the melody and immediately follow the chant, chiming in like a 'chorus' after the initial 'antiphon' sung by Pearl in the traditional way. I struggle to sing along, to follow the high falling melody and the syncopated and irregular double beat. The slow rhythmic repetition of a double stroke of the clap sticks makes it good to accompany the procession when people receive Holy Communion.

At the beginning of Mass, I play guitar and the song men play didgeridoo and clap sticks to accompany the singing of a special 'Our Father' which I had written and adapted to a more westernised-sounding Aboriginal melody I had heard in the Northern Terrritory. As the Mass progresses I repeat the Christian story and follow the life of Jesus and the coming of the Holy Spirit. I link the last with Pearl's new song. Then Pearl leads the new *Djaanba* song and the others follow. Later at communion time, I again lead the singing of the Our Father with guitar, didgeridoo and clap sticks. Pearl follows with the new *Djaanba* hymn for the communion procession.

The Mass comes to an end. The people disperse. Some get a ride with the sisters to their swimming and fishing place on the river. I pack up and load the boxes and guitar case back on the Toyota.

One of the older men, passing the Toyota, speaks approvingly of the *Djaanba* hymn: 'That a good song for church. That the little bird song from the *Djaanba*.' I asked him whether he understood what she was singing. 'I ought to', he said, 'I bin sing that *Djaanba* for a long time.'

So does that mean the new hymn is a part of the *Djaanba* song cycle, imported willy nilly into the Mass? I had been thinking it was a new song or at least new words. 'No', he said, 'that the little bird song from this country.'

So as I reflected, the image of the dove for the Holy Spirit had merged into the totemic bird of the red ranges at Kununurra. It was certainly nothing of my doing. The song from the *Djaanba* cycle has been given an additional setting. The Holy Spirit, hovering over all like a white dove, was now located, reborn in the little bird of Kununurra.

And so, had Pearl become a Miriwung theologian and liturgist? Had she overlaid a song of her 'country' over the more transcendent and mystic notion of the Holy Spirit represented by a bird no one had ever seen in the Kimberleys? In doing so, had she grounded and somehow brought together the Christian and Miriwung ways of being spiritual and religious, or had she confused one with the other?

In subsequent discussions and oblique enquiries from singers and authors, I never got a clear translation of the words of the *Djaanba* song beyond the original thematic allusions to 'bird' and 'country'. It subsequently passed into common Miriwung use at all Masses, not just the special Mass at the Aboriginal reserve. I am still not sure what meanings the people give to it when they sing it during Mass. I know it has important religious significance but I am not able to say much more than that.

PANEL III: Poetised reflection

The following poem uses several Miriwung words. *Ngarunggani winya* means 'in the time of the Dreaming'. *Warrana* the eaglehawk and *djalarang* the white-faced heron are totemic animals. *Warrana* is allocated to one of the two groups, or moieties, to which everyone in the community is assigned by kinship, and *djalarang* to the other. *Ngabang* is the Miriwung word for 'father' and is used to refer to God the Father and the Catholic priest.

Mass teaching

You're sitting cross-legged clothed in priest robes
with book and bread and chalice in the dusty circle,
cleared and designated for the people's Mass.

The Catholic mob, Miriwung people
from this, their mother country,
sit peaceful waiting on the circle's rim.

You give a welcome, play guitar;
you lead the people singing the 'Our Father' song
to focus their attention and call back watchful eyes
from dogs and restless children, passing trucks.

The men join in with didgeridoo and clap sticks;
women beat time with double hands on thighs;
the song goes up; the verse's repetitions
loop back once and twice
and at the end comes stillness.

You grab the silence for teaching,
to tell of *Ngabang*: Father God.
He made the Earth and later, freed it from sin
through His son Jesus' death and rising,
in times long past, but still in some way present.

You say the Miriwung word for 'dreaming'
that the people taught you for this time
of past made present, *Ngarunggani winya*.
The spirits of the people and their country
are honoured and evoked: *Warrana* and *Djalarang*,
eaglehawk and white-faced heron.
You set your teaching and your welcome
to negotiate a space for Christian *Ngabang*:
a heaven father to protect them and their country.

And when your teaching word is finished,
you give the signal for the *Djaanba* chant,
excerpted by the people from their dreaming songs,
for the procession at communion time.

The people take the song up from the leader,
dancing single file, weave a circle
like a slow snake moving round the Mass place.

And as they dance, like a garment,
they clothe the space anew; and bless the land
they always knew as sacred
before being stripped and cleared and consecrated
for the *Ngabang* spirit.

And when the *Djaanba* chanting rises,
grafted on your welcome and inclusion,
do other older ways and worlds come present?
And does this deeper resonation make your teaching
speak other words as well and meanings in this place?

PANEL IV: Intuiting the experience

As in the previous installation, the author/curator now attempts to intuit the experience evoked and made present in the previous panels.

The experience in body, space, time and social relations

As a *bodily* experience, adult education practice is sitting cross-legged on the ground. It is standing and then sitting on a Mass blanket, with the early morning sun slanting but shadowed by the strategically parked truck. There are corella calls, sounds of the camp waking up. As a bodily experience, it is my head turning either side to engage the audience.

There is a tension as I lean forward to maintain a sense of intensity, of engagement, watching, holding eye contact. I hold the guitar cradled over my lap. I have the Bible pictures on a stand near my knee so I can point to figures in each of the pictures. My ears are attuned to noises invading the space, breaking the link – passing trucks, barking dogs, etc. My body is thus attempting to 'tune in' to their bodies, to create a linked resonance. My consciousness is of tension – straining forward when I stand for the dancing, feeling relaxation in my body as the people take up the ritual and move rhythmically around the space.

Adult education practice as a *spatial* experience is being in the circle under the radiated rafters rising to their steel centre core with its cross. There is the sense of coming into the space and of locking into it: me to one side of the flat central circle, the people ranged opposite around the circle's elevated ridge, close yet distant, with the intervening space marked by stamping feet. The spatial experience is of a calling up, a flocking to this fixed Mass place. This flocking and settling at the rim is then, after the time of singing and instruction, continued inward when some of the people bring gifts to where I am standing and where everyone walks in procession to receive communion. Adult education practice as a spatial experience is about coming with people to one point, being together and dispersing. The space is in the people's land, in an unroofed structure that defined but did not cover the space.

Adult education practice as a *time experience* in this episode follows a rhythmic movement from establishing a relationship over time, built around visits and chats and knowing the children from school. This predisposing time leads to introductory time – the arrival at the Aboriginal village, the blowing of the car horn, the parking of the truck at the Mass place and setting out the altar on the blanket. The introductory time ends with the people flocking to the Mass place and exchanging greetings with the priest and the sisters. Introductory time leads to engagement time, when the celebrant orchestrates the musical and verbal processes which bind him to the people and set up a shared engaged time. Within the engaged time – nested within the ritual exchanges of the Mass – is the instruction time, which is followed by a ritualised acceptance time: in other words, the ritual compliance with the actions and songs of the ceremony that continue after the instruction time. The people ritually put into practice their acceptance of the teaching in the instruction time. The dispersal time is subsequent to the engagement time when the people return to their huts and camps and I to my house in the town. The experience as an 'experience in time' is about waiting and more waiting until people come. Everything flows from the waiting. Adult education practice is then experienced as waiting for a moment of focused attention mapped onto the predictable, measured, finite time of ritual.

As a *social* experience, adult education practice in this episode is an experience in social relations. The teaching/learning exchange is located in the social relationships and exchanges of the event. Some of these relationships are the church membership. They are 'the Catholic mob'. Their relationship with the educator priest they call *Ngabang* (Father), but who is also known by his classificatory 'skin' name as *djabidja*, places him in relationship to all the Aboriginal members where membership of other classificatory sections predicates kinship links. Besides these structured social relationships there are the informal links between the people and the priest who visits them often, takes them for rides and works with them on community development projects. There is a lot of affection and mutuality in the social relationships surrounding the teaching/learning exchanges in the Mass. Adult education practice in this episode is like being with quasi-kinfolk as father and weaving instruction into affirmations of filial and paternal affection.

Naming the adult education experience

Connecting in friendship and mutual approval celebration

Adult education practice in the ringplace Mass sounds to me like a kind of feast of friendship and mutual approval – the benign smiles and the enthusiastic entering into the ritual. The educational experience strikes me as being a funny kind of multi-level exchange of blessings – affirmations in which the learning agenda is promoted, modified and given a 'qualified acceptance'. It is like being welcomed and blessed in the beaming smiles of the Miriwung people and their children.

Seeking connection and response

What comes to light when I focus on adult education practice at the ringplace Mass is going through the motions – getting people's attention, making sure that the conditions for engagement are as good as can be, being given eye contact, laughter in response to a joke, being irritated by extraneous noises that pull the people's attention away. The experience was of the people always nodding and saying 'yes' (*Yoo*) in response to the often repeated 'Is that alright?' (*Warrang ngi?*); of the educator being totally accepted in a way that did not involve critique or interrogation. The teaching experience was like giving a church sermon – 'casting bread on the waters' – trying to keep a 'carrier wave' of laughter and eye contact upon which to carry the message.

Learning facilitation and ritual practice symbiosis

Adult education practice at the ringplace Mass feels like the music, ritual, laughter and learning being combined to carry the more difficult and less tangible Christian ideas. The phenomenon presents itself as a kind of symbiotic compenetration of ritual practice and learning facilitation: ritual being used to enhance learning facilitation, ritual processes being used to predispose for learning, and learning promoted to deepen engagement in ritual.

The phenomenon of adult education practice at the ringplace Mass teaching presents itself as revealing new significances in traditional ritual practices by encouraging old ritual forms in a new setting and expounding an augmented interpretation. The experience presents itself as the priest/adult educator attempting to provide not just instruction about new beliefs but how these beliefs are implicit in the existing Aboriginal ritual and beliefs.

Attention seeking; attention desiring; doing anything for attention

The experience of adult education practice is largely about seeking attention; desiring attention; doing anything for attention. Attention and then engagement – reciprocity. What comes to light in the experience is the priest/adult educator seeking engagement from the people and hoping for reciprocity, but at least attention and some engagement.

The phenomenon of adult education practice at the ringplace Mass presents itself as a desperate quest to generate a hush of attention marked by a cessation from alternative acts – playing with children, dogs, looking around, etc. Seeking engaged attention as a foundation upon which other learning facilitative processes can then be built is the key factor of the adult education experience in this episode. This experience is one of struggle – the diplomatic struggle for attention/engagement/being instructed without losing composure.

Multi-layered engagement built on successive agreements

The phenomenon of adult education practice at the ringplace Mass presents itself as multi-layered, interpersonal negotiation: instruction pursued within engagement; engagement pursued within attention; attention pursued following introduction to the new song and introduction pursued on top of a long-standing easy family-like friendship.

Adult education practice was experienced as a kind of terrier movement to maintain the nested agreements: eyes darting trying to keep the attention; out-manoeuvring potential distractions to allow the ritual to gain its momentum; an invitation to attend and engage and to stop doing other things.

Setting traps for learning

Adult education practice at the ringplace Mass was experienced as a pre-conditioning environment for learning, being constructed and maintained through time, waiting for the chemistry to take hold.

It was experienced as interpreting mixed reactions manifested in affirming smiles, accompanied by puzzled, blank looks and seeking to foreground the part receiving the affirmation. The experience meant redoing original interpretative remarks, at first using different words on the chance that the blank looks were caused by language difficulties since Aboriginal station English is not a rich medium. When different words seemed to make no difference, it was then exploring whether the rhetorical question, 'Now what do this chalice and this green vestment with its cross mean?', may itself have been meaningless. The experience was also about feeling reluctant to ask whether what the priest was doing was meaningful – sensing that the question itself was somehow unaskable.

Dialogue ping pong

What I see in adult education practice during the ringplace Mass at Kununurra is a kind of dialogue ping pong. The experience presents itself as a kind of action-reaction – action-reaction exchange: eye contact/smiles/greetings/jokes/words/song/sentences, all done in an interactive back and forward motion and the instructional challenging component woven into the forward and back of the exchanges. The experience presented itself as a feeling of concern that the ball stay in the air, to keep batting it back and forward.

Working on the edge of people's awareness

What unfolds for me as I dwell on adult education practice at the ringplace teaching at Kununurra is the multi-layered experience of working on the rim of people's awareness; being located outside people's private and unrevealed selves and finding the door opened only to reveal a benign friendliness but no intellectual engagement – a kind of faith without theology.

Taking the people into an experience hoping that they will get interested

What is also uncovered in this experience is taking the people into an experience hoping that their 'engine' will start – that the experience itself will be significant without too much need for explanation, like persuading people to march with a spirited band hoping that the participants will get into the swing of the experience and internalise its spirit.

An instructing experience

From another perspective, adult education practice in this episode presents itself as an instructing experience. Either as dramatised instruction – a show in which the priest is the main actor, commentator and interpreter of the processes – or a 'do and explain' experience, for example setting out the Mass instruments (doing) – chalice, plate, vestments, guitar, flipchart – and at the same time explaining their significance while keeping eye contact and making jokes to keep attention coming.

The experience of moving from amiable engagements and greetings to the ritual and attempting to explore significance is an experience of pushing for engagement, noting when the level of attention falls, attempting to call people to attention with jokes and laughter, and then pushing again once attention had been restored. As an experience it was dancing and pushing and dancing again, at the same time exhilarating and exhausting.

A working-in-the-dark experience

Adult education practice at the ringplace Mass is like working in the dark. Setting out predisposing processes, hoping for some 'take-up' from the people but not knowing if the instructional words have any deep impact, if there is a deeper acceptance of the ideas and challenges being promoted. It is also like not knowing what was getting across and yet receiving huge affirmations from the learners' nods and smiles and the piety of their participation in the rituals and prayers of the Mass.

I discover as well a sense of being welcomed but not actually invited in: being locked out from deeper exchanges; not knowing what the people think and not being told; a denial of direct discussion and exchange; a kind of wandering in the fog supported by the mutual esteem of facilitator and facilitated participants; wanting to include elements to be understood and committed to memory but impossible to assess; a permanent state of unknowing about what is getting across, what people are learning. It is like being held to what can be seen and having no way to explore further, like a priest giving a sermon and not knowing what people think of it or gain from it.

An energy-sapping experience

What shows up when I think of adult education practice during the ringplace Mass at Kununurra is an experience of entropy – that there is always less energy in the people than in the educator. This contrasts with the experience at the Outpost Inn, the previous installation, when the enthusiasm was reciprocal. Here the reciprocity is reciprocating minus one.

The experience had an element of endless pushing: that one needed to be on guard to protect the fragile attention and engagement which was always threatening to run down. At the same time, the experience was full of an energetic and reciprocal affirmation of affection, but not so much of engagement in the learning.

PANEL V: Distilling the phenomenon

The phenomenon of adult education practice intuited in the previous panel is now distilled into its major themes.

- A 'being with' and predisposing experience
- An orientation-to-learning experience
- An instructing experience
- A working-in-the-dark experience
- An energy-sapping experience

PANEL VI: Comment

As with the first installation, adult education practice in this episode is pursued in and with other activities on which they depend and in which they are entangled. The processes of identifying and attempting to contemplate the phenomenon of adult education practice are accordingly difficult.

The linked panels of this installation highlight elements in adult education experience, particularly the complex interpersonal exchanges which frame and colour adult education practice.

The notion of adult education as invitation receives strong endorsement in this installation, which foregrounds processes of predisposition and mobilisation within the adult education sequence, and manifests how little direct control over learning the adult educator has. He or she can invite but cannot force learning. The initiatory elements in adult education practice are foregrounded here as important elements in the sequence.

The limits of what can be revealed or assessed in adult education practice are also revealed here. The impenetrable privacy of the learner is pointed out strongly in this episode, where the ordinary silences and mysteries between learner and teacher are magnified inescapably in the differences of culture and language.

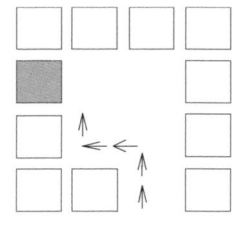

Chapter 4

Trucking with the Miriwung

The third installation relates to the experience of adult education practice with the same Miriwung Aboriginal people at Kununurra in North West Australia. The setting is no more than a hundred metres from the Mass place which, as was mentioned in the previous installation, had by law to be located outside the formal boundaries of the land gazetted by the Government for Aboriginal accommodation. This episode of adult education practice was very much a secular enterprise, the planning activities of which took place under a make-shift shelter in the middle of the reserved land.

PANEL I: Backgrounding

The Mirima council project was a community development project I established with the Miriwung people at Kununurra, North West Australia in the early 1970s. It centred on the establishment, resourcing and eventual collapse of a market garden project and the successful appropriation of its vehicles for cere-monial and social activities. The educational project I pursued with the people was directly linked to setting up and running two community projects: a repre-sentative community council and a market garden controlled by this community council. The educational activities pursued here were linked to understanding and carrying out the activities of the council and the garden project.

The adult educator: ideals and culture

I helped establish the programme as an extension of my pastoral ministry to the Miriwung people most of whom, as has been pointed out already, were affili-ated with the Catholic church. It was an intervention I initiated with them when they moved from affluent quasi-servitude on cattle stations in the Eastern Kimberley region, where I had first met them, to relatively autonomous poverty and social disintegration on the fringes of Kununurra.

I had two reasons for wanting to help them set up decision-making structures and economic enterprises. The first was that I thought by such action they
would become organised and therefore able to manage the many transitions
that were occurring in their lives. The second was that I had been informed by
the Federal Government that if any Aboriginal group formed itself into an
incorporated association and proposed to engage in positive economic and
social programmes, they would qualify for considerable Government resources
which this impoverished community badly needed.

I had recently been ordained and had no experience of, or training for, this
kind of work. I was, however, a member of the recently formed East Kimberley
Health Organisation that proposed ideas of community development to which
I was attracted. I had learnt the adult educational strategy I employed to pursue
this community development while working on Catholic residential missions in
the region.

The learners: Aboriginal settlers at the Kununurra Aboriginal reserve

The Miriwung learners described here are the same people mentioned in the
previous sketch. As was pointed out above, they considered themselves 'the
Catholic mob', so when I visited the Aboriginal reserve, which I did almost
daily, it was easy to convene meetings. It is significant that I was closely linked
with them. When I became involved in community development I changed the
emphasis of my ministry from directly religious matters to a social development
agenda: group decision-making, addressing social problems and working out
ways to find employment.

The sponsor

There was no official sponsor for this project. It was initiated by me as an
extension of my pastoral ministry but it had no specific sponsorship. Resources
were provided by me from the parish – fuel for the Toyota, stationery, the odd
phone call, second-hand corrugated iron for the shade shelter.

The arena and the learning-related processes

The Mirima project took place at the Kununurra 'Native Reserve'. The adult
education processes pursued in this project were held at a shaded meeting place
purpose-built by the group and myself with second-hand materials donated
from the parish and erected in the middle of the oval communal space between
the 12 pensioners' huts.

The educational strategy I employed can be called 'push-start action-based
teaching'. It traces its roots to a once often used 'top down' missionary
approach to indigenous people. The missionaries would establish an enterprise
for, and within, a target population, involving them as much as possible as
apprentices and co-workers in the project. The enterprise, once established,
was then supposed to be handed over gradually to the target people while the
initial support was just as gradually withdrawn.

I mentioned to the people that the local medical officers said the children should eat lots of fresh fruit and vegetables. I then pointed out that a local horticultural adviser, employed by the local agricultural research station, had said that it was possible to set up a large garden on land next to the reserve, which could be irrigated from the irrigation channel nearby. (Kununurra was the site of the Ord River Irrigation project.) I was able to point out that a project like this would very likely attract funds from the Government. There was a lot of interest in the project and the people voted to support further negotiations which I proposed to set up between them and the Government. I suggested that the people on the Reserve form a representative council. I pointed out that they would have more control over their lives and the Federal Government would reward their 'independent Aboriginal action' by under-writing their enterprises.

I had already seen mission projects in other places which were set up following the 'push-start action-based teaching' method mentioned above. I attempted to use a modified version of the same strategy by persuading the Miriwung to allow me to form them into a representative council which would run the proposed market garden, and which they would initially run with my assistance and eventually take over as their own. I pointed out that the Government would underwrite this project and provide money and resources for it, including a large truck for all the activities of the project and a four-wheel-drive utility for doing errands, etc.

The Mirima council eventually became an incorporated association. It attracted a sizeable grant for the project, including a large truck and a Toyota four-wheel-drive. The arrival of the truck caused what I thought was an extraordinary amount of jubilation for a work resource to cart fence posts, tools, fertiliser, etc. The Mirima garden was cultivated and fenced as long as the project money for wages continued. The vegetables grew, were photographed and flourished and died in the rows. They were never harvested or marketed. The truck became particularly useful for moving large groups to ceremonial meetings in remote places in the Kimberleys and western Northern Territory. The four-wheel-drive was appropriated by one of the council members who disappeared for several months (cf. Willis 1980).

Issues

Some of the major issues in this project that troubled Aboriginal people on the Kununurra reserve were widespread unemployment, poverty, alcohol abuse and domestic violence. For many of the people, living on the reserve at Kununurra was to be living in an out-of-control way without the familiar structures of the cattle stations, in close proximity to people of different language groups and different family affiliations who were relative strangers.

Another key issue relating to the educational process in this project was the difficulty of understanding proposed ideas, partly because of lack of a common language, but partly also because what was proposed had never been seen. Another issue was the habitual modes of opportunistic communication and decision making used between the educator and the people, both of which were pursued with huge amounts of ambiguity and lack of accurate knowledge about the real nature of proposed innovations.

Panel II: Sketching: reflections before the meeting

My sensitised mind, taken back more than 20 years and aroused by the backgrounding scaffold, once more relives and is saturated in the experience of setting up the learning experiences in the Mirima council and market garden project. Transported to the Kununurra Aboriginal reserve, I am aware of the flat grey of the earth pounded by thousands of Aboriginal feet; children running, walking. I am aware of the red Kimberley landscape – the dusty trees; red stone ridges rising behind the Aboriginal reserve; the smoke from cooking fires from the Aboriginal families camped nearby. Under the meeting place's corrugated iron roof, that we built in the early days, I am aware of the makeshift table and the three chairs brought over for the meeting. I know that if I sit and lean back into the chair's support I will lose my poised stance. I will have no place from which to maintain the intense engagement I need to keep the connecting link, eye contact and smile, to keep the mob together and on the track I am trying to take them. My belly aches with the tension.

I am aware that things need to come to closure. I am aware that I need a decision to warrant my continuing to act on the people's behalf. My tension is not a tension of depression or stress from outside forces. It is the stress of holding the threads of engagement and plaiting additional threads to make a 'rope of commitment' to the project which I can't really explain until there is something concrete to see.

I am stressed in trying to communicate with my basic Aboriginal English. I look for more concrete words to run alongside words like 'council', 'decision making', 'community development', 'project' and the like. I am working with a kind of guessed approximation. I can't demean these benevolent old men by asking them to tell me in their own words what they have just agreed to; to back-translate my language. I have tried it before with individual men and women and have found not much improvement in comprehension. So many of my words refer to things with no parallel in Aboriginal experience. I talk a long time to many of the people individually and I think we have a kind of understanding but I have never felt confident to ask one or other of them to give me an account of what has been said. I would like to, but in my exchanges with them English communication is so reduced and basic that I feel such a request would be an intrusion. So I work with the quality of eye contact and laughter. I crack jokes, looking for the laughter which I take to mean I have been understood, and in the moments of connected comprehension I try to insert related ideas and suggestions.

But it's not only living with vague comprehension. I am also living with vague 'agreement' to my proposals. I have been with them so long I have developed a sense of the quality of their acceptance of my proposals. They seem to agree with many of my proposals as long as I carry out the agreed action with them. When an agreed action is to be pursued in my absence, I know its execution will be contingent upon the absence of competing claims on their time by relatives or other welfare workers or, of course, other competing missionaries.

I build my agreement in the early months and years of my time with the people. I am negotiating a learning agreement with them to take up an unfamiliar script which, up till now, has been similar to the implicit learning in my Christian ministry where there is little demand on them to do or demonstrate their learning independently.

But there are differences. For one thing, the potential rewards are significant and tangible, for another, the people may be called upon to display some fruits of their learning if and when a government official wants to talk to 'the Aborigines themselves'.

In my Christian teaching with these people, I feel they have an enriched religiosity, a different way of being with God, which may well surpass the spirituality of Western Christianity. I can teach with a great deal of space for their own geist to fill the gaps. But here, in the teaching of social action, I feel the hard wind of challenge; to get through to the people and to generate a grounded assent evidenced in sustained action, at first with me and then autonomously.

My stress rests on the slippery nature of their understanding and compliance with the learning implications of the choices they have agreed to. I feel instinctively that it will be all right as long as I am with them and as long as my credibility with them is not challenged too radically.

This preliminary reflection, which foregrounds the attitude and misgivings of the educator, gives way to the following panel which is a poetised narrative of the educational exchanges in the Mirima council project.

As in the previous installation, there are a few Miriwung and Aboriginal English words. *Ngabang*, the word for father, again is used for the priest (and for God the Father); *killer*, a station word for a bullock killed for food; *rown*, Aboriginal station English for 'own'; and *yoo*, a Miriwung word signifying agreement, used in reply to the question *Warrang ngi?* which means, 'Isn't that right?' The word *business* was used by Aboriginal people to refer to an important Aboriginal ceremony, often requiring participants to travel long distances to attend.

PANEL III: Poetised reflection

Gone away

One more ride to the Aboriginal reserve;
you park the Toyota near the shade tree,
blow the horn – *time for meeting*! shout,
grab the briefcase and the papers,
settle back against the tree to wait.
Weary, weary, roll a smoke,
brush the ground dust from sweaty hands,
sweat marks on khaki cotton pants.

And wait, wait, puff the cigarette,
wait, shift, stand up, move, and now at last,
Bronson, the old Miriwung bossman, ex stockman,
walking to the meeting place: courteous, massive.
Manfred, his mate, won't be far behind
and others trickling up: greet, cough,
spit to the side, roll smokes, sit around and wait.

These are friends and congregation,
baptised last year, they endure hardship,
dispossession without self pity.
You won't mind if there's some slippage
between what is agreed and what is done
and who knows what will happen
around the garden project you are promoting.
On the missions, gardens never came to much.

What about Morris? You watch him sitting outside his hut.
He's another leader, more for younger people;
knows English better than those other station people.
He can read a bit – even write, from his time
in the Darwin leprosarium when he helped the doctors.
He's not as close to you as the other easy station blokes;
You can't work him out. Oh good, he's coming now.

He's got the briefcase you gave him
To keep papers needed at the meeting.
Why's he taking so long – is he just making you wait?

Eh you mob, this the different meeting:
this for project business not church business.
I bin tell you about this at the Mass place;
this not church word; this not Catholic word;
this different; this project word.
You mob living long time away from station now,
away from country, on this reserve.
You bin tell me lotta times, you lonely for country;
got no killer for beef, no rice, no flour.

This reserve got nothin, no store, no cattle;
people starvin. We bin talk lotta time for two way:
work for get back country – this the long time project.
But garden project we might be gettum straight away.
Gov'ment want to help blackfella set up rown projects;
might be they give you money for garden:
fence, water pipe, pump, truck, Toyota ,
make a big garden for fruit and vegies
make your kids strong.

If we do this project well,
Gov'ment might be givem back your country;
What you mob reckon? good idea or what?
You mob always say 'yoo'.
You sure you meanin that?

This gov'ment got different word now:
they want talk to blackfellas himself for projects,
not to their whitefella friends.
You mob gotta make a council to talk for you;
send paper to Canberra for that garden and truck.
No use whitefella word for this mob
gotta be blackfella himself.

What you reckon you mob? OK? OK?
What you reckon Bronson, Mr Bossman?
[Bloody hell, is he agreeing or what?]
What you mob reckon?
OK? OK? OK.

You want to send that word to Canberra?
OK? OK? OK.
I can write your word;
you gotta sign that paper.
What you reckon Morris, Mr. Chairman?
We can send that letter about the project,
about the garden? Is that OK?
You want me to write some notes for that letter,
OK? OK. Here's a draft letter. What you think?
Can you read the type words? OK? OK?
[this is driving me crazy]

Morris signs the letter with crabbed hands
and fingers from leprosy. He looks at you
and the group under the shelter.
'Finish the meeting', he says. Sun glasses,
white shirt, shorts and socks – a Darwin city black,
walking back to his tin shed.
You bet they didn't speak this weird station English
in Darwin.

Bone-weary from keeping the talking going
between you and the listening people;
Trying to stop answering your own questions;
Take the signed paper; post it to Canberra.

Hey you mob, [Toyota engine still running,
slam the door: news, news from Canberra,
the bait has been taken],

Gov'ment man sent that letter, coming for meeting;
you mob gotta talk.
I can sit with you but I can't talk;
this got to be your rown word.
When he coming for meeting,
you mob gotta talk.
It's your project OK? OK?

At the meeting place, introductions,
fingers crossed and waiting, waiting.
The Canberra man nervous of the silence,
Talking, talking. People looking blank.
Don't they realise all they have to do
is nod and smile – he's doing all the talking.
What's wrong with them, they drive you crazy.

A letter comes from Canberra.
There is guarded support for the project,
but some fear that the people
are being pushed by 'the priest';
they may not really want the project.
You rush to tell the people
about the Canberra man's report.

That Canberra man he reckons alright
but might be I pushen you mob too much.
What you reckon? You mob agreein'
for that garden project all the time isn't it?
You always sayin 'Yoo' when I say 'Warrang ngi?'
Might be something though. You mob don't do much
if I don't come for meeting. What that?
You mob laughin' for that, but I'm not head stockman.
I'm not boss for project, that your business.
I'm just helpin' get you started.
This gotta be your rown project all the way. OK? OK? OK.
Hey you mob, we got order form for the garden project;
letter just come from Canberra.
They gonna give us water pump and
that big truck, we bin ask for;
and four-wheel-drive car for people.
What you mob reckon? What kind truck you mob want?
What kind four-wheel-drive car?
Gotta put it on the order form.
You want bull bar, OK?
You want spotlights, cattle crate, long-range tanks?
Might as well: Toyota eight ton, what you reckon?
And Toyota four-wheel-drive ute – is that the one?
Gov'ment reckon OK. Comin' next week.

Jimmy drives the huge red truck
from the Toyota depot to the centre of the reserve.
Jimmy the only truck driver in the mob.
Morris, the meeting chairman, has a car licence;
drives the new Toyota four-wheel-drive ute.
A crowd surrounds the vehicles and shout and clap.
They praise you and line up to try it out.

What you mob clappin for me?
This not my truck for you.
This from Gov'ment, not me.
I was helpin' you mob just helpin'.
Gov'ment give you that truck not me.
That your truck for you mob.
That belong to you fellas proper way, straight up.
No-one can take that away; that's your rown truck.

You seize the time to strike – to ride the people's glee.
Now we got work; we got to keep the garden goin';
keep the water pump goin'.
Easy with that truck:
Jimmy good truck driver for that.
Easy to get fence posts, wire,
easy cart sand, cement for garden shed.
And easy pick up people for work
in that new four-wheel-drive.
Morris got licence; he can drive.
He can take people for garden work.

You won't need rides from me.
Won't be long: we gonna have tomatoes,
watermelons, chillies for all the camps.
Good for kids.
When we meeting for all this?
Must be next week,
I gotta go to missionary meeting in Broome,
be back next week ...

In Broome, you describe the project;
point out that the people own the project,
which is the key to its being taken up so strongly.
You are anxious to get back.

Where all the people? I'm back for meeting.
Garden got no water: chillies, watermelons
Everythin' dryin' out.

People gone for *business ngabang.*
Morris gone to country, got that four-wheel-drive;

big truck he gone too: big mob blackfellas
gone for *business*. People gone away, come back soon
after *business* – look around country.
Good truck that; lotta people, lotta swag,
water drum. No more taxi; no more lookin' for ride.
Mob got proper truck, *rown* truck.

They gone, *ngabang*,
all that mob gone.

Your 'ownership' words come back to you.
You drive back to the church house in the town.
Soon the people will be gone from church too,
they can travel far away all together on the truck.
Your congregation will disperse: to ceremonies, visits,
pick up and drop off friends, relations
in the big red truck they think you got for them.
Like a big ship almost an ark,
it will sail unchallenged, protected;
from station to station, town to town,
beholden to no-one: moving around country.

This poetised account completes the second section of this installation, which is followed by the intuiting account.

PANEL IV: Intuiting the experience

The experience in body, space, time and social relations

Previously, in the Mass place, where adult education practice was seen as a *bodily* experience, my body was in tension, so it is this time. But it is not the tension of pushing the ritual. It is the tension of sustaining and drawing out a more positive assent. I am not seated on the ground but on a small chair leaning forward, smoking often and poised to focus and arrange the varied reactions of the stakeholders.

As an experience in *time*, adult education practice is weighed down by the need for quick decisions and consequent action. Learning facilitation as a briefing for decisions is governed by outside time factors – visits of government officials; requirements that agreements be reached. The embeddedness of this adult education practice in finite time is one of its features, experienced as time-dependent practice looking for decisions, permissions and planned actions to be pursued *on time* and within allocated learning time.

As a *spatial* experience the community development programme is organised around meetings at the centre of the Kununurra Aboriginal reserve. It is stated by the use of space – the makeshift shelter made by the men, which defines and amplifies the educational processes. As a general rule, the level of engagement is reflected in how close the participants get to the desk for the Aboriginal executive and the educator. The educator's task, defined spatially, is to get the participants to move closer to the desk rather than remaining on the fringe. Adult education practice involves inviting the people forward while at the same time informing and challenging them to decide. As a spatial experience, the adult education practice is sometimes 'being close' and sometimes 'being far'.

Adult education practice as a *social* experience is an experience of developing and maintaining relationships; of respect for people, friendship and protection of people's feelings. It is also about redefining and renegotiating the educator's role. Since I was already established as priest and pastor with authority, but above all with connections, the experience of facilitating learning about councils meant persuading compliance with my plan to step down so that the project could be taken up by their own executive.

Naming the adult education experience

'Being with' the learners

The phenomenon of adult education practice in this episode is experienced as a calling to meeting, proposing and laughing and 'being with' *en route* – like getting people into a boat and then pushing off and staying with them. It is experienced as an invitation to accompany the educator on a road that only he can see clearly; to learn procedures about meeting management and validation of group decisions, the reason for which is understood by the educator alone.

The experience of adult education practice in this episode is similar to the Moscow circus performance when a juggler rotated dinner plates on the tip of long rods held in a rack so that at one time about forty plates were spinning on their individual supporting rods. The circus performer had periodically to re-spin or realign one or other plate on its supporting rod as it threatened to slow down and fall off. In a similar way, the adult education experience is like constantly looping back, 'putting out fires', overcoming or managing confusion, conflict and lack of understanding.

The experience is like being a minder, hovering over the Aboriginal chairman to assist him in the unfamiliar territory of white bureaucracy. It is also like a lawyer talking, laying out the planned activities, setting up the garden, paying the workers, meeting the government representative.

It is thus uncovered as a one-man band with all kinds of slightly bemused dependants, exhilarating at first and increasingly exhausting as the elaboration of the project requires more work and more dissembling. It is like being a friendly sheep dog gathering the people together and keeping them there, then attempting to get them to learn about opportunities, gain skills in meeting management and group decision making, and negotiating with white officials.

Dealing and counter dealing

What I see in adult education practice in community development with the Miriwung is dealing and counter dealing – of the educator and the Miriwung people chasing each other to get a result, of consciously risking incomplete compliance with agreements for the sake of benefits to be gained, and even letting the learning agenda fade behind the entrepreneurial agenda. It looks to me like a chain of initiatives, reactions and subsequent actions followed by counteractions, almost like two fencers sparring for advantage.

The experience is the learning facilitator setting people up and the people in their way setting him up too, by not really buying his intervention but not discouraging him from persevering.

The phenomenon of adult education practice also looks like hunting for the 'learning button' in the participants while pushing the 'potential benefits button' at the same time. It means initiating and maintaining preliminary agreements to assemble; to make corporate decisions; to negotiate with white officials.

Adult education practice in this project with the Miriwung is also experienced as the people being attracted and held by scenarios and promises of benefit while being kept away from other white missionaries and social activists.

Grabbing and dancing, pushing and laughing

What comes to light when I focus on adult education practice in the garden project with the Miriwung is grabbing and dancing, pushing and pulling, laughing and remonstrating. The experience presents itself as huge outputs of energy from the learning facilitator and a kind of earthing of most of the energy in the minimal compliance from the learners, mixed in with an affable courtesy and friendliness.

It presents itself as a social steam-roller catching up and sweeping the people along – a kind of hectic high time with the educator talking and cajoling and dancing and challenging and reminding and repeating and acting out agreed actions in the company of the people, then looping back to explain and re-explain; and the people approving but not comprehending, going with the educator's enthusiasm in general without focusing on elements in particular. It shows up as a fast swoop, almost a stampede through a series of community organisation establishment processes – a kind of headlong rush to meet external deadlines proposed and approved in a non-negating kind of approval; the classic 'Isn't that so?' calling for an affirmation.

Kidding to learn

Adult education practice in this community development episode with the Miriwung people at Kununurra was like trying to kid them along to learn. It is like trying to wind them up like a self-starting device and letting them go. It is like trying to get a kid to learn to ride a bicycle and letting go before they realise they are on their own; like pushing a car with a flat battery until it gets up enough momentum to turn the engine over and get started.

The experience is noisy greetings and joking and suggesting and people being challenged to learn what they have been inveigled into agreeing to. The experience of adult education practice presents as cajoling and dancing and kidding and remembering and setting out procedures for the learners and prompting them. The experience looks like organising a huge marching band, engaged in amiable and benevolent passivity by the Miriwung people. I see adult education practice as the group looping into a kind of inward spiral, leading into a central point of focused attention, confronting community problems of poverty and malnutrition. I then see them spiralling out to generate agreement to the garden project, to forming a decision-making group, and negotiating with funding agencies to get financial support for machinery and wages and transport.

The phenomenon of adult education practice presents itself as getting people to carry out agreed roles and 'waiting for their learning engine to start' – for the members of the council to take initiative and responsibility for learning about the processes of the council and the garden project.

Making spaces

What shows up when I think of adult education practice in the garden project with the Miriwung is making frames and not filling in the details – suggesting activities outlined boldly in general and winning approval, in general, but not going into detail; leaving that to work itself out over time and leaving room in trust for the learners to fill in ways in which they might put into practice what they had been part of.

This experience of adult education practice was also one of trying to resist the temptation to 'do it yourself'; of initiating and standing back – of taking an initiative then letting the idea be shaped by the Aboriginal participants – backing and advancing, while knowing that at least in the beginning, the project is not of their choosing.

The experience tended also to be one of being alert and attuned to every sign of acceptance, distance, rejection – a turbulent process of constant checking and rechecking confidence and commitment – of selectively amplifying responses detected to various proposals.

This making spaces experience is like cooking a feast of linked possibilities – learning possibilities, enrichment possibilities, endowment possibilities – and offering them, garnished with jokes and promises of ongoing support, to the participants, hoping to entice them to try agreeing to one and then the other until a full consent can be made and built on.

Utopian colluding and concern

The experience of adult education practice is also like being in a fog of collusion. The experience of collusion also went to the ownership of the project that, while in the hands of the Miriwung, is again dependent for its survival on the adult educator's energy and commitment.

The amiable togetherness and the possibility of receiving resources in and with the project are accompanied by unspoken tensions between a host of feelings: fear, superiority, irritation, frustration, and not knowing the Miriwung language. Accompanying this as well is the still deeper sense of colonial superiority expressed in the unconscious assumption that 'what I know and do is better than what you know and do'. There is also a tongue-in-cheek feel to the experience, as if the educator and the educated were colluding in a kind of wishful fantasy – acting out roles on cue, writing letters, discussing tools and machinery as if vaguely hoping something would surely come of it. Adult education practice in this episode is also experienced as lip service, without full assent being given to the educator's assertions. Adult education practice means putting out the energy and tact required to protect the project from internal conflict and lack of continuity. But it also means allowing the project, which is developed in collaboration with them, to remain tacitly under the educator's entrepreneurial control.

Caught in one's own whirlpool: chaotic and stressful

Adult education practice is like setting up a kind of whirlpool and being caught up in it; experiencing contradictions in directly persuading people to take on a project defined and promoted as an enterprise of 'the Aboriginals themselves'. This adult education practice is experienced as chaotic and stressful: proposed actions being tabled and immediately implemented under time constraints; agreements being hastily secured almost after the activity requiring such authorisation had taken place. Adult education practice is like steps being retraced, explaining and re-explaining, people grouping and regrouping, deciding and re-deciding. It is like discussion and generation being overlaid with, and challenged by, unforeseen reactions, rejections, conflicts and tensions between group members and between emerging Aboriginal leadership.

The learning facilitation project, held up by the infrastructure of council meetings in which the learning is embedded, is experienced as slippery and risky and dependent on agreements and compliances also requiring energy, tact and support.

PANEL V: Distilling the experience

The following are themes that emerged in the adult education phenomenon.

- 'Being with' the learners
- Dealing and counter dealing
- Grabbing and dancing, pushing and laughing
- Kidding to learn
- Making spaces
- Utopian colluding and concern
- Caught in one's own whirlpool: chaotic and stressful

PANEL VI: Comment

As a lived experience, the limits of adult education practice, portrayed here as pursued using action-based method, are revealed strongly. The risks and enrichments of such initiative and cajoling strategies are manifest and humbling. Adult educators who aspire to control in their learning facilitation will need to reflect on the essential 'out of controlness' of adult education practice.

The experience of adult education practice in this episode foregrounded a sense of ultimate lack of control in learning facilitation. The learners' choice to use the truck as a general-purpose bus for the stakeholders in the project indicated that the continuance of the learning processes around the management and continuance of the Mirima council were not perceived to be as pressing as the immediate requirements of ceremonies and links with family and relatives.

While the process is revealed as chaotic, learners seemed to have managed to gain an important vehicle largely by learning how to keep the educator interested, and thus how to gain access to his resources.

As far as I was concerned, the experiences surrounding this project had a profound influence on my learning and later life choices. As a coloniser, a person placed over Aborigines, whose authority came from non-Aboriginal sources, my role impeded much that I wanted to do. I did not really object too much to being 'taken for a ride', since the truck was so evidently a hugely important resource deemed otherwise unobtainable. It was used for so many significant activities hitherto postponed due to lack of transport, and facilitated their moves to understand and engage meaningfully in their post-colonial world.

Nevertheless, I didn't want my educational role to be always subverted according to unspoken other agendas. I realised I could not readily pursue my community education vocation while I was located in a clerical position which was useful in many ways, but not in the egalitarian educational work. I needed to change the relations I had with the Aboriginal people and other non-Aboriginal people to something more equal and elective, but even if a more equal relationship developed, there was still the question of developing appropriate ways to work in response to Aboriginal people's real needs.

In terms of adult education practice, the experience left me with a desire to continue to support community development processes, while at the same time looking to establish programmes that would teach specific skills – literacy, maths, etc. – in a contractual and specific way to those who had developed a clear learning agenda.

Allied interpretations

The meanings emerging from the phenomenological account being worked towards in these pages complement meanings generated by more analytic approaches from social science. The question is to what extent such diverse approaches can serve to enrich each other and the reader. The following is a brief account of these interpretations where it is argued that the research approaches actually enrich each other.

The first interprets adult education practice as influenced by being a type of action-based teaching. The second looks at adult education practice in this setting as deeply shaped or even destroyed by the patterned ways Aborigines had developed to manage the encounters and agreements with their white mentors.

Action-based teaching and assumptions

As an enterprise to facilitate learning, the setting up of the Mirima council and the Mirima garden were, as we have seen, a form of 'push-start action-based teaching' – an activity set in train with a group of people under the initiative and direction of the educator. Ongoing engagement and simultaneous learning from the people were then expected until the project was finally handed over to them.

One of the challenging dimensions of experiential learning is that it can generate different outcomes from different participants. Educators usually attempt to prepare participants, and debrief afterwards to identify predicted learning outcomes. The further away the culture and background of the participants from the facilitator, the greater the likelihood that different outcomes will be experienced. This is particularly the case when large numbers of assumptions are made.

In the case under consideration, there were considerable numbers of assumptions that were not verified. One was that the thing being done would be 'valued equally' by initiator and follower, and that the follower would in fact want to give it the same priority when the initiator was not there.

The status of activities relating to the Mirima garden was also affected by the 'presence or absence of the initiator'. If he was present, activities related to the garden also related to the political relationships between the initiator and the Aboriginal men. If he was absent, the ordinary routines of gardening tended to be left to women who were not prominent members of the executive committee that had made the decision to establish it.

Patrons and riders

In reflecting on the exchanges of that period (cf. Willis 1980), I coined the phrase 'patrons and riders' to represent the character of the relationship. My patronage was generated by my clerical role and my capacity to bestow resources in a paternal way to those people identified as my 'clients' – those belonging to my group or mob. My capacity to bestow such favours was augmented by my capacity to broker agreements and goods and services from the Government. I was interpreted as would-be patron, inviting the Miriwung to participate in the action learning I had set up, from which Government benefits would come. I was not consciously aware that within the discourse of relationship such an invitation would be linked to earlier invitations to religious activity, and their acceptance of the invitation would be perceived as 'making me happy'. It would therefore depend on my being there and would have little meaning if I was absent.

The Miriwung people were called 'riders' in the phrase and not clients since, while at least partially accepting my invitation, they never totally accepted my patronage. They refused to become my grateful clients responding to my wishes, but because they did not want to offend me and because something good might eventuate, they 'went along' with the activities I proposed. They 'went for a ride' on the energy and direction of the project and got off when its course deviated from the path they wished to follow.

The failure of the action-based teaching approach in this case can be at least partially explained through the general 'Patrons and Riders' interpretation. This gives some rationale for the ambiguous collaboration and compliance of the Aborigines with their would-be educators and service providers. Applying this interpretation as a kind of code provides some rationale for the ambiguous collaboration and compliance of Aborigines with their would-be educators and community. What it does not show is what the experience of being an educator in such a situation is like. This is the contribution of the general phenomenological approach in its interpretative and intuiting forms.

This brief commentary, which juxtaposes the expressive phenomenological approach with the more analytical interpretations in the final Comment panel, gives a brief example of how each approach can enrich and serve the other.

The next installation moves from the East Kimberleys in North West Australia to Alice Springs in Central Australia.

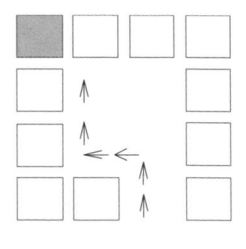

Chapter 5

Dead words and live politics

This fifth installation is set in Alice Springs. It relates to the experience of class-room teaching with a group of Aboriginal adults enrolled in a full-time pre-tertiary and pre-vocational programme sponsored by the Institute for Aboriginal Development (IAD) in the early and middle 1980s.

PANEL I: Backgrounding

IAD is an Aboriginal-controlled and owned adult learning centre in Alice Springs, originally established by the Uniting church to promote intercultural understanding between Aboriginal and non-Aboriginal Australians in Central Australia. It came under Aboriginal control in the early 1980s. It originally ran homemaking, nutrition and basic literacy courses for Aboriginal women who came into Alice Springs to have their babies. It also offered language and cross-cultural courses for non-Aboriginal people seeking to understand, and interact appropriately with, Aboriginal people in the course of work or community life.

The pre-tertiary, pre-vocational course under consideration here was introduced during my time of employment at IAD as an extension of the adult basic literacy programmes already offered. The subject I taught was called community education. It was an expansion of community development workshops already offered to Aboriginal groups. These explored the processes required to run an organisation within the larger community and societal structures of Australia. The courses looked at organisation processes such as meeting management, public speaking, organising a campaign and using the media. They also examined the social context of Alice Springs by looking at major service and commercial institutions, their structure, activities and decision-making processes, and their attitude to, and engagement with, the Aboriginal community.

The course was being offered during an unprecedented development of Aboriginal education and employment opportunities in the early eighties. There were opportunities for tertiary study for Aboriginal students who were not required to matriculate and who were able to receive additional tutorial assistance during their studies. Employment opportunities were growing as the Aboriginal health, housing, land and legal services expanded and pursued an active policy of recruiting Aboriginal workers. There was opportunity, and some pressure, for Aboriginal people to gain the skills the jobs required, beginning with basic literacy and numeracy combined with knowledge of the structure and function of the Australian society.

This full-time course was developed to meet this need. It was located in an airy, purpose-built building on the IAD grounds in Alice Springs. It was an approved course of study for which Aboriginal people could receive a weekly study allowance from the Federal Government.

IAD was required to furnish progress reports on the progress and attendance of students receiving the study allowance and other benefits. In the eyes of the Government, students were required to attend their course in a similar way to attending paid work when they gained employment.

Attitude and culture of the educator

By 1982 I had been employed at IAD for more than 2 years and had felt dissatisfied with the educational outcomes of small courses which I ran with Aboriginal communities about Australian society and ways of functioning within it. I felt that the required depth of communication skills and information needed a more sustained time, and supported the proposal to extend these workshops and combine them with extended work on literacy and numeracy development to make a full-time course.

I was excited at the prospect of working alongside Aboriginal adults in a deeper way. I saw this as having huge benefits to their self-esteem and to their opportunities for work and further study. I was hoping to adopt a facilitative style as an 'employed tutor' since IAD was an Aboriginal-controlled centre and I was employed by them to resource their learning projects.

I did not see myself as a didactic teacher or as having authority over the students. I saw myself almost as someone they had paid to provide assistance. I felt I would be free from the constraint I had experienced in adult education work at Kununurra when, as a missionary priest, I had felt unable to collaborate on an equal footing. Here, I felt, would be a way to avoid the sense of oppression usually characterising the relationship and exchanges between white teachers and Aboriginal students.

Attitude and culture of the learners

The recruited learners were men and women ranging from their early 20s to late 40s. A number of the women had extensive domestic duties they had to carry out while they were doing their study. The younger men and women had been unemployed for several years. They felt that their Aboriginality, as well as their lack of required skills, worked against them when competing for jobs.

On first meeting, their most noticeable feature was their buoyancy. They were merry, friendly and socially inclusive, and somewhat nervous about the possibility of having their lack of knowledge and expertise exposed.

Their attitude to me was open and accepting. When I defined myself as their employee, they pounced on the idea gleefully and often brought it up, partly in jest and partly as a demonstration of their awareness of strength through their affiliation with IAD and its Aboriginal management. Their attitude to learning and being a student was more ambiguous. In many cases they had major deficits in English writing and spelling which weighed on them and made their academic work seem very difficult, if not impossible.

Being a student had difficulties as well. The regular attendance required by the curriculum and the Government department responsible for their student allowances proved difficult. A number pointed out that they moved about a lot; that they were usually without money and depended on friends and acquaintances for transport which was unreliable. Managing the attendance requirements of the course tempted several into a range of deceptions and ambiguities that threatened the teaching/learning relationship.

The sponsor

IAD has been introduced already. The additional sponsor was the Federal Department of Education that funded the students' allowances on evidence of attendance and some progress in the course. Agents of this Government department visited regularly but were kept at arm's length by the IAD administration and individual students, all of whom were concerned to protect their privacy and ways of doing things from Government intrusion.

Issues

The major issues in this assisted learning programme have been mentioned in passing. There was widespread absenteeism and the consequent cover-ups and dissembling injected considerable ambiguity and instability into the teaching/ learning relationship. There were related issues of ill health, stress and alcoholism. Another issue was misunderstanding and fear based on experiences in the past. It was not uncommon for Aboriginal students to suggest that the teacher was 'thinking like a white' in moments of disagreement.

The adult educator seeking to be a 'contracted facilitator' was often placed in the position of arbiter and advocate. Some Aboriginal students would repeat patterns of irregular participation of their past school times. A related issue was the difficulty of maintaining the 'contracted facilitator' stance in the exchanges of the classroom. There were times when it seemed that the students had lost motivation to continue their studies. Some would arrive for class exhausted, sometimes with a hangover. At these times they would give no signal to indicate a continuance of the contract where I would be alongside and facilitative. This would tend to dispose me towards a mentoring 'reminding of our agreement' stance, which was a slight departure from the original agreement.

Another source of ambiguity was that the Aboriginal Board of Directors had expectations that the adult educators they employed would educate their students by the overall philosophy of Aboriginal control at IAD. There was thus an occasional issue of contradictory expectations in style between the students and the board of directors.

PANEL II: Sketching: health politics and visiting the hospital

It was about 8.30 a.m. The 14 or so Aboriginal students had gathered in their usual classroom for the day's activities. The morning would be a look at health ideas and systems in Alice Springs. The afternoon would be a planned visit to the hospital where the students would meet staff and be shown through the wards and operating theatres and other places and functions of the hospital.

The students took their accustomed seats in the carpeted one-room class-room. Outside, the Central Australian sun was already heating fiercely and the water-cooled air from the air conditioner vents in the ceiling was pushed down by ceiling fans, flapping loose papers and making their constant 'fwap, fwap, fwap' sound in the room. The women spoke to each other, exchanging news of family and friends. There was laughter over minor mishaps – cars breaking down and long walks in the dark. Someone's baby was sick; a young man had been gaoled for drinking in a public place. The students feared he would be mistreated by the police and listened to hear if his mother, auntie, grandmother had been able to visit him and see if he was all right. The assignments from last week were handed back with pencilled notes and comments. They would be discussed in private study time.

It was time to introduce the new topic: the health system in Alice Springs. Inside the community education curriculum, this topic explored Aboriginal and western ideas of health and healing, the various medical and dental services and the hospital where most of them had spent some time. Students were familiar with the Aboriginal Congress, a flourishing Aboriginal-controlled medical and dental service with a number of Aboriginal health workers, working with non-Aboriginal nurses and doctors. A number of Aboriginal students had been employed there as drivers and cleaners. The public hospital was not as well known, although a number of students had relatives who had worked there as gardeners and laundry hands. Arrangements had been made for the students to be given a guided tour of the whole complex.

I gave out some notes on health systems and services and pointed to a major distinction between preventative and therapeutic services. There was a pause and then Alan said,

'Peter, what's that word you just said, "thera-something"?'

I repeated it and said it was a version of the word 'therapy' which was pretty common. Alan said, 'Therapy eh.'

He turned to the other students and said, 'Do you use this word?'

There was a pause. He laughed and said to me, 'It's no good, Peter, that's not one of our words. That's a dead word. It's no good for us. Have you got a live one?'

They all laughed and I laughed with them, thinking on my feet. I then said, 'Well, it means there's one system to help people avoid getting sick. That's the preventative one – prevents illness. Then there's another system for curing people when they get sick (giving therapy), to make them well. That's the therapeutic system.'

Alan said, 'You mean this "thera-something" is all the services for healing people, making them get better?'

'Yes', I said.

'Well', he said, 'what's wrong with "healing services"? That's a live word.'

I grinned at him. 'Good point. You might need to know the word "therapy" though. You know, "physiotherapy", etc. But I suppose we can do without therapeutic.'

It was one of our constant amicable battles to maintain, extend, ground the lexicon of appropriate English which they could use in speaking (or already did), and could learn to write and use in their letters and essays. I found I could argue the case for the inclusion of a word provided I did not presume that it would be automatically accepted, and that I respected the cry of 'dead word' and argued for it or worked with them for a substitute. I would then be able to elicit an agreement so that I could refer back to the contract (or they could) where I was there to help them with *their* learning, which they assured me meant the learning they were choosing to pursue.

The key to this process was the constant referral back to the learning agreement about what the students wanted to learn and the nature of learning as the permanent taking on of particular forms of knowledge and skills which required some struggle to achieve.

We spent time preparing for the visit to the hospital which was planned for the afternoon. I had been discussing 'ways of being' in society – how men had staked out a claim for privilege over women in many things and that women, in order to reduce their inferior status, had had to analyse the way society was structured in language and decision making. We thought about how the class worked: how I was answerable to the Aboriginal director and he to the Aboriginal board. We talked about how IAD was structured to give Aboriginal people access to its board and decision making, and how it was concerned that people at the centre were treated respectfully. Pejorative words or 'put-down language' were frowned on.

Each student spent time formulating questions they wished to ask in preparation for the visit to the hospital. These were their own work and not discussed as such, nor were questions prescribed. It was to be their own inquiry. After lunch we took the IAD bus across town to the hospital where we were met by a senior registered nurse who had been deputed to show us around. We were ushered through various wards – the outpatients' clinic, the kitchen and huge laundry, where again some of the students or their relatives were or had been employed. We took the lift to the operating theatre, were shown the scrub-up room and the disinfecting machines and were then escorted to the maternity section.

At this point the sister gathered the group into an alcove and said that we had been shown most of the places and activities of the hospital and were there any questions. There was a pause and then Anna, one of the younger women, who had been making notes in her folder, said that she had a question. The sister turned to her expectantly.

'Who makes decisions in your organisation?' Anna questioned. 'I mean the decisions about policy and staffing and things like that?'

There was a pause. The sister, somewhat taken aback, said that she really didn't know. She herself answered to the matron but after that she wasn't sure. She thought that there was a board of directors over the whole hospital but she really wasn't sure. Anna reflected and then asked how people got to be on the board, and how many Aboriginal people were on the board. The sister said she would ask and let us know.

We returned to IAD and were able to pursue the question of what difference it makes to know about decision-making structures and processes, and how such questions had become important. The same young woman said she was employed occasionally by the Central Australian Aboriginal Media Association (CAAMA) which ran the local Aboriginal radio station, and that questions of decision making for Aboriginal people were of immense importance. She smiled at me and said the IAD had given her the chance to use her newly found skills and to think strategically about being Aboriginal – in other words, to build on the IAD course. Anna pursued her questions of the hospital and the class built up a small file on the decision-making structure of the health system.

PANEL III: Poetised reflection

Live words dead words

From fringe camp and state house
Aboriginal men and women come,
driven in their own minibus,
to start the day at college
with their tutor.

Some are missing,
(don't know where they are),
and some are back.
The group is different every day,
a different game, a different set of strings
in this guitar of learning.

And how to link, engage them
in their own learning place.
They grin and frown and call you in.
It's their own dance and learning,
and you've been hired to help.

Don't call it learning just like that.
Who's to say what all of us will do
with all that stuff you're serving up to us?
What's it mean? Where's it from?
How's it fit with what we know,
how we feel?
Don't give us dead white words

to make us feel bad, feel stupid
in our own place;
we want to learn to write
the words we use,
our own live words.

Well go on, it's ok.
We'll tell you when to stop
and how we feel – it's ok.

And you turn back to the lesson, careful
like taking a shy horse through traffic,
tense and eager, moving ideas forward gingerly,
ready to respond to eye, body, voice.

The energy momentum winds up,
moves laughter back and forth;
ideas from the teacher
batted back and challenged,
accepted, rejected, reinvented, renamed,
as appropriate knowledge,
made clear, distilled, revised, approved.

Then, moving from discussion's noisy space
to the private work of writing,
you are dismissed. Students,
caught up in the group's momentum,
push out into the unfamiliar textual lake
launched on a cockle shell
of new-found confidence and interest.

And as you come in turn to each,
words on paper hidden
by the writer's crooked arm.
The artefact of their learning,
Half-formed half-made,
pushes the limits of their new-found skill:
first try, second or third;
never tried it before,
never thought I could.

You try to hold a gossamer touch,
to safeguard confidence, enterprise.
You point to grammar, spelling,
work the sculptor's chisel. You assist
but keep back, careful not to come between
the writers and their final work
emerging from a sea of drafts.

Crushed in the minibus
for learning trips in town,
you cross the country
to factory, hospital, gaol,
drawing closer in the travelling hours.
You feel their lives of poorness and neglect;
their grace and courage in hard times.

And you see as well, a sharp attention
as they start to see, to know
that their life feels bad because they are excluded;
because they're black;
that there's nothing wrong with them;
the hurtful rejection and disdain they resist
is not just in their imagination.

In the bus's dark, enveloping fug,
an ark of safety feeds their optimism,
and you are honoured to be made
in Aboriginal house and land,
their guest and mentor.

PANEL IV: Intuiting the experience

The experience in body, space, time and social relations

As I dwell on adult education as a *bodily* experience, I see the experience as constant bodily movement. I am in motion, particularly back and forward to the students at their desks and up and down, sitting and standing: upright to communicate, to be free, visible and mobile; sitting to be less elevated, more receptive and on a level footing. I experience adult education practice also as backwards and forwards between the blackboard where I write and draw, and the middle of the classroom, where I read blackboard notes and headings I have just written, from a position among them.

The bodily experience in the one-to-one review, when the student discusses written work with the educator, is close and turned inward, protective of the student's privacy. The teacher's body is attuned to the student's body: attentive to and often partly unconsciously mirroring the student's bodily state. The body, tense to avoid offence, can become somnolent when the movement of ideas and language slows down.

In the frequent journeys in the IAD minibus, the bodily experience was of being compressed; of being initiated into close living with blankets, children, cigarette smoke and noisy conversation over the engine noise.

Adult education practice as a *spatial* experience is linked to the body. It is strongly influenced by being pursued in an Aboriginal-controlled adult learning centre. The experience is framed in the broad experience of being a guest/paid employee, allowed onto the employer's land to perform designated functions, after which to leave the space. In this context, the space is felt as somewhat constraining. Whereas in the cross-cultural education programme the educator is aligned with the Aboriginal people in charge of the centre and feels like an insider, here the experience is more ambiguous. In general bus rides and meetings, the space is friendly and welcoming. When tension mounts between ideas or procedures, however, the experience of adult education practice as a spatial experience carries with it a strong sense of being a stranger in a strange place.

Adult education practice as an experience *in time* has a sense of many starts and of interrupted and contested time. The experience of linear time, of lesson and curriculum planning and routine daily implementation, meets the experience of episodic time where time is interrupted: where there are many beginnings and repetitions as new people join the group, when some are absent for a few days, when others return. Adult education practice as an experience in time then becomes an experience of broken time. The experience of building up confidence to attempt a difficult task has to be built and rebuilt in the moving times of attendance.

Adult education practice as a *social* experience is perceived as seeking membership; being on trial; being welcomed; being challenged; receiving confidences; sharing sadnesses and bereavements. Adult education practice in this episode is to be incorporated into the group and to receive honour and obligations within that relationship. It is also about continuing the traditional teacher/pupil relationship inside the larger relationships of Aboriginal control of the learning centre. The experience includes that of assessing Aboriginal students, albeit under their invitation, but still to some extent in the traditional manner where the teacher is given the authority of expertise and provides some kind of grading assessment of the students' work.

Ways of naming the adult education experience
Building a utopian space
Adult education practice in this episode strikes me as being like a utopian space, laboriously constructed and defended for people who experience day-to-day life as hard and oppressive. It is like a reassurance that the educational process is OK – that it is honourable and possible.

It is like building a safe space in which the learning facilitative processes such as questioning, discussing, testing one's knowledge and skills, doing forecasts of what might be involved if a person were to engage in study, can be carefully and respectfully introduced.

It means inclusive waves of confidence and conversation being made, and the learning agenda being floated onto it without losing impetus and without losing its exchanges back and forth – questions, comments and the like.

A complicated, volatile coming together around learning
The phenomenon of adult education practice in this context presents itself to me as a complicated coming together around learning: a mixture of all kinds of invitations, appraisals, rejections, challenges, family-style fighting centred on

learning experienced and expected; a control-resisting phenomenon; the experience of control being wrested from the adult educator and somehow experienced as reassuring.

It is experienced as a positive and enthusiastic adult educator-reactive, participant-responsive, conversation-immersed confidence and optimism-building phenomenon.

It is like a protracted conversation in a noisy pub where people are forever joining and leaving the group, and where the point being pursued in the conversation is contested noisily, exuberantly and confidently by members of the group.

Being valued and challenged to make learning happen

This experience of being an adult educator is like value being given and a welcome extended to the educator with the belief that, with the help of this professional resource person, things can be made to happen.

It is like the Aboriginal students' world being opened, and quizzes and challenges offered, building on the affirmation and acceptance offered to make learning happen.

Diplomatic negotiation: making connections

I recognise the experience of adult education practice being like diplomatic negotiation. It is like connections being attempted with the participants to persuade them that learning is OK and possible; like negotiations being carried out to engage in the classroom processes, to write and to learn. This dimension remains a constant element in this episode of adult education.

Practising adult education with Aboriginal people in this episode is as a contracted tutor giving feedback and assessment to the contractees because it is in the contract and nothing to do with the contractor's status or inclinations.

Reassuring and protecting continuance

Adult education practice in this episode is also like a collaboration to generate trust between the educator and participants so that participants can feel able to interject, debate, disagree, joke, expose their knowledge and lack of it. It seems to be like keeping a conversation going to allay fear and build confidence; to shore up and strengthen the teaching/learning relationship; to protect it from being destroyed in the appraisal and assessment processes.

Making and maintaining momentum

The experience presented itself as keeping buoyant exchanges going in which ideas and experiences are discussed. It is like people picking up confidence, with the momentum generated in the exciting conversations giving them enough energy and confidence to attempt the otherwise unnerving solitary work of writing, and to see their writing work as drafting, with space for change and improvement.

Working with a draft means suggesting alternatives rather than saying things are wrong. It is like sculpting a text while it is being written so that learning facilitation is experienced as the gradual shaping of a text.

Madness and exuberance

What comes to light when I attend to practising adult education in this programme at IAD is an experience of madness, of exuberance; a maelstrom of good humour, debate, anger and political contestation.

Exposing, threatening and challenging

Adult education practice is like feeling unsure about the appropriateness of educational processes. The experience has a dimension of working with rawness. A sense of being exposed in the Aboriginal environment, unsure of the weight which might be given to remarks or comments about the assignment work when the students might have been traumatised by insensitive or hostile feedback during their previous schooling.

What unfolds for me when I dwell on adult education practice in this set is the experience of the teacher's cumulative sense of self revelation – as being there for these students – frustrated by absenteeism and fostered by bus trips and lengthy time together.

Flying a hang glider

I depict adult education practice in this context as a group of wounded aviators, persuaded to launch a hang glider big enough to hold them in the air, but leaving them vulnerable to many forces, unable to recover if something goes wrong and with the knowledge that an accident would open old wounds.

The experience of adult education practice is like a soap bubble of confidence and inter-racial collaboration, inflating with huge hopes and excitement married to extreme vulnerability. In its fragility, the experience is like flying a hang glider knowing that sudden turbulence could collapse it beyond retrieval; or like riding a skittish horse through heavy traffic – the simile used in the poem.

PANEL V: Distilling the phenomenon

The following list of recurrent themes emerges in the intuiting process.

- Building a utopian space
- A complicated, volatile coming together around learning
- Being valued and challenged to make learning happen
- Diplomatic negotiation: making connections
- Reassuring and protecting continuance
- Making and maintaining momentum
- Madness and exuberance
- Flying a hang glider

PANEL VI: Comment

This experience of adult education practice was significant in my professional history since it was the first episode where the adult educator was not accorded largely uncontested authority over both the processes and the content of the educational project. Here the adult educator had a kind of conditional authority that had to be constantly renegotiated. Another significant feature of this episode was that unlike earlier examples, there were considerable expectations about the project's outcomes. Aboriginal students wanted to gain skills and knowledge so they could carry out a range of tasks in their world. They enrolled in the course and placed expectations on the process that it would provide them with the needed skills. In their minds, the success or failure of the process was directly linked to the action of the teacher. The experience was thus far less open-ended in its direction. In the end, the learning experiences were required to generate skills and knowledge to a certain standard of performance.

This outcomes-focused agenda was linked to strong expectations as to the deportment of the teacher who had to fit in *and* make a difference. The experience was most fraught as well as most rewarding, leaving vivid and touching memories.

A major issue in this experience was the contested nature of learning and its facilitation. The experience brought out complexities in the 'teaching and being taught' experience and highlighted emerging themes in the experience of practising adult education.

This installation also highlights the importance of the preliminary and then constantly renewed engagement between adult educator and the enrolled participants, as well as the influence of the contextual elements: the sponsor, the course itself and the physical and socio-political environment. This experience of adult education practice was to bring out considerable additional complexity when the project involved inviting defensive but hopeful participants to become active learners, with clear skills and knowledge to be learned to a recognisable standard.

One of the significant elements in the experience of adult education practice was the central part played by momentum generation: the importance of getting a process going that would encourage participants to engage in learning generative processes like writing, reading and calculating. This seems true especially when, as is often the case in literacy, the teaching/learning processes are experienced as difficult and mysterious and enormously time consuming, and where improvement seems to take such concentrated effort over such a long time.

This episode of adult education practice brought out its dimensions as a kind of warming-up and psyching-up for the battle of learning. On reflection, this seems to recur in many if not all episodes of facilitated adult learning, only not necessarily in so visible a fashion.

We move now to an episode of cultural awareness education which also took place at IAD.

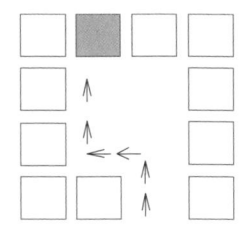

Chapter 6

Dusty journeys at IAD

This form of adult education practice was a cultural awareness programme to assist people understand the Aboriginal world. Like the previous event, it took place in the early and middle 1980s at the Institute for Aboriginal Development (IAD) in Alice Springs.

PANEL I: Backgrounding

Context

Besides the courses for Aboriginal adults, which were the main concern of IAD, it also sponsored several cultural awareness programmes each year for non-Aboriginal people to get to know the Aboriginal world and to gain some insight into ways of improving communication and collaboration between Aboriginal and non-Aboriginal people.

The immediate sponsor of the programme to whom I was immediately responsible, was the Aboriginal director, a Yankunytjatjara elder who had been an interpreter with the founder of IAD. He valued the opportunity for open conversations between Aboriginal and non-Aboriginal people, particularly to foster empathetic understanding of each other's cultures, values and customs, and to dispel misinformation and misunderstanding.

The early 1980s were a time of great political development for Aboriginal organisations. There was considerable movement in land claims and an upsurge in Aboriginal confidence and political power. During that time Aboriginal people in Central Australia learnt how to use legal processes to protect their rights and advance their interests. A backlash movement called Citizens for Civilised Living attempted to mobilise public opinion against Aboriginal people and generated considerable national criticism.

The educator

As mentioned earlier, I had come to IAD very much wishing to work in an environment where there would not be too much white dominance. IAD had an Aboriginal director whom I admired, and an interest in win-win collaboration with non-Aboriginal people. My attitude was optimistic. I believed that empathetic conversations between Aboriginal and non-Aboriginal people, combined with serious reflection on one's possible unwitting collusion with prejudice and racism, could lead to a change of heart and changes of behaviour in civil life.

The learners

Participants in these cultural awareness workshops were recruited largely from human service organisations in Central Australia and beyond. There were people from government and private service providers such as the police, the health and welfare departments, the Commonwealth employment service and a number of churches and education providers. There were also socially aware activists and interested citizens in the group. The attitude of participants ran from sentimentalised glorification of Aboriginal culture from a small number, to hostility from participants required by their employer or superior to attend (also mercifully, a small number).

The processes

The cultural awareness programme took about 20 participants (which was the maximum) in a bus to spend a weekend with Pitjantjatjara people at Finke, an Aboriginal settlement several hours drive from Alice. The group was met by an Aboriginal guide who showed the people where to camp and organised conversations and visits to various points of interest on the settlement – store, clinic, church, school. The visitors were also taken hunting for kangaroos and digging for honey ants and witchetty grubs. There was a barbecue in the evening with some traditional Pitjantjatjara dancing and singing. On Sunday morning there was a Christian church service to which the visitors were invited, followed by a discussion with some of the Aboriginal people, where questions could be raised.

The people returned to Alice Springs on the Sunday evening, and then spent the next week in discussions, debriefings, films and presentations from Aboriginal leaders in Alice about matters of health, law, land, religion and civil life. At the end of the week the group again took the IAD bus, this time to a local restaurant to celebrate the completion of the programme.

Assessment was left to the individual person. It was rather like attending a church retreat, which of course had been one of the sources of the workshop's original design and impetus. Towards the end of the course, the participants carried out an evaluation in which they reflected on their experiences and their learning, and made written comments about the course. Most of these were favourable, although from time to time the irritation (particularly of those constrained to attend) would come out.

Issues

There were two major issues. One was that the curriculum of the cultural awareness workshops aimed to generate empathetic conversations around issues of misinformation and misunderstanding. This was appropriate for favourably disposed participants seeking information about facts and figures and an understanding of the different emphasis given to cultural practices like funerals, borrowing and lending, being on time, etc.

There were, however, often one or two irritated or angry participants, particularly from those who had been directed to attend, who were resistant to, even prejudiced against, any empathetic feelings or insights that might otherwise have arisen. The course was then challenged to cope with considerable negativity and resistance for which it was not fully designed, and to cater for the distress that some brought to the group, which required deeper and most probably almost therapeutic processes for which the programme was not prepared.

Besides those with negative feelings, there were others who had experienced a range of encounters with Aboriginal people, some of which they interpreted in ways that differed from the approach of the course presenters. These alternative interpretations would often convert the times allocated to small group discussion and meditative reflection to strong debate. The workshop was also not well equipped to understand, argue for and insist on the empathetic stance required, and to persuade those wishing to argue and debate to pursue their agenda elsewhere.

With the background in place, the set moves to its second component, the sketch. It is called 'Tickets for the Harley'.

PANEL II: Sketching: tickets for the Harley

There were about 20 people in the IAD course. A number of missionaries on their way to their first posting with Aboriginal people had registered. There were men and women employed in welfare and service organisations: Commonwealth Employment Service, Community Health, Community Welfare, the hospital and the gaol; a small group of women who had come to Alice Springs to a women's camp-out protest at the American surveillance installation at Pine Gap just outside the town; two police officers, one an athletic young man who had been recently posted to Alice Springs, the other older, with some years' experience in the region.

The young police officer was extroverted and articulate. He offered his opinions confidently about the importance of having 'one Australia' for everyone; that anyone who really wanted a job could always find one; and that there were certain things, 'pursuits' in the world, which naturally fell to men, like public life, engineering, medicine and police and military work. There were others like cooking and rearing children that were best done by women. He was puzzled why Aboriginal people could not just get out and get a job and a house like he had done.

His comments appeared to be founded on an unshakeable assumption that the way society was set up was good as it was, and the way things were was the way they were supposed to be. He had difficulty going through the reflexive processes of the course and, in one exercise in which participants were invited to explore what being 'white' meant, complained that he couldn't see the point. His frequent reference to the women on the course as 'girls' (to correspond to his reference to himself and other men as 'boys') irritated some of the women, who more than once attempted to suggest alternative language and points of view.

The length of the workshop – 5 days plus the introductory journey and 'camp-out' at an Aboriginal settlement, gave time for people to get to know each other and for some disagreements, friendships and their opposites to emerge.

As the facilitator, I had confidence in the workshop's formal processes which I had developed from earlier programmes. It had talks from Aboriginal leaders and experienced non-Aboriginal community workers and anthropologists, with linked discussions around set and open-ended questions. The open discussion times were designed to provide an informal process through which the aims of cultural awareness could also be achieved. On the last day of the course there was an evaluation session in which, again, the young police officer asserted that he couldn't really believe there really was such trouble between Aborigines and whites. He suspected it might have been a 'beat-up' from the city journalists.

During one of his loud, cheerful remarks, it became clear that the three women who had come to Alice Springs for their Peace camp were being goaded almost beyond endurance. During the coffee break, one of them said to me that the young police officer's remarks were offensive and irritating and had really made the workshop difficult.

I then asked the women in their small cluster if it was possible, in the spirit of cultural awareness, to develop a way to understand police, and in this case male, culture. There was a disconcerted pause and then one of the women said that although this might assist her in understanding where he was coming from, it was clear to her that the white patriarchal regime privileged his culture and aspirations. It was unfair and oppressive to women, and of course to Aboriginal people, and that she had better things to do with her time as, she felt, had Aboriginal people.

I pointed out that, at least in this course, Aboriginal people whose current situation was indeed linked to the inequities and prejudices of the white system allocated some resources and time to expressing and explaining their way of being in the world to members of the white culture, even though it was evident they had much to work on with their own people.

At this point we were interrupted by the young police officer who joined the women from the side while I moved some distance away. I could see him animatedly showing a photograph of a shiny Harley Davidson motorcycle which, he explained, was the first prize in the police raffle being drawn soon, and would they like to buy some tickets.

The women during the week had explained the ideological stance that drew them to the Pine Gap protest camp. They had spoken of attempting to develop inclusive, more ecological symbols for their life and work together, like certain flowers and moving water. They spoke of the great circle in which each was accorded space and time to be heard. The Harley, with its black and gleaming chrome and its surrounding aggressively male 'bikey' culture as a symbol, beat across the women's sensibilities. They refused his offer with the coolness which had characterised their earlier exchanges with him over the week, once they felt they had not been able to achieve an understanding. On the bus going out to the final celebratory dinner, the officer, although with few tickets sold, pronounced the week-long workshop a great idea. 'Everyone should do it!'

As the adult educator presiding over the last moment of that course, I had to realise that there was still plenty of room for improvement.

With the sketch completed, the next element in the set is the poetised reflection, with much to think about.

PANEL III: Poetised reflection

Cross Culture

You greet the latest student group,
at the Aboriginal learning centre.
The Yankunytjatjara director, dignified and friendly,
bids them welcome; bids them listen.
At the course's start
you invite introductions, expectations,
and look for hints of predisposing stance:
interest, resistance, collusion.
Your agile eye, including smile and joke,
moves to form the learning group,
find out what they bring
to mix into the course's alchemy.
You spot reluctant learners
already shaped by years with Aboriginal people
on station, settlement or town;
directed by their employer to attend,
suspicious and resistant in the course.
Others you reassure
who bring interest, hesitation,
whose paths have never met or crossed
the Aboriginal world; excited and
alive to possibility,
bringing nothing to forget.
+ + +

You share the long bus journey
and camping near the settlement.

You walk with the visitors past Aboriginal houses
and store and church: children playing easy
in the sand, dogs in every camp.
You invite the learners to be open;
you watch for the signs of doubt or question.
You listen as the Aboriginal speakers
welcome all the guests and talk
of 'country' and their culture,
what they do and what they hold as sacred
in their world. And you keep watch
as the strangers are attracted
or enchanted, repulsed or confused.

+ + +

In the classroom back in town,
reflecting on the settlement visit;
attentive to compassion, insight, irritation,
you listen for puzzled half-formed questions,
hoping for resolution in the days ahead.

And now you hope the Aboriginal speakers,
commissioned to explain
their life in white Australia,
show eloquence and forbearance
as you sit tense and watchful.
You note the students' comments and reactions
as the living landscape of life together,
Aboriginal and white, begins to show
its tracks and intersections and its scars.
You try to move from information and debate,
listening for how the people feel
in the course's different times and places.
You lead them to confront whiteness:
privilege entrenched in race,
uncomfortably exposed, contested,
in the stories and reflections of the week.
And at the workshop's end, most speak of moments
of awareness and change. An angry few write of wasting time,
of being gracelessly subjected to exercises without meaning
and being harangued by angry Aboriginal leaders
whose jobs, they think, are paid for
by the 'white system' that they, at least verbally, reject.
You know heart movements are hidden unless displayed;
you look for signs of empathy and attunement;
like when conversation or debate
resonates in compassion
with Aboriginal voices once briefly heard.

And then you bring the risky two-edged meeting
to an end; hoping for some signs
that all the conversations, visits and debates,
have made a mark and wrought
some soul change, compassion, transformation.
You pack up the textas and butcher's paper
ready for next time's people.

PANEL IV: Intuiting the experience

The experience in body, space, time and social relations

As I dwell on adult education practice as a *bodily* experience, I feel tension, dust, mobility. The experience involves me standing, greeting, sitting in the bus, greeting and setting out the camp site, walking around the settlement, walking with the gathering women and riding with the hunting men. In the classroom, the body becomes the instrument of order, standing to welcome, to take questions; and the instrument for engagement, sitting to join groups moving in various simulation games.

The *spaces* in this experience are not constant. The original settlement experience confronts me with expanding and contracting spaces between the educator and the participants. They contract when the participants huddled in a circle with the educator leading discussions. They expand when the learners move around the settlement and become opened to each other and the messages and spatial experiences of the settlement: when they watch the plastic bags and papers blowing and caught in the piled-up sand at the sides of graded dirt roads; when they feel the red dust and see the corrugated iron fences, unpainted sheets of house and shed walls; crows, black shapes near the store rubbish bins and their desolate cawing in the early afternoon.

Adult education practice as a *time* experience has lots of waiting in it. The waiting at the beginning and then the long trip in the dusty bus and then waiting in what shade can be found when the bus first arrives at the settlement, until an Aboriginal guide can be roused. There is also the sitting on rolled swags at the camp site waiting for the planned programme to get under way. In the subsequent classroom interaction, time has a different, more urgent feel, linked to the experience of risk and the sense of building tension on the one hand, and the experience of tedium on the other, when speakers go over time and the engagement of the participants seems to evaporate into a kind of torpor.

The experience of *social relations* in this episode of adult education practice is characterised by the unstable interactions of various groups. The participants do not have a stable relationship with one another or with the educator or the Aboriginal presenters. The Aboriginal presenters have an unstable relationship with the educator, the participants and the groups with which the participants are affiliated; for example, some Aboriginal presenters find it difficult to treat police officers and correctional service workers from the gaol as if they are just participants in the course. The trust, respect and affection the educator gives to the participants tend to be spasmodically reciprocated and mixed with episodes of hostility and distrust.

This episode of adult educational practice manifests what can be experienced when the educator is attempting to generate a particular kind of learning by exposing participants to direct experiences and attempting to shape their responses. The following comments explore some of the emerging themes in adult educational practice that are strongly evident in this episode.

Ways of naming the adult education experience

Contesting hearts and minds

Adult education practice in this episode is intuited as being in fierce contest for minds and hearts while at the same time struggling to display inter-cultural respect; of dragging, mobilising people who are physically present but may be ideologically removed from the necessary empathetic disposition required for the course to be useful.

Adult education practice in this context is experienced as highly normative in the way processes are set up and the 'right' way to engage is modelled by the educator.

Trusting the process and the learner

Adult education practice is like being immersed in an orchestrated group experience and subsequent debriefing processes with limited control and authority. It is where the learner's ability to choose the outcome preferred is respected, and a gamble taken that reluctant participants can learn empathy from the actual experiences of living alongside Aboriginal people.

Offerings: things close to one's heart

The experience of adult education practice in this episode is like introducing a friend to another friend and hoping they will like each other; standing tensely as they engage and, at least in the early stages of the encounter, trying to clear up misunderstandings and facilitate clear communication.

The experience also feels like offering fine old wines to new drinkers and having to educate their palates and their taste at the same time as exploring the wine.

Indirect pedagogic tact and opportunism

The experience of adult education practice presents itself to me as oblique and indirect. Desired changes are modelled, described, discussed but never demanded.

The experience is also one of 'pedagogic opportunism'; of 'going with the flow' that is generated by putting people together under the 'cultural understanding rubric'; of working to shape the flow as it evolves, trying to protect participants and Aboriginal resource people involved while supporting the energy of the process.

Working within conflict

The phenomenon of adult education practice in this episode is like sponsoring discussions between conflicting Aboriginal and non-Aboriginal people during a fragile 'cease fire'; attempting to broker and moderate conversations between the participants, permanently risking conflict and withdrawal from the exchanges due to memories, prejudices and fears of both parties.

The experience is also like being vulnerable to being taken over by relevant hostile participants in the course, who might resist the party line and argue against tolerance and collaboration.

Having little control

Adult education practice presents itself as being in a new and strange world at close range; seeing learners react to encouragement to overcome their reluctance to get involved.

The adult education experience is like accepting helplessness; of having little influence over what the participants think, judge, conclude and learn; of surrendering control for the sake of the experiential process; of risking misunderstanding and resistance and having low control over the learning outcomes.

Needing to please and no assessment

The experience is like being put on trial by the participants, who of course pay money to attend. It is like putting out different elements from the learning facilitative menu, seeking to engage their learning palate while not offending them or directly assessing or measuring their learning.

PANEL V: Distilling the phenomenon

This panel now provides a space to distil major themes.

- Contesting hearts and minds
- Trusting the process and the learner
- Offerings: things close to one's heart
- Indirect pedagogic tact and opportunism
- Working within conflict
- Having little control
- Needing to please and no assessment

PANEL V: Comment

This installation was long in its gestation and has raised considerable challenges in writing. In the cumulative backgrounding, story telling and poetising, the phenomenon of adult education practice was made vividly present. The phenomenon of attempting to generate specific kinds of learning from an orchestrated set of experiences in the workshop is shown in all its risk and energy and complexity.

In the 'mobilising for learning' of earlier sets, adult education had no class-room and the participants were grouped for action as well as learning. The adult educator's experience involved all the things occurring in the attempt to expand the focus on action to include learning.

By contrast, this installation presents the experiences that took place with a group of participants already mobilised to engage in some kind of learning. The learners were enrolled in a gazetted course but there was still a strong element of passivity and persuasion. It was not the same change agenda as had been in the earlier episodes. The change agenda involved attempting to persuade participants, who had deliberately enrolled in a learning course, to adopt a learning stance offering respect for Aboriginal people, their culture and their history at the hands of white colonisers. The experience was thus about the attempt to generate deep and empathetic learning, rather than surface or rote learning (cf. Biggs 1989), within an agreed learning generative activity.

The drama metaphor

The experience of adult education practice in this episode calls to mind setting up and running a stage play – a dramatic presentation. The adult education activities parallel those of the playwright, producer, director and one of the lead actors. The adult educator can also be the master of ceremonies, intro-ducing new acts and possibly interpreting their significance to the audience; the stage hand moving the props; the front-of-house usher making sure patrons are seated and comfortable; and an internal critic, appraising the play and the performers for ongoing improvement and consulting members of the audience for their reaction.

Following the stage play metaphor of the experiences surrounding producing a stage play, the adult educator is not only positioned as writer and director, but also as one of the main actors, seeking rapport with the audience; communicating feelings, ideas and information; and generating response from heart to heart, to mind and to feelings. Whereas drama tends to stop with the footlights, adult education can lead to change being chosen and acted upon after the play is over.

The actor adult educator is also revealed as part evangelist. The agenda is to inform, to reassure, to recruit. The adult educator experience also includes prompting patrons to be aware of the genre of the workshop – 'this is a listening with the heart', not just an arena of debate and information. This precarious monitoring experience involves observing, interpreting and guiding participants about the weight, import and significance of things seen and heard.

The adult education experience also involves carrying out a critique of the performance of the stage performers and the learner participants. From this perspective, the adult education practice in this episode is like street theatre, where the actors recruit participants from the audience to play informal parts and become part of, rather than spectators of, the action, and where the agenda is to inform, to critique and to generate change.

Thus, if expressive research of this kind can be presented using the metaphor of an exhibition, the adult education practice being researched in this way has a parallel metaphor as a stage play.

With this installation completed, we move to an experience of workplace training: a third episode of adult education practice also pursued at IAD.

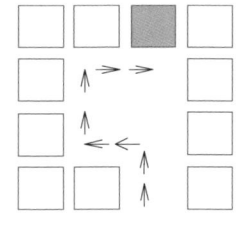

Chapter 7

The flight of the pelican

The following installation is the third adult educational experience located at the Institute for Aboriginal Development (IAD). It concerns training Aboriginal IAD employees to become adult educators. The sketch from this set is derived from a paper written closer to the event and published under the same title as this chapter (cf. Willis 1986, p. 32). This installation has been modified to allow the format of the sketch to include various contextual elements that were woven into it in its original form. The backgrounding section is reduced to a brief exploration of the adult educator's attitude.

PANEL I: Backgrounding: on-the-job training at IAD

By the time this episode occurred, I had been at IAD for 5 years. I had run community development and community management programmes, and cultural awareness courses like the one described in the previous chapter. I had also run community management programmes for isolated Aboriginal groups, as well as being involved in the community education programme described earlier. The IAD community had wanted to increase its Aboriginal adult educators, a policy I strongly supported, thinking this would help to overcome difficulties and complications due to most of the adult educators in the Aboriginal-controlled adult learning centre being non-Aboriginal. The experience of adult education practice in such a context was challenging and fraught. Aboriginal adults, while entering various learning projects which would strengthen their ability to manage their personal and work lives, often resented being taught by non-Aboriginal people in their own centre. Working with Aboriginal trainees was thus an innovation I had welcomed. The senior trainee was a relative of one of the leading Aboriginal students in the community education course and was a confidant and mentor to other students as well. I was pleased and honoured that he and his colleague would join our programme but I was worried about how the transition from 'colleague' to 'trainee' would be managed.

The sketch that follows tracks the learning facilitative strategy that emerged from within the training exchange of offering a space where the trainees could almost manage their own training. The experience of adult education practice was largely making a space and clearing the obstacles so that the trainee, like a pelican in a shrinking waterhole, could find enough room to spiral into take-off.

In Australia's remote regions, towards the end of the dry season, pelicans (large water birds with long wings) are forced to smaller and smaller water holes in search of food. When a pelican takes off from a small lagoon, it puts out tremendous effort as its huge wings thrash the water and air. The bird traces a wide spiral in the narrow water space to gain maximum runway. Once airborne, even slightly, it seems to relax immediately as if to rejoice in the achievement of flight. The pelican will often fly in slow, graceful, concentric circles as if savouring its achievement and deciding whether to continue upwards or to return to the water. If it decides to fly, the bird spirals upwards, effortlessly gaining height until it catches a thermal wind and then floats serenely on its way. Two things seem to help in the struggle: the memory of the joy of flight, and the consciousness that even when one inch above water it is already flying.

This case study is a personalised account of the discovery of an inductive method of adult education training for Aboriginal adult educators which has helped to get them 'airborne'. Trainees may be hesitant if they do not know what it will be like to take on the role they are being trained for. In this case, there were no Aboriginal adult educators to share experiences, and the experience and testimony of white educators was not always seen as relevant, due to differences in culture and status. This was the situation for the first Aboriginal adult education trainees in the Community Development section of the Institute for Aboriginal Development in the middle 1980s.

The community education programme at IAD was one of the programmes concerned particularly with skilling Aboriginal people to make up for unsatisfactory schooling and preparing them to take the many jobs provided by Aboriginal organisations. Aboriginal and non-Aboriginal educators from this programme taught a one-year, full-time, social action course in the Institute's community education programme for Aboriginals wishing to update their literacy, numeracy and general social knowledge.

The Institute had an active policy of Aboriginalisation. Suitably qualified and experienced Aboriginals were urged to apply for vacant positions. In addition, under special provisions of the central Government's job training scheme, Aboriginals could become adult education trainees. It was hoped that eventually they would inherit positions then held by whites. During their training, trainees received wages equal to the base grade of the salary they would receive if they were qualified. This introduction to employment status was thought to be a major incentive for Aboriginal people who had no similar prior experience.

To be a trainee as an adult can be difficult, particularly if one's fellow workers are not. One may feel like a second-class citizen, a poor cousin or not quite an adult. Feelings of being marginal can destroy other positive feelings, especially when the training programme looks complicated, heavy and parental, and when the person in charge of the training comes from a different background.

The following story explores this experience.

PANEL II: Sketching: training at IAD

Many things can go wrong when the trainer belongs to the colonisers and the trainees to the colonised. This was the case at the Institute for Aboriginal Development in 1984 when two adult education trainees joined our Community Development section. We had to cross barriers of race, class and culture between trainer and trainees. I was Anglo-Australian, middle-class, almost over-educated, from an urban background where class segmentation meant I had never met Aboriginal people, let alone people who were not somewhat like myself. Both trainees had known poverty and hard times. They had left school early and had grown to adulthood in the central part of Australia where community relations were often hostile and where Aboriginals and whites seemed natural enemies.

The two trainees had high ideals about Aboriginal development. The senior trainee had been profoundly influenced during 2 years of study at a city college far from Alice Springs. He had a highly developed sense of rightness; a taste for beauty and goodness. These assets, which he brought to a job about which he knew little at first, formed the basis for his commitment to adult education training.

The training programme was organised in two parts. The trainees were to enrol in a part-time formal course in adult education, teaching at a local community college. The rest of their time was to be spent in on-the-job training as adult educators in the Institute's programme. The trainees enrolled in the teaching course for adult educators at the community college and attended the first of the weekly lectures. The course was designed for tradespersons who had taken teaching jobs at the college and needed qualifications and skills in adult education.

The lecturer was courteous. He explained that the course used a competency-based approach and identified the expected outcomes of the course: the things graduates would be able to do that they could not do now. He talked about various types of learning outcomes, about attitudes and knowledge and skills. The trainees vividly remember his reference to psychomotor skills. This specialist jargon seemed to symbolise the alien and unapproachable nature of the enterprise, at least in the way the trainees experienced it. The trainees never returned to the college, although they still came to work. It was to be on-the-job training or nothing.

When back at the Institute, the trainees were not sure what to do. Not only did they not know at first how to perform the adult educator's duties, but they did not practise my 'white' kind of time and task planning. It was difficult for them to plan ahead and commit themselves to future action on a certain day. I was torn in two ways. I had to care for my work in the growing and turbulent community development section and, at the same time, provide training to the trainees. Moreover, neither I nor the trainees seemed very happy about our training relationship.

Even though we all lived in Alice Springs, our worlds differed radically. As a white middle-class man from another part of Australia, my home life, my interests and my language were different. Neither did I have the same network of relatives whose history and needs would impinge on mine, whose family disagreements with other families would involve me and affect my work. In close quarters, other variables intruded on the trainer/trainee relationship. Our office was crowded. There were lots of phone calls, and activity requiring action for which they were not prepared. The trainees were not happy. They complained they did not feel 'located' in the sense of knowing where they were going. I was not happy, either, feeling that the trainees were not being trained, were not changing into my idea of adult educators.

This sense of dissatisfaction lasted until we became involved in the events surrounding the National Aboriginal Day. This was a turning point because it introduced a more inductive method of training, more suitable in cross-cultural situations. It was like the beginning of the flight of the pelican.

The NADOC parade

National Aboriginal Day is important for all Aborigines and yet at the time of this episode in the mid-1980s, many Aboriginals did not participate for a variety of reasons.

In 1984, the adult education trainees were approached by the IAD board of management to set up a community development exercise to increase the assertiveness and confidence of the Aboriginal students attending the various courses at the Institute. The project was to centre around the preparation of a float to head the NADOC procession through Alice Springs. The trainee adult educators were to use community development techniques to mobilise the students. The hope was that the students would make a declaration of support for the Aboriginal community of Alice Springs and a claim for social justice, equality and respect for Aboriginal culture. The challenge for the students was to stand on the float, with all its statements and banners, to show their pride in being Aboriginal and their commitment to improving community relations. Many were reticent about such assertive behaviour. They used the phrase 'shame job', meaning shameful. They were non-committal.

The senior trainee went to the adult educator in the home management course and asked if students in her sewing class would make banners 'for the march'. He also asked to have the banner making take place in the main seminar room since most students went through it to the tea-room. The chosen decorations were symbols of the Arrente people to which the adult education trainees belonged and on whose traditional land Alice Springs was built. Many Aboriginal students had links with Arrente people.

When the students stopped to look on their way to the tea-room, the senior trainee gave them paint and asked for ideas. The junior trainee passed the word that all students could make a symbol or poster. The seed grew. More people stopped to draw a poster or to paste up photographs. The senior trainee was unobtrusive. He asked for ideas, looked for assistance, praised those who helped. Work on the decorations pre-empted regular classes. Students freed from study were buoyant and creative. The day before the march, a giant semi-trailer arrived to be transformed into a float. The poster makers and decorators wanted to see how their decorations would go over, but some still hung back from the great display float as their children swarmed over it. The two trainees climbed aboard and within seconds the trailer was full of people on their way to celebrate their own 'coming out'.

There was no doubt that the two trainees had pulled off an adult education exercise concerned with 'social integration' and 'social responsibility'. But they had not formulated a plan, nor had they identified themselves categorically as adult educators. They had not drawn up a programme. This was to come much later. They had hesitatingly begun the *process* and, like the pelican, they had taken off first in a small spiral with the option of returning to the water (withdrawing from their educator role) and then, with increasing confidence, expanded and intensified the initial process which widened progressively with gathering support. The direct feedback from the growing adult learning group encouraged the two trainees to put more energy into the process until the exercise became a fully fledged learning exchange attuned to the Aboriginal style and with the pitfalls minimised. Carrying out the exercise gave the trainees direct access to the reality of adult learning. It was experienced directly rather than mediated through the eyes and words of the white trainer.

In some ways, the gradual involvement of people – the doors left open, contracts unsigned – was to unleash a sense of glee: to do something because it is good fun, beautiful, great! In that aesthetic moment the difficulties in communication and collaboration between coloniser and colonised, lower class and upper class, white and Aboriginal, were lifted. We were no longer looking at each other. We were focused on the shared task of raising consciousness and involving the Aboriginal students in an adult learning/becoming enterprise. It was as if in the space and encouragement provided to develop their own adult education programme with the Aboriginal students, a strategy emerged that they could use with the Aboriginal students and I could use with them.

I then tried to follow the same strategy in which hesitancy could be transformed into confidence. I tried to provide the trainees with ways to 'taste' processes as well as outcomes, and then to evaluate them before being committed to them. This meant putting a spiral in place of the linear path of western technological decision making, where the value of the outcome is the main criterion for acceptance or rejection of a proposition.

The trainee adult educator was able to identify and experience the actual processes of the tasks of adult education: to participate as an associate in consultations, programme planning, teaching, administration and evaluation –

not as an assistant but as a consultant associate. By providing a taste for the processes of adult education, trainees were attracted to gain greater knowledge and skills in promoting adult education. They subsequently became keener to address the mysteries of 'psychomotor skills' and 'behavioural objectives'. They had a sense that there may be something worth knowing behind these words, or that other more useful knowledge might give them better skills to achieve real and sought-after goals that they had come to strive for and value.

I already knew that the trainees possessed strong views on integration, wanting their students to take their place alongside other Australians without losing pride in their Aboriginal identity. To become adult educators they needed to be able to convert such a goal into a programme. For motivation, I referred to the trainees' generalised hopes that the students would take on confident behaviour and that this could result from the planned education programme. We agreed on the general outcome to be sought. The question was which processes to use. The senior trainee was a skilled and tactful negotiator. My task was to show that the goals could be achieved by using the skills he already possessed and that the activity itself would be interesting, exciting and fun. I knew that his aesthetic sense of what was good and fitting had been refined, and that without this sense there would not have been the same foundation on which to build. Thus the adult education practice portrayed here was experienced largely as a matter of letting go. This is explored more fully in the poetised reflections below.

PANEL III: Poetised reflection

Making spaces

To be needed
and hated;
to be valued as resource,
hated as a white fella
and, in times of cultural off-duty,
crammed together
in the truck (him driving),
not bad mates.

Can your apprentice
be your boss?
Can white ways
so easily translate
into Aboriginal ways?

Always seems different
when you do it
and he does it;
nothing stays the same.
It's not just replacing him for you.

All the classroom games
are changed.

And he's no young apprentice –
the students call him uncle.
He is sure-footed in
the Alice Springs cross-cultural jungle;
knows how to manage;
hard to call him trainee.

Besides, in our coffee talk
he wraps the word 'trainee' with distaste.
Oh sure, it's a way
for a meal ticket, job, career,
but it's too bloody demeaning;
and the white bloke,
employed by our own Aboriginal board
is the trainer.

He knows trainee money won't come
without him as the trainer;
it's enough
to make you hate him.

Are you supposed to track your trainee
into the Aboriginal classroom,
watch as he works and nurtures
the student's fragile trust?
He doesn't need any of that;
can come in heavy like a fruitcake,
heavy, chewy, reliable, predictable.

We'll have to go easy;
let the trainees train themselves
while the trainer takes the risk,
attends and listens,
clears the way, a runway
for take off.

PANEL IV: Intuiting the experience

The experience in body, space, time and social relations

My *body* recalls this episode of adult education practice as being cramped and crushed, sharing an office with three people: two trainees and a secretary. It is also being crammed into the minibus with participants and their swags, driving several hours to the Aboriginal settlement for the cross-cultural workshop field trip (discussed in the previous installation) and having coffee round a table with four or five in a space comfortable for two. The experience is one of heightened sensory awareness, trying to read the body language of the trainees, their level of attention, engagement and optimism.

In regard to *time*, the training experience is like waiting for the teachable moment while pursuing one's work accompanied by the trainee. The training project sees time hang at some stages when a proposed project is not taken up, or the trainees do not turn up for work. At other stages, time becomes fraught around attempts to negotiate with the trainees and fear that any misunderstandings might precipitate conflict and consequent loss of ground. At those times the experience of adult education practice in time is one where time moves very slowly.

As a *spatial* experience adult education practice is correlated with physical distance. When people sit close (even when forced by circumstances, like driving in a crowded car or bus) there are amiable discussions about non-controversial things. At other times the trainees keep distant, so that adult education practice is about trying to get close and trying to be close comfortably. Adult education practice as a spatial experience is about trying to get close and feeling closeness or distance as an important component of the experience.

As a *social* experience, adult education practice is experienced as difficult and fraught. The social relationships involve coming together, being friends, exercising authority over projects, giving directions and explaining requirements, rebuking and being rebuked. Adult education practice in this context is experienced as contradictory – of being welcomed as friend and colleague and rejected as a person 'placed above'. It is thus experienced by participants wanting the relationship to be different, as fraught, not agreed to and in constant tension – the trainer wanting the training/mentor relationship to be accepted and for the trainee to act within this; the trainees wanting the trainer to give them space and leave them alone, but still collude with their self-training.

Ways of naming the adult education experience

'Being with' in ambiguity

I depict adult education practice in this training episode in graphic form as a 'being together', with trainer and trainees each representing, and affiliated with, radically different groups who are largely opposed to each other and have a history of conflict, attempting to share knowledge and expertise. I depict adult education practice in this training episode as people with multiple attitudes and moods coming together, and each not being sure which personality of the other group members is presenting at any one time. The adult education phenomenon presents itself as an experience of ambiguity: of nothing being clearly spelt out; of apparent agreements not meaning the same to all.

Friendship/working links' tensions

What shows up when I think of adult education practice in this training episode is the invitation to learn being overlaid with the invitation to friendship. What appear are complex ways of reaching out and being received in: mobilising the trainees and fielding their complex reactions. What shows up is greeting and befriending, reacting, listening, trying to take some action on responses deemed suitable and trying not to take up and run with angry responses deemed unhelpful, while protecting self from rejection and disappointment. Adult education in this training experience is like trying to get your brother or sister to learn something without offending them or appearing superior to them, but at the same time being anxious that they do learn skills to a high degree and feeling reluctant to point out shortcomings. It is also about the experience of constantly fearing rejection or challenge when demonstrating the way a particular task is to be carried out.

The metaphors that best convey the experience of adult education practice in this training episode are: teaching someone with bad sunburn (whom you can't comfortably touch) to ride a bicycle; teaching someone to ice-skate in the spring when the weather is turning warm; teaching ballooning in a cyclonic sky; riding a bicycle blindfolded; dancing with a wizard who can change shape; accidentally turning up to a funeral in fancy dress or being dressed for a funeral and ending up at a wedding.

Struggling for learning

Adult education practice sounds to me like ongoing self-critique and struggling for learning – like attempting to explain the learning tasks in more detail while at the same time attempting to out-manoeuvre negative reactions; attempting to clarify objectives, disclaim unintended racist slights and build a clean training relationship; struggling for ways to collaborate in learning.

The experience is also like sparring for advantage: listening to responses; trying to convert the energy in anger into energy for learning while at the same time preserving one's own sense of humour and worth.

Reluctance and concealment

Knowledge and lack of knowledge being hidden is another dimension to the adult education practice. Trainees reluctant to discuss their learning with the trainer and reluctant to engage strongly in the planned programme. I see the experience as a kind of cover-up, with the educator trying to encourage the people to expose their shortcomings, then being confronted with having to admit to his own.

The experience is like spending time getting up to the start from a handicapped position.

It means greeting, and talking about proposed tasks, and appreciating positive, constructive reactions to my initiatives, and enduring angry reactions, attempting not to fuel the flames or exacerbate the anger.

It is like winnowing for the learning agenda in the trainees' anger, resentment and backlash, and the trainer's self-doubt and constant self-suspicion of hidden racism embedded in the ways of training being pursued.

Kidding the trainees along

What comes to light when I focus on adult education practice in this training episode is the experience of jockeying or 'kidding the trainees along' – like helping someone ride a bicycle and knowing that learning the combined acts of balance and pedal pushing and steering and braking cannot actually be achieved by a direct transfer of information from trainer to trainee in a direct lock-step manner, but has to be done by the learner him or herself.

I recognise adult education practice in this training episode as talking and joking and picturing the proposed learning in as favourable and accessible a light as possible. I see it as trying to get the trainees to make a commitment to learning while at the same time continuing to invite them to participate in learning facilitative activities, hoping again that the 'engine will start' and that the trainees will come alive.

The experience of training, then, is of trying to get the trainees to engage, to 'have a go' and to stay with the experience. It is to allow learning to take place: saying positive things, avoiding taking umbrage at hostile or fearful or cutting remarks, and, as far as possible, removing extrinsic barriers to the actual learning which might serve to make the learning task more difficult.

The experience is like constantly steering a conversation to stick to the point and avoid unhelpful digressions which could weaken the learner's resolve and provide a reason for postponing effort and application to the learning. The experience of adult education practice can be described as resisting distraction and offering constant support while being challenged and befriended by turns.

Trying but not knowing

Adult education in this episode presents itself to me as trying but not knowing, suggesting but not sure if the suggestion is adopted or rejected, being preoccupied with whether the trainees are happy with my engagement with them or whether they are withdrawn or resistant.

What unfolds for me when I dwell on adult education practice in this training episode is the experience of being well meaning and out of control. The experience is like being in a cycle of introductions, engagements, agreements, disagreements, decision making, action and review, with the different components of the experience becoming more and more multiplex and blurred.

What I detect in adult education practice in this training episode is a monkey mind, darting in every direction, trying to find a way to proceed while keeping control over the process. It is like trying to avoid confrontation, to avoid going backwards; of feeling a sickening sense of the naivety and crudeness of the training programme; of being impeded from getting to the skills required to be learned by the demands of the relationship.

I detect in the experience a feeling of being set against the trainees: of experiencing myself as trainer being exposed as incompetent; of being insensitive to the trainees' experience and at the same time experiencing waves of anger, irritation, frustration at the permanent difficulties which surface and resurface.

Feeling one's way to learning

Adult education in this episode sounds like feeling one's way towards learning or feeling one's way to a learning facilitative agreement – working in ignorance and working in tension; feeling the demands of the management on the one hand and the resistant distress of the trainees on the other.

I depict adult education practice in this training episode as getting in close; enduring the strain; taking on hope, being unsure, trying and trying and laughing and trying and not knowing.

Adult education in this training episode looks to me like hunting in the dark for an acceptable way to proceed. It seems like letting pre-judgements and pre-planning go; using huge amounts of time to talk and plan and talk and ask about feelings and irritations. Adult education practice is also about feelings and aspirations being exposed, and set tasks that have to be completed somehow being managed.

The experience looks to me like slowing down and braking; finding nothing useful in the training repertoire; coming to a halt and eventually finding a way in 'no way', where the training consists of making spaces.

Becoming invisible

Adult education practice in this training episode feels like working to become invisible – working to minimise 'angry-making' exchanges and letting the tasks to be performed by the trainees emerge. As an experience, it feels like what John the Baptist said of himself and Jesus: 'He must increase, I must decrease.' It feels like being diminished, even violated, in the struggle to get the trainees to engage with the learning tasks in the contract and to disengage from resisting and resenting the trainer. It feels like a mother letting a child go to enter a new phase of life without thanks or a backward look.

The experience is like coming together to look at a project and to tease out its requirements, then stepping back and handing over to the trainees.

I picture the experience of adult education practice as waiting for openings. By that I mean waiting for moments where it seems possible to initiate some learning exchange for the trainees which would be accepted.

Becoming silent: teaching by non-teaching

I picture the experience of adult education practice in this training episode as a kind of non-teaching: of becoming silent and allowing the tasks to speak for themselves. I see it as the need emerging to background the interpersonal exchanges in favour of encouraging the trainees to address and make transparent the tasks of their training in all their details: of making spaces where the trainees can make their own learning.

Darkness, suffering, healing and frustration

What I see in this adult education practice is darkness, suffering, feelings of anger, healing, frustration, achievement, exhaustion and irritation.

It is about an increasing tension to find an honourable resolution to the permanent confusion and opposition of feelings and expectations.

It is about the educator being personally exposed and challenged: about finding his or her opinions, tastes and preferences exposed, challenged, belittled, praised.

PANEL V: Distilling the phenomenon

The following is a list of major themes in the structure of this experience of adult education practice drawn out from the intuitions above.

- 'Being with' in ambiguity
- Friendship/working links' tensions
- Struggling for learning
- Reluctance and concealment
- Kidding the trainees along
- Trying but not knowing
- Feeling one's way to learning
- Becoming invisible
- Becoming silent: teaching by non-teaching
- Darkness, suffering, healing and frustration

PANEL VI: Commentary

This installation looked at on-the-job training as a form of adult education practice. There are considerable differences, at least in emphasis in the learning facilitative practices and the roles of the educator and the people being educated, between this form and the more detached adult education practices in classrooms and formalised training rooms.

The question of what motivates a person to want to help another to learn seems to be linked to his or her interest in caring for his or her fellow human beings. This seems also to be based on a person's internal qualities – aesthetic and moral sense – that assess things as good or bad, beautiful or ugly. This is what provided the foundation of the hope shared by the trainees and myself – that we would work out a way together since we had so many similar ideals and goals, and the same 'taste' in important matters.

Does this point to the importance of the aesthetic sense and the need to refine and develop it? Aesthetic development and affirmation refer to a set of educational outcomes through the achievement of which people are confirmed in, and develop, their ability to feel, to celebrate, to rejoice. Those who have wisdom and good taste can be motivated and drawn to activities not because of what they lead to but because they are good in themselves. In the last analysis, the struggle to be truly human is the fight to respond to the good and not the expedient. The road to most learning outcomes is easier if, besides setting a goal, the learner develops an appreciation for the goodness of the journey. The aesthetic agenda in adult education may be perceived by some to create an additional burden on adult educators. What in fact seems to emerge from this installation is that the experience of adult education practice, particularly when it is concerned to motivate participants, does to a greater or lesser extent attempt to harness the aesthetic sense.

A noticeable feature of this experience which flows, among other things, from the above, is the level to which the adult education experience becomes fraught. The experience often has elements of personal revelation and risk taking: of getting in close perhaps in less physical ways than in the installation here. The adult education exchanges are not experienced as 'cool' information exchanges or the detached 'here are some ideas for your consideration if you find them interesting' attitude. The experiences seem to be warm to hot and more encompassing than reduced. They tend to drag in and somehow involve the adult educator's opinions, sense of goodness and value, prejudices, passions, fears and style. Such experience of 'having a lot riding on' the educational activities is often felt in the passionate way the adult educator discovers her or himself putting out the learning invitation. It can also be felt in how he or she reacts to the kind of reception manifested by the engaged learners to the offered learning facilitative processes.

This 'hot' dimension of the experience of adult education practice, foregrounded in this installation, is not uncommon in much adult education experience.

A final element in the adult education experience highlighted here is the strange sense of sometimes succeeding when you fail, and vice versa. The nature of learning facilitation as 'creating opportunities' and removing barriers but not actually doing anything proactive or directly transitive about the actual thing or things to be learnt, highlights its essentially non instrumental dimension. This installation resonates with Heidegger's (1968, p. 15) notion of teaching:

> ... whether or not a cabinet maker's apprentice, while he is learning, will come to respond to wood and wooden things depends obviously on the presence of some teacher who can teach the apprentice such matters.

> True. Teaching is even more difficult than learning. We know this; but we rarely think about it. And why is teaching more difficult than learning? Not because the teacher must have a larger store of information, and have it always ready. Teaching is more difficult than learning because what teaching calls for is this: to let learn. The real teacher, in fact, lets nothing else be learned than learning. His [sic] conduct, therefore, often produces the impression that we really learn nothing from him, if by 'learning' we now automatically understand merely the procurement of useful information. The teacher is ahead of his apprentices in this alone, that he has still far more to learn than they – he has to learn to let them learn.

This completes this installation of the flight of the pelican. As we move through the gallery to the final installation, we are moving from Alice Springs to Adelaide; from the IAD to the University of South Australia; and from the challenges of getting people airborne into learning, to the following challenge of keeping them there.

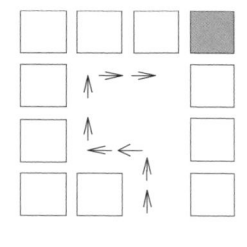

Chapter 8

Starbursts and shocks at the Uni

The final set in this exhibition relates to my current practice as a lecturer at the University of South Australia. I have worked there for nearly a decade in awards-providing professional education for adult educators already engaged in some form of adult education practice in TAFE colleges (Colleges of Technical and Further Education), community learning centres and workplace training.

PANEL I: Backgrounding: University teaching

Attitude and culture of the educator

In this episode, my attitudes and approach to adult education continued to be similar to the approach and assumptions and values of earlier episodes. The approach still tended to focus more on educating the learner than transferring the skills and information required in the learning. The emphasis of this approach was not shared to the same extent by some of my colleagues in the university who had a background in trade instruction, and we had useful conversations comparing and contesting approaches.

My attitude is to some extent resistant to an instrumental ideology whereby students at university are perceived by teachers, and the students themselves, as having things done to them so they will become different. If tertiary education were being imagined as a kind of factory producing skilled people for industry, it seemed to me that the wood was being lost for the trees. If I saw the difficulties of the push-start action-based learning that I attempted in the Kimberleys (cf. Chapter 4) because it seemed not to have enough direction, I saw tremendous difficulties in current tertiary education because it seemed to have too much. And if, in the Kimberleys, it was left to the participants to subvert the process for their own ends, it seemed to me that, at universities and TAFE colleges, academics needed to resist the temptation of literalism and instrumental thinking. 'If learning is a symbolic activity', I thought, 'then surely the process to facilitate it should be of the same order.'

I was also conscious of the transactional dimensions of formal award-bestowing education, where the educational project is coloured by processes of selection, admission, assessment and graduation, all of which I saw as having a tendency to modify the student's freedom to pursue knowledge for its own sake in favour of slavishly following the curriculum guidelines. At the same time I saw lecturers occasionally constrained to teach things they did not value because it was 'part of the course'.

I was interested in creating a process within which students could seek to resist restrictive forces. In a similar way to the challenge felt by non-Aboriginal participants to 'become cross-cultural' in the cultural awareness programmes described above, mature-age students in this programme, I thought, needed to think themselves into a positive and empowered frame of mind – to 'become academic' without losing their self-esteem. If they could become public speakers, abseilers, presidents of school councils or Rotary, there seemed no reason why they should not also be able to become academics. This was provided of course that they wanted to – and of course sensible people only want things they think are valuable and achievable. It was clear to me that my agenda would have to include making the goal achievable (which I thought it was anyway) and making the path to it interesting, even exciting. I planned to set out to capture their imagination: introduce them to exciting writers and thinkers.

I was preoccupied with ways to set these tertiary students on a quest for retaining and developing their adult autonomy while under the direction of their lecturers. I wanted the programme to introduce students to assertive participation in tertiary education. This involved understanding it as a contractual service, paid for by taxpayers, which purported to offer students possessing prerequisite academic skills and who had been admitted to the course, effective tuition in subjects which were then to be examined according to an agreed criterion. Students have always enjoyed the story of the assertive student from Victoria, who, having conscientiously done the required work and received a low grade, demanded that the tutor be directed by the head of department to improve his teaching. While the story is a salutary reminder of various accountabilities, most students still felt at a disadvantage in exchanges with their lecturers and benefited enormously from clear guidelines of appropriate practice in order to keep the road in sight.

I also wanted to encourage supportive and respectful linking of students to one another in a community of scholarship and often friendship. My interest was the theory that people in transition need to find a supportive community where they can feel comfortable and supported in their struggle to manage the changes they have chosen to make or have accepted as inevitable. Bernie Neville (1989) talks of the importance of a spirit of love and acceptance in education (symbolised in Greek mythology by Eros), in which humans find community and support. My agenda was to work towards generating that spirit in the group.

At the same time, I wanted to make the classroom environment a place where the transformative journey would be confirmed and celebrated. For me the classroom could also be a place of high time, a time of intense exchange and discovery. It can be at least sometimes a place of visions and dreams; of what might be or what could be inspired by Dionysus, god of enthusiasm and the joy of change in Grecian mythology.

As a student of Berger and Luckman (1971), I had been influenced by the notion that a person's world is socially constructed and that one of the most effective ways to manage personal change is to join a group of people engaged in a similar transition. And so when a student's study enterprise might not receive support from family or work, he or she could gain support from others in the same boat. I believed the class could be a supportive learning environment for just such students.

Attitude and culture of the learners

The learners in this episode were adult educators enrolled in the then Associate Diploma in Adult Education. Many had applied for the course in order to advance their career and not, as they said, just for the knowledge. A substantial number of these adult educators turned students were clear that they already knew all they needed to know in their education and training work, but were constrained to attend and came for the 'bit of paper'. Others said simply they had come 'to learn more'.

Many had considerable gaps in their academic knowledge and skills they needed for tertiary study. This was often combined with a strong fear of failure. Many students had also entered tertiary education as an important life transition – a chance to be different, to become more educated, well read, intelligent etc. I was to discover that many mature-age students entering tertiary study in Australia suffered a lack of self-esteem and self-confidence in their new setting. This was also the case in America (Perry 1968; Daloz 1986).

I then found that while the outcome may have been seen as an exciting goal, the path often seemed difficult and daunting. In the eyes of many students it wasn't so much rocky or difficult, it was incomprehensible – it kept disappearing. Students slaved over a piece of work to find it unaccountably rejected. Others seeking a pass grade were equally perplexed to find their work highly graded and praised.

Many students thought the education they were looking for would occur through a kind of linear expansion of their existing knowledge and skills rather than a radical change in the way they addressed knowledge, some or much of which they in fact already had. Perry (1968) discovered recurrent patterns in the way students who had entered tertiary education to 'get an education' participated in the academic processes. According to his research, many were confronted with the need to become different. They felt the need to develop different ways to assess ideas rather than to merely memorise them: to realise that in lots of cases there was no right or wrong answer to problems, just more or less useful ways of addressing and interpreting them.

This approach was often perceived as threatening and strange. This judgement seemed unavoidable since a change in perception cannot be directly taught. It has to be arrived at. Jack Mezirow (1977, 1985) carried out research subsequent to Perry on the experience of women returning to tertiary study. He listed a series of predictable stages they passed through on the way to achieving a form of consciousness that suited their newly constructed selves and their academic and social environment – a process he called 'perspective transformation'. A few wrote in their evaluations or in letters that they had become fired up and inspired through the lectures and the interactions of the group.

There were, however, a few students who found this kind of education interesting, even inspiring, but not what they came for. They had clear expectations of what they wanted and how what they wanted could or should be provided. They were interested in clear information and preparation for action which, from a reading of the prospectus, they understood would be provided. For these students, who have been to date in the minority, the interventions and challenges of the subject tended to generate more puzzlement than enlightenment.

Processes and arena

The teaching arena was a ground floor classroom with students clustered around circular tables, restaurant style. The introductory class had nearly thirty students.

I was teaching an introductory subject in the Associate Diploma that provided opportunities for self-reflection and assessment. One of the early assignments invited students to reflect on their experience as a learner during various stages of their life. This proved an important step for them to position themselves in their life stage development and to reflect on themselves as adult learners. A central part in this process was the reflection on how perspectives change over time and could be expected to continue to change.

During the early exchanges in the course I was careful to stress the contractual nature of the teaching/learning relationship between us. I prefaced remarks with phrases like 'as we agreed' and 'this is part of the agreement we established'. I felt that this would give me licence to negotiate quite stringent academic standards. I could provide feedback to students with comments like: 'I know we have contracted for honest and careful feedback on this or that point and my feedback is that this is well presented and argued', or 'that this is weak and unsatisfactory and should be repeated'. There was a lot of going over work and resubmitting, as students were sometimes encouraged and at other times directed, to take the opportunity to improve within understood parameters. I was able to point out that I was under contract to them as their tutor and that it was understood that they would not want me to let any shoddy work go unchallenged.

Issues

There were two central issues. The first was that, as has been pointed out, a considerable number of students were angry at being made to enrol in the course and they wished to fulfil the minimum requirements to graduate. The second related issue, also mentioned earlier, was the university structure of teaching and learning processes: lectures, tutorials, assessment, and their influence on the kind of learning participants were pursuing. A third issue was the tension between the lecturer's agenda to persuade students to become scholars and some students' agendas to do the minimum and depart with the diploma. The working out of these issues forms the background to the sketch which follows.

PANEL II: Sketching: the end of friendship

They were ebullient, bright-eyed men and women aged between the middle 20s and early 60s seated around tables at intervals in the classroom, with five students to each for this first preparatory subject concerned mainly with orientation and engagement with the course. He had a hard time getting their names right – too much research and committees were eating at this magic stuff that grew and congealed around the students and himself. He knew he was different when he was with them and wondered if they too suffered or felt a change in their souls when they came together each week.

Of course some students had already foregrounded the contractual elements in the subject – assignments, assessment, grades. 'Is this part of the assignment?' He needed to slow down – thought back to the great time when, loaded with summary sheets and handouts, he had launched into a long lecture on Durkheim, to be met with his first question when he finally drew breath: 'When is our first assignment due?' He had laughed confusedly because he hadn't really paid attention to the full architecture of a course and the roads and fences that bounded the field and built up pressure forward.

Recollections of learning

He wanted to take them with him out and above to the whole universe of learning and then back to the tiny bailiwick in that universe concerned with teaching. He asked them to write down something they had learnt or a learning experience they had had. There was a pause. There were clarificatory questions – what kind of learning, what kind of 'thing'? But they were not answered. He said the exercise was designed to let them discover their own definition in their own way without being shaped by academic frames. After discussing their experiences around the tables, he then asked if any would like to provide a brief note on their learning to contribute to a matrix he had laid out on the whiteboard.

A number spoke of 'learning to do something': ride a bicycle, use a piece of computer software; others spoke of learning 'that', where learning meant gaining new information. One student said he had learnt that despite all the scientific breakthroughs for human betterment, violence and persecution of people have continued. Another mentioned learning that burying metals under certain bushes would cause their flowers to change colour. Another group reported another kind of learning which was a kind of 'realisation'. They spoke of realising that although they had come to university to assist their employability, there were very few jobs around and that their university degree might not in fact be a ticket to a job. A woman said she had been nervous about the course but had realised she had the strength and purpose to pursue her studies. At this point another woman said she had realised that life could go on after the murder of her son. He had been killed while backpacking in Europe. There was a silence, then a young woman in a wheelchair, who had been nearly killed in a car crash the previous year, spoke about learning to live with what you've got – in her case her only hand to push the wheelchair wheel and drive the car, a will of iron and an aversion to self-pity.

The lecturer, as always, felt privileged and on sacred ground – he felt a kind of germinal force already stirring in the classroom. The next question was whether they had learnt by 'being taught'. A few who had learnt a skill spoke of someone who had shown them. Most of the realisations had occurred without a teacher because of some event, some critical incident which had demanded that they work something out/make sense of something in their life. At this point the woman in the wheelchair spoke warmly of a man in the rehabilitation centre she had attended, who had gone with her through her long time of despair and clumsiness. She spoke of his ability to push and to leave go, which, she said, had kept her spirits up. The lecturer was uplifted; he felt honoured that such revelations would have come forward in his class. He then prompted the class to consider what kind of learning was facilitated in their own teaching. At this point he digressed to introduce some of the specialist terms of the adult education profession that classified and clarified meanings of learning and education.

Remembering what you were told

The lecturer handed out a sheet with definitions of formal, non-formal, informal and incidental learning and a matrix of different kinds of learning: gaining skills, gaining and memorising information, making meaning, becoming transformed, realising, critique. He then said that these definitions were needed as a kind of professional language. He then spun around and asked the students to close their books, take a fresh sheet of paper and write definitions of the four kinds of adult education and six kinds of learning. He did not check them, just grinned and said that in every profession, you must put to memory its categories, terms and its essential processes.

He then returned to the theme of learning and of naming the kinds of learning the students purported to facilitate. There was a pause. The group was so diverse. Some were teaching hairdressing, computing, cooking, music, business management, dance, life skills. It was clear that much of the learning they had valued in their own lives had not been assisted by a teacher; nor was it often about gaining some kind of objective skills and knowledge. Was there some way to make sure that such deeper learning could happen in the course of their teaching? That perhaps spaces could be left for such to occur?

A couple of participants asked how they could leave meditative spaces if everything was locked into a rigid format of instruction and assessment. There was considerable discussion about the current interest in competency-based education (CBE) which many adult educators enrolled in the course were required to implement in the workplace that sponsored their teaching. 'What kind of learning comes from a bloody module?' yelled one frustrated tradesman educator who had prided himself on knowing his trade very well and transferring his skills and 'know-how' to the learners in his care. Another adult educator horticulturalist said that her area had been hugely assisted by a modularised 'teach-yourself course' on the classification of plants. Her comment was echoed by two computer software instructors who praised their competency-based 'teach-yourself' packages: 'We can spend time alongside the learners as they go through the programme, keeping their confidence up – saves us doing the same thing over and over and over, used to drive us mad.' At this point Colleen, a music teacher, said: 'I can't teach competence in music, I've got to teach excellence. If I tell someone their playing is competent, they will feel like a hack, a clapped-out performer who never made it. You might be able to be a competent truck driver but being a competent artist means you have never become fine-tuned and no one will want to listen and neither will you.' The class could see her point. She then said that excellence meant putting hours and hours into practice until the work emerged in its magic and perfection.

The discussion surged around how one could teach such magic and perfection. It became clear that more than technical perfection was meant, though it seemed always built on technical perfection. This placed serious demands on the learner: 'you can always do better'.

In the ensuing weeks, what had begun as a predictable objectified 'course' became more contested and more exciting as various students from a range of approaches and ideologies felt able to claim some space for what they wanted from the course. That left the educator in a quandary. It was evident that the group was well aware of the basic assessment requirement of the subject, the dates for assignments and the criteria for grades. That was clear. It was the processes that were contested. Students obviously expected the processes somehow to dovetail with the assignments but apart from that, the processes to be followed had been opened but not closed. Had the educator laid out a formalised, detailed lock-step programme as some of his colleagues did, it would have been accepted. The sense of jeopardy had been summoned up in the invitation to clarify learning goals since various students began to sketch out their expectations. Only a very few were prepared to say that all they wanted was to be competent.

As the course continued, the adult educator was conscious of huge differences in the expectations and engagements of individual students. It was one thing for him to set out expectations; it was another to take on the tasks needed to meet them. He was confronted with conflicting expectations, largely linked to contested notions of the function of the three-hour teaching session each week. For some, the class meant getting clear information that could be understood, and further clarification sought. That would mean that by the end of each session the student 'had' the information relevant for that week. The lecturer, whose style had never been in that mould, referred back to the kinds of learning the participants had mentioned as significant in their lives. He asked them to remember the desires of some that spaces be left for them to take on ideas, mull them over, check additional readings and construct their own version of the ideas in dialogue with him.

On top of this was the open-ended style of the assignments. There were no right answers. Students were required to voice and substantiate their opinions but there was a required format: the essay had its own rules that had to be mastered.

At the coffee break the lecturer returned the first assignments that had been handed in two weeks earlier. He had always a sense of difficulty, of how to distribute them to the students while respecting confidentiality and the students' sensibilities. He never wrote on the outside of the assignment cover. He had decided that assignments should go directly from lecturer to student without other students seeing them. This would be a departure from the time when he had put all the assignments in a box and students picked theirs out at the coffee break. He had decided to give them out so he walked around the classroom handing the assignments to individual students. Once that was completed, he returned to the desk at the front of the class while the students read their grades and the feedback comments. There was a noticeable shift in the atmosphere. He made some general comments about the assignments and noted some good points and some problems that had occurred in a number of papers.

During the coffee break, one student asked him to decipher his hand-written comments on their paper. Another challenged his assessment and he said that he would take her paper back for a second look. He said he would mention that option to the class after coffee. Two students thanked him for 'giving a distinction', to which he replied that the grade was not a gift: their work was worth the grade. As the group walked over to the cafeteria, he noticed a change in the interactions. Instead of continuing the discussion with him around points emerging in the day's topic as was usually the case, the group members seemed more distant and seemed to prefer to talk among themselves.

When the group returned he made a point of mentioning that students were welcome to query his assessment if they felt they had not received the assessment they were expecting. At the end of the class, one of the students said that although he, the lecturer, was amiable and flexible in the classroom, he seemed strict and much more demanding in his assessment. It seemed to the lecturer that this was a crucial moment in the subject, when the learning generative processes he had put in place met the learning appraisal processes he had also arranged. These were expected but they seemed to relate to the more classical, technical world of the essay genre. He had not addressed this since he understood the students were familiar with the essay form, and of course the focus of his teaching had been on making spaces for deep reflection. Was this most important part of the teaching/learning process to be left out – or was it beyond assessment?

The matter was returned to the classroom – the contract between lecturer and student seemed to need revisiting. It was not as if the matter had not already been dealt with; it was just that now the blanks had been filled in and the terrain had become more clearly marked. The lecturer could feel a subtle change between the easy, exploring environment that characterised the dialogue and reflections of the first classes, and an emerging, more contained, less adventurous style of the class.

Over the subsequent weeks the latter spirit tended to increase. Students gave evidence of less initiative, less reading between classes and less reading of suggested but not required texts. The lecturer, who regarded the educational enterprise as an adventure, was reminded that it was also a transaction. It was dancing indeed but also dealing, and he was once more aware that for teaching to work in that environment, the two processes which contested each other needed space to flourish and find a balance.

PANEL III: Poetised reflection

Moment of truth

With boxes, folders, markers
for the class, you push
through the door and thread
a pathway through the students
clustered at their tables.
You claim the desk in front
and turn to welcome,
bring the place to life.
And, as you turn, the students
break their talk
and turn to you and,
in that same turn of eye,
note the assignment box
with graded work returned;
themselves drawn out on paper
flattened between the leaves
and now returned with your assessment.
Standing to the front and side
you field and fill out half-formed thoughts
and feel their bright engagement;

and look for ways to cherish and entice
the laid-bare heart and mind and soul,
to go in deep, to struggle and to know.

When students claim their papers,
your grade, with comments
of what you see and value,

sits inside the assignment cover
away from others' eyes.

You watch as their
seeming casual glance to grade
and comment, hit and skid away
and in that instance,
or so you think and fear,
their open space for you
is closed and gone.
No easy comrade smile
of fellow knowledge workers at their trade;
those gleams of recognition,
of thought and insight shared,
which warmed your heart
and made the lesson lift,
are damped and doused.

The music's stopped, the dance is gone,
And poetry is come to prose.

PANEL IV: Intuiting the experience

The experience in body, space, time and social relations

Adult education practice as a *bodily* experience in this university teaching
episode is about being weighed down with boxes full of papers and readers and
handouts. It is about ceaseless motion: standing at the lecturer's desk, moving
to the whiteboard to write a word or phrase, walking through the seated
students, sitting down during students' tutorial presentations or during discussion between students. Bodily movements are quick and energetic, the voice
loud, optimistic, even joyful and always challenging. The eyes scan the room,
catching and linking with each student, seeking response, attending to signs of
affirmation, engagement or resistance. Looking to make eye contact, looking
for alert or slumped bodily posture. The ears are attentive again seeking
sounds: murmurs, laughter at jokes, chuckles of affirmation, or of conversation
between students.

As a *spatial* experience, adult education practice in this university teaching
episode is framed by the university classroom with tables and chairs, facing the
whiteboard and the lecturer's desk at the front. As pointed out in the background to this installation, this classroom space is broken by large, round café-
style tables with students sitting in groups of five and six around them. This
spatial distribution shapes the experience in that the students' attention is easily
diverted to their table companions so that the space itself carries a challenge to
the lecturer seeking sustained attention from the students.

The varied distance between students and the lecturer is a characteristic of
the experience of adult education practice in this episode. The most dispersed

experience is during the formal lecturing when the lecturer moves to the lecturing table and faces the students, who turn from their tables to face him. The spatial experience is closer when the lecturer joins one of the table groups during group discussion, and closer again at irregular intervals when a student seeks to engage one to one with the lecturer. This spatial concertina modifies the adult education experience.

In the most distant spatial configuration, the experience is equivalently distant and the student participants are experienced by the lecturer as an audience to be managed 'as one thing': to be handled and nurtured almost as an organism. The lecturer experiences himself as responsible for the quality and focus of this audience group, required to care for it to keep it together and to shape its curriculum so that it is learning and attentive and not hijacked into becoming punitive or destructive. The students are experienced as this 'one thing' – an 'audience' requiring to be managed and entertained and helped, manipulated into paying attention and responding to the ideas, feelings and images of the lecturer.

When the space contracts to the tutorial configuration, adult education practice is experienced as less predictable and controlled by the lecturer, more constructed of conversations between students and the lecturer and between the students themselves. During face-to-face interactions between the lecturer and one or other students, the experience of adult education processes is qualified by the closeness of the space which puts lecturer and student face to face. Refusals and low assessment grades made in this space are experienced as fraught, while approvals given and high assessments revealed in this space are intensified.

As a *temporal* experience, adult education practice in this university teaching episode is felt to be bounded and constrained by timetables: times for assessment and times for assignments to be returned. Time in this experience runs out on some occasions; at others it is given. Students are 'given time' to finish. At other times they can be invited in tutorials by the words 'take your time'. Such invitation is given because the experience of adult education practice in this context is that time is out of the individual's control and possession. When students approach the lecturer they will often apologise for taking up his or her time.

As a *social* experience, adult education practice is carried out in a network of formal and informal relationships. One of the major relationships is the lecturer/student relationship. This is then embedded in the students' peer relationships through which they group and cluster, and which often shape the lecturer/student relationship. As a social experience, adult education in this episode is also shaped by age relationships: older middle-aged lecturer and younger middle-aged students; and gender relationships: male lecturer and male and female students.

Naming the experience

Opening-out and closing-in

What I discover in adult education practice in this university teaching episode is the experience of the lecturer giving out and being received, the experience of students giving back and being received, and all the exchanges constantly under a kind of scrutiny and adjustment.

The experience is a kind of opening-out and closing-in. The opening-out experience accompanies giving lectures and fielding questions; experiencing strong interested feedback, intelligent comment and challenge where the topic is taken, seized and interrogated. The closing-in experience (which seems also to include a closing out of the lecturer) is students pushing back to the lecturer to explore what is required of them: requests and demands for clarity for assignments, details of assessment, times of assessment being due, criteria and the rest.

The experience is a twin action. It is firstly an experience of proaction: the adult educator putting out and checking the 'take-up'. It is also the experience of being reacted to, and appraising and attempting to mollify the anxiety about assessment.

Adult education practice experience in this university teaching episode seems to be like throwing out burley (ground bait used to attract fish) near shoals of different fish and attempting to attract them. It is also linking with every student, building cross-links between lecturer and student, and between students. Burley throwing is experienced as a mix of self-revelation, explication of central points in the subject matter of the course, hints on ways in to further learning, elements for assessment and interesting things planned for the sessions of the course.

Instructing and testing

What I discover in adult education practice in this university teaching episode is the experience of instructing and then testing students' retention of key ideas and skills: of passing on clear information and demonstrating analytical skills, checking that they are understood, requiring they be committed to memory and then testing several times to ensure their retention.

Being constrained and held responsible

Adult education practice in this episode presents itself as being held responsible for clarity and direction; as the lecturer being confronted with administrative deadlines for assignments to be marked and assignments returned, and changes to assignment grades recorded. It is also like being bound down by the weekly three-hour teaching format.

Being on a tram you can't get off

I recognise adult education practice in this university teaching episode as like being on a tram one can't get off, or being caught in a bus with no brakes, running down a hill with the lecturer and students stuck on it, holding on until it comes to rest: a sense of being caught without control in a longitudinal process so that the experience feels different at different times – beginning, middle and end.

Tension between inspiration and assessment

What shows up in the experience of adult education practice in this university teaching episode are two channels: one of inspiration and one of assessment.

What shows up in the inspiration phase is experiencing 'putting out to be accepted'; of following and building on the track of approval; of being attuned to what brings smiles, laughs, approval – and trying to take the seduced, smitten, engaged students into new ideas and processes of the course. It is a kind of getting up momentum in the early engagement. What shows up as well is a parallel force: an invitation to discovery, attempting to allay student fears of being exposed, ridiculed, abused, assessed too punitively, failing, but at the same time a force calling to prepare them for assessment.

Amplifying student responsive voices

The experience of adult education practice in this episode presents itself as the students' voices being amplified and integrated into the general teaching/ learning agenda, speech being invited from all participants to 'get them in'.

Dealing and dancing

I recognise adult education practice in this university teaching episode as 'dealing' and 'dancing' – as a double-winged experience. One wing is the experience of all kinds of agreements being set up – assessment, structured tutorials, dates of assignments – from lecturer to student and from student to lecturer; the rails of the enterprise, the skeleton, the road, the frame. The second wing is the experience of the juice: the dancing, the sense of energy, of 'clicking' – resonation when it comes, a sense of harmony, spiral of knowing, a kind of domino effect of enthusiasm and illumination.

I recognise adult education practice in this university teaching episode as 'no deals, no dance' and 'no dance, no learning' as an experience comprising agreements being sought, attempts being made to allay fears, benefits to be gained being outlined and considerable effort being put out to make the journey enjoyable.

Being held accountable for classroom moods

I recognise adult education practice in this university teaching episode as an experience of being made responsible for the quality of this high time – praised when the experience is felt as exhilarating; blamed and withdrawn from when the classroom activity is flat.

A dinner party of appraising guests

It is like having a dinner party of invited guests who are actually invited to sample and share the fruits of the host's catering but, at the same time, become engaged in appraising the food and its presentation while having their own consumption monitored.

PANEL V: Distilling the phenomenon

There are six main themes that can be distilled from the intuiting of this episode of adult education practice.

- Opening-out and closing-in
- Drilling and testing
- Being constrained and held responsible
- Tension between inspiration and assessment
- Amplifying student responsive voices
- Dealing and dancing

PANEL VI: Comment

This last installation resonates with commonly encountered classroom-based adult education scenarios. The significant element in this experience is the adult educator being confronted with the structural constraints of formal education and the need to take its dynamics on board.

The profile of the experience in this episode tends to foreground the dialectic that in fact seems to be a constant element (in sponsored adult education practice) in the interests of the sponsor, the educator and the learner.

As a phenomenon, adult education practice, viewed through this window, has a constant element of judicial and prudent dealing, compromising, clarifying, etc., like the sound of the drone in bagpipe music that permanently colours whatever melody is being played.

The transactional quality of formal education has created an opening where contemporary technical rationalism can require more and more information and stipulations that the course, and particularly the assessment, be clearly laid out with more and more detail and the lecturer/tutorial episodes integrated with it. Educational approaches of a more exploratory and collaborative nature are challenged to cater for this transactional dimension which, as became apparent in the sketch in this installation, exerts great pressure on the students' engagement and performance.

Where the students are established adults seeking a qualification to underpin their professional pursuits, adult education practice with a strong interest in deeper, transformational learning is not necessarily the preferred approach. Pursuing such learning requires negotiating with students in order to integrate reflection on the quality of learning being pursued and the nature of the learning facilitative processes offered.

When democratic adult educational and learner-centred ideals are embraced, they need to inform the approach that the lecturer takes when he or she wishes to challenge behaviourist, assessment-driven learning, and to resist reducing the reflective exploratory classroom into a training room only.

If adult educators wish to hold to and promote democratic and respectful principles, they cannot just act unilaterally. They cannot dismiss or ignore narrow instrumental curricula, even in the cause of democracy and critical thinking. Respectful and careful processes are needed through which the underlying assumptions and ideology behind mechanistic approaches can be interrogated – a kind of mini cultural and critical awareness course – within and ancillary to the formal programme. A related requirement in this experience seems to be forbearance, perseverance, tolerance and 'coolness'.

Conclusion

This concludes the visit to the Main Gallery. We have experienced the seven installations and journeyed with the curator over more than 20 years of adult educational practice in a range of sites and contexts throughout Australia. After the introduction to each episode, there has been a cautionary tale from the experience of practice, and a poetised reflection. This has been followed by processes to intuit the lived experience of adult education in each of these locations and to distil major elements of each. The commentary process in the sixth panel has offered some reflection on the significance of the experience in the related episode.

In the presentation of these installations under the rubric of 'expressive research', there has been a strong invitation to attempt to contemplate them and let the experience portrayed 'speak' to the person looking at the installation. It is now time to bring into play the complementary 'explanatory' mode of thinking to address questions about the theoretical foundations of the approach used in this thesis. This will take us out of the Main Gallery and into the Gallery of Method.

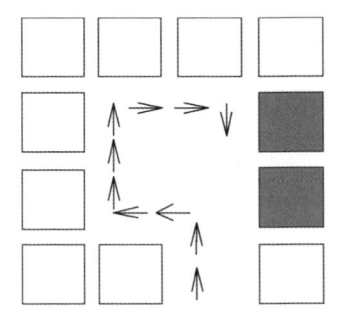

PART III
THE GALLERY OF METHOD

Orientation

Having moved from the Main Gallery, visitors are now invited to enter the Gallery of Method, a very different location with 'dialogue' rather than 'portrayal' on its agenda. This gallery uses two chapters to argue the case for the method employed. The first looks at the background and dimensions of the 'expressive' method, a form of interpretative research used in the installations. The second explores phenomenology in its complementary 'empathetic' and 'intuiting' forms, as a major philosophical foundation of the Main Gallery's expressive method.

The visitors, emerging from the Main Gallery full of the images and metaphors of the expressive approach, were encouraged to adopt a 'contemplative' rather than 'analytical' stance and allow the installations to 'speak' in their own language (as it were). Here, as was pointed out above, the Gallery of Method adopts the 'explanatory' stance to the 'inquiring' visitor and attempts to argue the case for the validity and usefulness of the expressive method adopted in the Main Gallery.

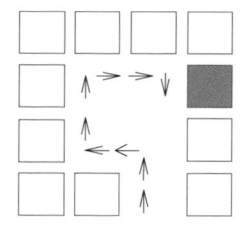

Chapter 9

Expressive method in qualitative research

Introducing the expressive method

As was pointed out in the opening chapter of the thesis, the aim was to write a reflective academic text that would be a portrayal of the lived experience of adult education. In the reflective processes of writing and rewriting, the expressive interpretative method employed in the Main Gallery emerged. The process of selection of method and techniques of portrayal used in the Main Gallery was a matter of testing and judging whether something of the lived experience of adult education practice was made visible. There is a similarity between the 'try and see' approach used here and the experimenting an artist might do with paint or texture or sound, seeing whether by using a certain approach the lived reality of a particular experience might be in some way made visible. A number of representative approaches were viewed and critiqued. Eventually a final clustering into the installations of the Main Gallery was made. Departing from the pictorial simile to one of harmony and resonance, the process of selection of approaches was similar to an orchestral composer grouping instruments, looking for the most satisfying mix for the expressive work planned.

This Gallery of Method begins with elaborations of the expressive research approach introduced in the first chapter of this thesis and linked initially to the work of Reason and Heron, and then to that of Eisner and Barone.

In this study the expressive approach is located and developed as a phenomenological form of interpretative research, which is the main argument of this Gallery of Method. Before this exploration of its interpretative and phenomenological roots, the study needs to consider summarising work by Barone and Eisner (1997) which elaborated the meaning and dimensions of the expressive research. For these writers, another way to name and describe this expressive form of research was to look at it as 'arts-based research'.

Expressive and arts-based research

Barone and Eisner list seven features of arts-based educational inquiry which have huge resonances with the work pursued in the Main Gallery. The first feature is that arts-based research *creates a virtual reality*. They suggest (1997, p. 75) that 'the author acutely observes and documents the telling details of human activity', but within a work of fiction which nevertheless mirrors the lived world and somehow makes the familiar fresh. This is the aim of the Sketching panel in this study.

The second feature is *the presence of ambiguity*. The arts-based researchers try to leave spaces in the text which can be filled by the reader in a kind of dialogue with the author, but adding his or her own insights and images to enrich the reading (Barone and Eisner 1997, p. 76).

> The aim of the literary artist is not to prompt a single, closed, conver-
> gent reading but rather to persuade readers to contribute answers to
> the dilemmas posed within the text.

The third feature is the *use of expressive language*. Barone and Eisner mention writing that is metaphorical and creative. They quote Dewey's comment that artists *express* meaning, whereas scientists *state* meaning. As he says (Dewey 1934, p. 84):

> The poetic as distinct from the prosaic, aesthetic art as distinct from
> scientific, expression as distinct from statement, does something
> different from leading to an experience. It constitutes one.

There are significant links between this feature and the poetised texts in the Main Gallery.

The fourth feature of arts-based research is the use of *contextualized and vernacular language*. Arts-based research wants to use 'non-technical, everyday vernacular forms of speech that are more closely associated with lived experience' (Barone and Eisner 1997, p. 76). Barone and Eisner stress that such language is not abstract and theoretical but vernacular. In the following chapter, where intuiting phenomenology is explored, it will be suggested that the approach used here does use vernacular non-technical, non-jargon language, but not necessarily as commonly employed. The use of poetic forms for example, as seen in the Main Gallery, tends to mould ordinary vernacular language in a *new-making* way so that the familiar becomes strange and somehow re-seeable, as if with new eyes. The use of Aboriginal English in two of the installations is a good example of the use of this vernacular feature, illustrating how the language of the time and context is adopted. The poetised reflections from the same installations use vernacular words, but this time compressed and angled in a new way so that they can 'catch the eye' of the reader.

The *promotion of empathy*, the fifth feature of arts-based research, refers to its capacity to represent the viewpoint and feelings of people involved in an experience. As will be explored below, interpretative research that seeks to understand things from the other's perspective has needed a way to express this inter-subjectivity. The use of literary devices and approaches has some capacity to evoke empathetic feelings, images and insights in the reader.

The sixth feature refers to the writer's *personal signature*. Arts-based inquiry has a strong individualised feel to it. The writer has, to a greater or lesser extent, put her or his unique intuiting of a phenomenon into text. It is the artist's genius that something so individualistic and specific to the writer can have (to a greater or lesser extent) the power to evoke in the reader an analogical resonative experience.

The seventh and final feature is the *presence of aesthetic form*. Barone and Eisner suggest, as does this thesis, that expressive genres like stories and poems have special aesthetic requirements which must be followed to generate the desired evocation and portrayal. Good arts-based research must, as far as possible, be good art as well – a good story, poem and the like.

These seven features can be found in abundance in the Main Gallery of this study and serve to make apparent the arts-based character of this thesis. This and the following chapter examine the foundations of this expressive approach.

The exploration begins with a consideration of the *interpretative dimension of expressive research* method and its links with adult education research. This expressive method, as a whole, is shown also to be phenomenological when taken in the broader, more contemporary sense (cf. Crotty 1996a). It encompasses the ideas and methods derived both from the narrower classical and the broader interpretative approaches to phenomenology – or the 'intuiting' and 'empathetic' approaches, as they are referred to in this study.

The classical approach which underpins the Intuiting and Distilling panels in the installations of the Main Gallery is considered in the next chapter. The rest of this chapter confines itself to the general expressive research method within the interpretative phenomenological tradition and then introduces four significant elements in the project which need to be acknowledged and their influence noted.

The first element is the *contextualised* nature of adult education practice as it is pursued in various times and places. The second is *the interest and bias of the researcher*. The third element is the *autobiographical character* of the study, since it builds on the writer's own experiences of adult education practice. The final factor influencing the expressive interpretative method used here is the *reflective practice* element, in that the author revisits past events of his adult education practice, seeking to learn from and understand them.

With this introductory overview completed, the following begins with an exploration of the nature and location of 'expressive' interpretative research among forms of qualitative research.

Qualitative research and the expressive approach

Qualitative research

The expressive research pursued here, which draws on germinal work by Bruner, Reason and Heron mentioned in Chapter 1, is a particular version of so-called qualitative or interpretative research concerned with 'perception' rather than 'explanation'. Qualitative research is concerned with meanings that humans develop and place on their worlds. Qualitative researchers, according to Denzin and Lincoln (1994, p. 2):

> ... study things in their natural settings, attempting to make sense of, or interpret, phenomena in terms of the meanings people bring to them.

As Miles and Huberman (1994, p. 6) suggest, the researcher tries to gain information about:

> ... the perceptions of local actors 'from the inside', through a process of deep attentiveness, of empathetic understanding (Verstehen), and of suspending or 'bracketing' preconceptions ...

This approach is also described by van Manen (1990, p. 4) as '*human science* which aims at explicating the meaning of human phenomena ... and at understanding the lived structures of meanings (such as in phenomenological studies of the lifeworld)'. Lifeworld refers to the way a person experiences the world.

Much qualitative research concerned with meanings is also often referred to as 'hermeneutic'. Hermeneutics as a research approach was originally linked to the interpretation of religious texts in an attempt to come to understand their original meanings, rather than those 'mapped onto' it, as it were, by later readers. This approach was later extrapolated to life and experience and ways of knowing the world.

The interpretative approach, as Merriam (1991b, p. 48) points out, grows out of this hermeneutic orientation based on interpretation and the search for deeper understanding. She goes on to say that, in the interpretative approach:

> ... reality is not an objective which can be discovered and measured but rather a construction of the human mind. The [perceived] world is a highly subjective phenomenon that is interpreted rather than measured ...

Hermeneutic approaches to human science research were developed in radically different ways by Dilthey (1987), Heidegger (1962) and his student Gadamer (1975). The expressive phenomenological approach developed in this study is located within a general hermeneutic approach, as will become clear.

The qualitative approach thus defined encompasses a variety of research approaches concerned with meaning in one or another way: in other words, with developing a hermeneutic of human action. In the same passage quoted above, van Manen points out that science tends to taxonomise or explain while human science wants to explicate or unravel the meaning of experience and understand its structures. The distinction used in this thesis between expressive and explanatory approaches is an attempt to follow the same track.

Explanatory approaches to qualitative research

Explanatory approaches in qualitative research can be linked to certain forms of empirical or post-positivist inquiry. One of the meanings of the post-positivist approach to qualitative research, highlighted by Garman (1996, p.14), is its explanatory one. It is linked to a desire, inspired by a kind of possibly unconscious scientism, to use so-called 'objective' tools of positivist science in qualitative research. She quotes Lincoln's comment that empirical post-positivist researchers seek to explore human meanings and significances, adhering to the principles of objectivity, validity and reliability as their canons for rigorous findings (Lincoln 1994). Some of these approaches seek to categorise human phenomena and then explain them in terms of the categories to which they are assigned. Others seek to discover causes for a human experience and thus explain it by examining the origins and nature of the causes. Both of these approaches and their limits are reviewed briefly below.

Explanation by categorisation

Explanatory inquiry can also generate knowledge by the processes of abstraction and categorisation, through which humans name the world they experience by relating experienced phenomena to general ideas they already possess. The implications and values of the broader category can then be attributed to the specific entity under consideration. The explanatory agenda for conceptualising interpretative research is to classify phenomena and link them to theories and information developed around the general categories to which it is assigned. In adult education research of this kind, the researcher seeks to generate new knowledge by classifying particular adult education activities according to existing categories.

For example, a student in a technical college may be puzzled by experiences in the classroom where the lecturer always seems so concerned to spell out exactly what students are required to do. Researchers can gain a particular insight if they classify the educational interactions of the classroom as 'transactional' behaviour – in which the students exchange specified performance for grades. By referring to it as transactional behaviour, the researcher can gain or create an insight into how the interactions of adult education practice, now named as a series of transactions between instructor and students, becomes considerably modified. Naming the interaction as a transaction highlights two features of the TAFE (Technical and Further Education) course. One is its power to confer grades and certificates in exchange for specified student performance, the other its need to attract and retain students and to qualify them according to established criteria. The researcher can then revisit some of the puzzling experiences in class and see if they can be made meaningful by being reinterpreted as 'transactional' behaviour. For example, could the obsequious behaviour of otherwise forthright people be explained as transactional strategies by which they, perhaps unconsciously, present the 'gift' of compliance to the lecturer, hoping to draw the return 'gift' of a high grade? Alternatively, could the obsessive directions of the instructor as he tries to get all the students though their competency tests before the end of term be interpreted as strategic transactional acts to ensure that they, the students, as consumers of the service, will be satisfied with it? Using this abstracting, conceptualising method, the lecturer's unusually defining behaviour is explained by naming it as an example of the broader category (i.e. transaction) to which the particular experience is assigned.

The act of categorisation in this explanatory conceptual process is revealed as a process that names 'this' (e.g. the students' compliance and the lecturer's unusually directive behaviour) for 'that' (e.g. transactional behaviour). In other words, it explains the particular in terms of the characteristics and features of the general category to which it is attributed.

This act of categorisation, which often generates huge amounts of knowledge, has a downside in that it moves the mind away from the 'livedness' of the actual experience. For example, the actual experience of being instructed in an unusually mechanistic, almost legalistic, way will tend to be blurred when it is categorised and interpreted as a type of transaction. To account for the lived experience of what it is like to be meticulously instructed by the TAFE lecturer needs a different approach which will capture the tension, fears and irritation in the teaching/learning exchanges. An expressive rather than explanatory interpretative approach aims to provide such a window onto this dimension of the human experience being researched.

Explanatory approaches by searching for causes

One of the common agendas of approaches of this kind is to attempt to explain a phenomenon in terms of its *causes*: to approach the thing being studied as something that was caused by particular forces which the research process seeks to uncover.

Denzin and Lincoln (1994, p. 8) mention a qualitative research study carried out by Howard Becker and his colleagues, published as *Boys in white* in 1961, which is an example of the 'cause seeking' approach to qualitative research. It is a study of the intern processes in medical school by which medical students take on the identity of doctors. His rigorous, meticulous data, collected from interviews and triangulated with participant observation, was analysed to look for factors causing young interns to take on so-called 'doctor' behaviour and attitudes. He wanted to understand medical students' behaviour in terms of its causes. Such a process frames the phenomenon under consideration as 'something which is caused'. This places medical student behaviour somehow in the same category as certain physical phenomena, for example lightning. Discovering the causes of something can lead to a discovery of general rules governing such causes. Thus, looking for the causes of lightning led to the discovery of electricity. Looking for the causes of medical students' recurrent behaviour confirmed and expanded some sociological theories of socialisation.

From another perspective, anyone looking at dramatic lightning patterns in a humid sky before a thunderstorm, and hearing the comment, 'Yes, that's caused by static electricity building up in the clouds', may feel a strange sense of let-down. To explain an event in terms of some of its *causes* may not account for the phenomenon in terms of its *significance*. In other words, for what the bolt of lightning means to a person experiencing, witnessing and reflecting on it. In fact, in the expression 'bolt of lightning', where 'bolt' is a metaphor refer-ring to an arrow from a crossbow, signifying immediate explosive action from a distance, the lighting is referred to as an experience – that is, as something which has been perceived and named. There is thus a subjective element that is picked up in the word 'meaning'. As the old saying has it, 'matter wouldn't matter unless there was a mind to mind'.

Critical explanations

The causes behind social events and processes have also been traced by critical theorists to the influence of hidden interests and inequalities embedded in the social discourses people use to construct and interpret their lives. These so-called hegemonic interests are alleged to be responsible for the unproblema-tised assumptions people can hold about the nature of the social order and various uncontested inequalities between social groups and categories defined by race, class or gender.

As David Little *et al* write (1991, p. 3):

> Critical theory shows how the pre-eminence of instrumental reason
> has impoverished social interactions and created inequities in material
> and social wellbeing ... The concern of adult educators is directed to
> change in the practice of adult education as a basis for penetrating
> unquestioned vital cultural traditions and creating the milieu for
> members of society to engage actively in the transformation of society
> along just, humane and equitable lines.

The expressive interpretative approach pursued here has not taken the directly critical approach. It does not explicitly 'look past' the phenomenon to the interests being served in its promotion. Nevertheless the expressive agenda, by keeping such a strong focus on 'the thing itself' as a lived experience, does attempt to 'look past' accepted interpretations of a phenomenon and the culture in which it is embedded. As Crotty (1996a, p. 89), has put it:

> Culture may make us human but it does so in a quite definitive and
> circumscribing way. In imposing these meanings, it is excluding
> others. And we should never lose sight of the fact that the particular
> set of meanings it imposes has come into being to serve particular
> interests and will harbour its own forms of oppression, manipulation
> and other injustices.

What this study argues is that there are elements in an experienced entity, with its meanings and significance, which emerge only with representative rather than analytical treatment. This differs from that which is achieved by explaining it as a type of 'something' and attributing to it characteristics of the type to which it is assigned. It also differs from that which is achieved by seeking to identify some of its causes, and it is a different kind of knowledge from that which emerges from seeking to uncover hegemonic interests that underpin its assumptions and values. The representative agenda needs an expressive approach to complement these explanatory ones.

The expressive approach

The distinction between Reason and Hawkins' explanatory and expressive modes of knowing (1988, p. 79) can be elaborated using a parallel distinction between two general camps called, in this study, 'conceptualising' and 'perceiving' (cf. Merleau-Ponty 1974, p. 196). The expressive interpretative approach used here, with its strong influence from phenomenology, attempts to name direct experience by what the philosopher Merleau-Ponty (1974, p. 198) calls perception: 'Perception does not give me truths like geometry but presences.'

The 'presences' refer to the outcomes of being constantly in the world as part of it; of being awake and aware of the world in which, and of which, one is. Presences are generated by getting back to a first level of awareness before engaging in conceptualising processes to become aware of 'what is present' in their life world, and what experiences are present to them.

Perceptual research seeks to portray these presences; to generate expressive, so-called 'immediate' knowledge of the researched entity, seeking to 'bracket out' received views and namings; to provide a vivid portrayal; to represent phenomena as far as possible as lived, contextual experiences. This use of the word 'perception' to refer to so-called pre-philosophical, pre-analytic forms of knowing follows Merleau-Ponty's usage in his work *Phenomenology of perception* (1962).

Reason (1988, p. 80) suggests that meaning is interwoven with experience and that the inquirer will discover the meaning the experience has been given when he or she engages in ways to make it manifest:

> ... to make meaning manifest through expression requires the use of a
> creative medium through which the meaning can take form. This is
> not to be confused with a conceptual grid which divides up experi-
> ence, it is rather the creation of an empty space ... which becomes a
> vessel in which meaning can take shape.

He goes on to mention the languages of words (stories and poems), of colour and shape (painting and sculpture) and of actions (mime and drama) in which meaning can be created and communicated. He makes a significant point that meaning in this sense is never directly pointed out but rather is demonstrated 'by re-creating pattern in metaphorical shape and form'.

Reason then links the expressive process to the personal journey of meaning making, in which a person's expressions of their experiences through story and other aesthetic artefacts may become linked to the great stories or sagas of human kind.

This journey into personal meaning making raises the issue of truth: of ways in which the expressive process can be in some way accountable to its accompanying experience. The possibility of self-indulgent narcissism has to be addressed in this form of human inquiry. It is clear that what is being sought is not explanatory truth but expressive truth which joins the experience and its expression, and needs to be understood and judged in those terms.

Reason's two categories seem close to those proposed by Bruner (1986), who suggests a distinction between the *paradigmatic* and the *narrative* forms of knowing, saying that the two approaches are radically different but have complementary functions (p. 11):

> A good story and a well-formed argument are different in natural kinds. Both can be used for convincing another. Yet what they convince of is fundamentally different: arguments convince one of their truth, stories of their lifelikeness.

As Reason develops his approach, it emerges as a form of interpretative inquiry in which an experience is reflected upon in such a way that it is not categorised or analysed but rather expressed in a variety of ways in search of its meaning. The word 'meaning' tends to include the notion of significance, and represents a considerable investment of thought and imagination by the reflecting expressive person in attempting to portray the wholeness of the experience.

Expressive research is then the version of qualitative research pursued in this study, since it is concerned with making explicit our perceptual understandings of events of practice as experiences, prior to further analysis. It is pursued on two fronts. The first is via the *empathetic* expressive road that gives an account of the adult education practice as experienced by the author in a specific context with the interests, prejudices and dispositions he possessed at that time or place. This expressive project is examined later in this chapter. The second is via the *intuiting* expressive road, drawing on classical phenomenology with a focus on the 'whatness' of the experience of adult education practice in the episodes described. This is explored in the next chapter.

The following table graphically illustrates the method developed for this study, which is located in two cells of this matrix. The axis along which the expressive and explanatory modes of knowing are located is intersected by the axis along which the varying foci of inquiry are located.

Table 1: Location of research method

INQUIRY FOCUS	MODE OF KNOWING	
	Explanatory	Expressive
POSITIVIST		
QUALITATIVE		
● Post-positivist		
● Interpretative (phenomenological)		
● Empathetic		* * * * * * * * * * * *
● Intuiting		* * * * * * * * * * * *
● Critical		

The study turns to locate its approach in the general field of adult education research before pursuing the use of the expressive method in this study.

Expressive approaches in adult education research

In earlier times, it would have been difficult to find a qualitative discourse community in adult education research since there were few interpretative researchers. Merriam (1991b, p. 44) mentions that:

> ... most research in adult education has been based on a positivist paradigm which assumes there is an objective measurable world which can be described and plotted.

John McIntyre in his recent essay on research in adult education and training (1995, p. 122), confirms this and then refers to the qualitative reaction to this tradition. Citing Usher and Bryant (1989, p. 23), he points out that the positivist empirical approach has been vigorously criticised as being based on limited assumptions about science, persons and society that deny the power of human beings to make meanings and create a social world.

Qualitative approaches and expressive research

In the last two decades, adult education researchers have also focused on questions with a more interpretative approach. A considerable number of projects have explored the way adult learners learn and adult educators teach (Deschler and Hagan 1990; Titmus 1989). A number of adult education researchers in the last decade have explored epistemological and philosophical questions concerning experience, knowledge, learning, practice and research (cf. Boud, Keogh and Walker 1985; Brookfield 1987; Usher and Bryant 1989; Warner-Weil and McGill 1989; Mulligan and Griffin 1992; Boud, Cohen and Walker 1993). The interpretative agenda pursued in this thesis is placed in this general area.

There is also a range of writings concerned with theoretical and practical approaches to adult education practice with an experiential flavour: Brookfield (1990a) on teacher education practice; Miller (1993) on group work practices in adult education; Heimlich and Norland (1994) on teaching style; and Vella (1994) on listening in teaching. These also represent interests closer to the question of practice pursued here.

A larger community of researchers has centred on critical approaches to adult education, seeking in particular to identify and resist collusion in false consciousness embedded in adult education policy, provision and practice, caused by the influence of hegemonic interests shaping the common discourses of personal and social life. Writers and practitioners such as Jack Mezirow, Phyllis Cunningham, Michael Collins, J.E. (Teddy) Thomas, Griff Foley, Mechtild Hart, Mike Welton, Stephen Brookfield, Mike Newman and Jane Thompson are some of the more prominent researchers. Selected titles from their major works are listed in the bibliography. Many of these researchers worked with groups of learners from oppressed and resistant groups, making considerable contributions to critical research. Their own research was often grounded in references to teaching/learning experiences with these groups. There has been considerable debate among these writers and practitioners contesting various versions or emphases of the critical approach. Some approaches have tended to locate the site of so-called 'false consciousness' in the learning individual locked into a flawed 'frame of reference' and requiring 'perspective transformation' as a way of delivering critical knowledge through transformative learning (cf. Mezirow 1977, 1985, 1991b). Others following a more Freirian approach have seen the site of false consciousness as the oppressed group and the road to critical knowledge through the praxis of political and social collective resistance (cf. Newman 1993, 1994). As has been pointed out above, the phenomenological approach pursued in this study claims to complement and enrich the critical approach.

A small number of adult education researchers have already formed a phenomenological discourse community. There are major contributions from Stanage (1986, 1987), Collins (1984, 1985) and Brookfield (1990a, 1990b). Each uses the approach in different ways. A detailed summary of these approaches and their relation to the present project is provided in the second chapter of this Gallery of Method where the two major approaches to phenomenology suggested in this study are explored extensively. At that point their contributions can be more readily located and evaluated within the matrix of approaches suggested.

Suffice to say at this point that, as a generalisation, it is suggested that Stanage and Collins have used phenomenology in its classical or intuiting version to analyse the structures of adult education experience. Their approach, with its analytical rigour, contributes to what, in this thesis, is referred to as 'explanatory knowledge' of the experience of adult education. Brookfield on the other hand has used the later, so-called 'empathetic' version of phenomenology and his contribution uses expressive and explanatory approaches. The approach in this study is mostly expressive and uses empathetic and intuiting forms of phenomenology in pursuit of this agenda.

The expressive method attempts to allow the adult education practice to stand clear from imposed meanings. As such, while not actively seeking to name oppressive interests at work, such a project serves the critical agenda indirectly by freeing the researcher's eye from hegemonic interests that shape the way it is presented. Critical theorists, presented with a phenomenon-for-itself, may be able to more readily get a better view of the inequitable forces embedded in discourses that attempt to shape the actual educational events and practices to their interests. Having thus located the approach of this study within the general categories of adult education research, the study now turns to an exploration of how the expressive approach is pursued in this thesis.

Applying the expressive method

Reason's theories of expressive qualitative research underpin the installations of the Main Gallery. The six panels of the installations use two complementary forms of expressive method. The *empathetic* expressive method was used in the development of the first three panels. It attempted to bring the lived experience of each episode of adult education practice to mind and to life by attempting an empathetic and narrative portrayal of the event as a contextualised and person-alised experience. In this approach, the author tries to 'get into the shoes' of the person engaged in the experience (which of course in this case is the author himself, some years back in time). He does this in order to see it, as it were, with his eyes, and to describe it as what he was seeing and making sense of during the episode. This draws directly and easily from Reason's 'verstehen' approach. It seeks to be an explicative 'connotative' process which is the 'elab-oration of feeling and emotional imagery and intuition into created form and expression' (Eckhartsberg 1981, p. 83).

As will be elaborated later in this chapter, the Backgrounding panel's func-tion will be shown to frame the chosen episodes and provide a contextual map of some of the social, cultural and personal forces exerting their influence on adult education practice at the time. The Sketching panel will be shown to be a way to portray each episode as a narrative experience built into a story with colour and complexity and richness. The Poetised reflection panel will be explained as the form of rich imaginal writing with the most freedom to convey what the experience in these chosen episodes of practice was like for the author. In the building of these panels in the installations, the 'verstehen' methods of the first three panels were an attempt to give an account of an experience from inside the person having it. It was aimed to make the experience of adult educa-tion vividly present with all the interactive subjectivities and feelings and judgements that were part of it.

The expressive project then made a space for a complementary *intuiting* approach in the Intuiting and Distilling panels. This was an attempt to intuit the structures of the adult education practice experience, built on the classical phenomenological agenda of Heidegger and Merleau-Ponty. The intuiting expressive method was used to contemplate the experience itself, made present in these empathetic texts but letting go the defining images and ideas just gener-ated, and attempting to go back to 'the thing itself': to the structure of the lived experience of adult education practice. These ideas will be explored at greater length in the following chapter. At this stage it is now necessary to return to further elaborations of the empathetic expressive approach and its links to the first three panels in the installations.

The detailed discussion of the contribution of the three panels to the empathetic expressive approach is built on four significant elements of the empathetic expressive projects that have already been alluded to in the text and which now require explication. The first two belong to the nature of this kind of research. Of these, the first is its contextualised character, since empathetic expressive research which seeks to present an experience as 'lived' needs to cater for the way that experience is given meaning and significance by the person experiencing it. According to the empathetic tradition, attribution of significance to an experience is done through all kinds of interactions with members of one's proximate and remote social environment, who therefore need to be given a place in the research explorations.

The second dimension – the personal – is again linked to the nature of empathetic research. As will be shown below, it is not possible to attempt to get into the shoes of the person being researched without being aware of, and to some extent factoring in, the researcher's mindset and dispositions as well. Expressive qualitative research which wants to include the personal and subjective as real elements in the phenomena being studied, needs to be somewhat reflexive as well and to include the personal interests and biases of the researcher as part of the research text.

The other two elements are linked to the particular phenomenon being explored by the expressive methodology. Adult education practice pursued by the author and so described has a strong autobiographical flavour since the installations are, as it were, based on episodes of adult education practice engaged in by the author himself. Finally the experience of adult education practice, the phenomenon under examination, is a combination of thoughtful learning facilitative activities, their reception by the would-be learners and the educator's ongoing response to their reaction in turn. There is thus in this phenomenon a strong element of reflective practice. The following looks at the significance to the thesis of these four qualifying elements.

Qualifying elements

The contextual element

The social nature of empathetic qualitative research, with its intention to get inside the person having the experience so as to see it with his or her eyes, needs to be attuned to the contextual and interactive nature of this kind of seeing. This contextualised nature of human subjectivity and the essentially social nature of named human experience differ considerably from more positivist and functional approaches. Usher and Bryant (1989, p. 146) have pointed out that one of the heritages of adult education literature has been a:

> Knowlesian decontextualised concept of the 'self' in relation to 'knowledge' ... they deny to adulthood both the role of the self in authenticating its own knowledge and the role of knowledge in contributing to a responsible sense of 'selfhood'.

The contextual element in this project is linked directly to the nature of empathetic 'verstehen' research which, as has been pointed out above, wants to 'get into the shoes' of the person encountering the experience that is being examined. Getting into the mind of the person experiencing the phenomenon under study also requires an awareness of the social and cultural environment of the experience. This is a key point in this method since one of the foundations of empathetic, interpretative research is that, when a person names her or his experience, the act of naming, of using language, is pursued in interaction with the current ideas which are a major constitutive element of that environment. The experience becomes what it is named, and what it is named is constructed in and through a dialogic process with the people of one's social universe through what George Herbert Mead (1962) called 'symbolic interaction'.

One of the foundational assumptions of this study is thus the historical, social and of course symbolic 'embeddedness' of the human self that influences its engagement in activities (such as in this case adult education) in different times and places. Usher and Bryant (1989, p. 150), referring to Mead, explain this socially constructed self as 'a developing entity which *arises in the process of social experience and activity*' (Mead 1962, p. 135).

The expressive approach of this project with its agenda to portray the phenomenon of adult education practice will need to provide a space to describe elements of the practitioner's environment that contribute to his embeddedness in the changing historical contexts of the experience. This will tend to include elements of various social and cultural forces active at the time, and largely as perceived reflectively by the person having the experience.

Thus, in the Backgrounding panel explored at length below, the author will describe some of the significant circumstances of each episode and something of the participants in the episode's teaching/learning exchanges. Of course he cannot stop there. He has to stand back for a moment from the person having the experience and look to see what stance and dispositions he has brought to the experience which would constitute another ingredient in its interactive nature.

In the same way that the adult educator's personal and professional dispositions need to be mentioned as a component of the background of the episodes of practice in the installations of the Main Gallery, his personal influence on, and interest in, the structure and approaches of the whole thesis, which is coloured by such a similar personal element, need brief acknowledgement.

The personal element

The personal element refers to the importance of the text being located as coming from a particular writer, located, as has been pointed out above, in a social context but also possessing concerns and predispositions which will serve to influence the emerging text in one way or another. The following introduces the author once again, following his brief appearance in Chapter 1, giving a brief account of the significance of his interests and predispositions in the shaping of the emerging text.

While not seeking to elaborate and defend exhaustively every aspect of this inquiry, it is important to acknowledge the personal quest element in this project. It emerges in the introductory chapter where I identify myself and indicate my interest in the project. It recurs throughout the study in the moments where I position my 'self' and explain that to the reader. Although this is not an autobiographical thesis in which I adopt centre stage, but rather a study about adult education practice (as has been said in the introduction), there are from time to time remarks I make as the author and curator of the exhibition which signify the quest element in the study, and as such, some acknowledgement is needed.

Two implications follow from the research quest element in this study. The first is that it is an exploration rather than a testing of hypotheses or grand theories. The second is that it has some bias embedded in the interests and stance of its author/researcher that the author acknowledges, but for which he does not apologise. The stance of the author/researcher emerges at different times throughout the study, for example in his choice of definitions of adult education practice. These represent his preferred approach and arguably are appropriate in this research since the episodes of adult education practice are actually *his* practice. Nevertheless, one can see that the presence of some personal preference and interest in the research, which tends to be influenced by a kind of continuance of the author's autobiography off stage, here influences the shape of the research. As Reason and Rowan said (1981, p. xv):

> Researchers give off all sorts of messages in all kinds of ways. They
> try to direct scenes on the research stage, but they are actually part of
> the play.

The personal quest to explore and understand adult education experience is small scale and low key. It does not purport to have answers. It has a big question about what adult education practice is like and how that experience can be understood and represented so that others can get an idea of what it is like. The metaphor of an exhibition carries the meaning of the thesis well, provided it is understood that the installations are set up not as triumphalistic conclusions, but as contributions to an ongoing collaborative search by the curator in dialogue with those entering the gallery to contemplate the installations.

Having admitted the presence of the researcher and his agenda, the text now turns to two related qualifying elements which characterise the research being pursued: its autobiographical and reflective dimensions which qualify and illumine its practice. These elements have considerable significance in the general agenda of the thesis. The autobiographical elements restrict the episodes of adult education practice to the author's own. The reflective practice dimension serves to focus the text on adult education practice, and to contribute to the agenda of the thesis to focus on what the author/adult educator was doing, rather than on the author who was doing it.

The autobiographical element

Autobiography as a form of social research has been explored by writers such as Armstrong (1987); Faraday and Plummer (1979); Gusdorf (1980); Olney (1980); Reason and Marshall (1987); Reason and Heron (1986); Salmon (1989); and Usher and Bryant (1989). Much contemporary writing has tended to explore autobiography within more general categories. One of the most common is *narrative research* (cf. Richardson 1990; Carter 1993; Casey 1995). Another locates it within *personal experience methods* (Clandinin and Connelly 1994), while others have explored autobiographical studies under studies of subjectivity or *emotional sociology*. Ellis, for example (1991, p.126), speaks of emotional sociology as:

... consciously and reflectively feeling for our selves, our subjects and our topics of study and evoking those feelings in our readers.

Many of the aims of this thesis bear pretty close resemblance to such research. The preoccupation here is not to produce a comprehensive review of autobiographical approaches to research, but to identify and understand elements in autobiographical approaches to research that might serve to shape the empathetic expressive research being pursued.

Armstrong (1987), looking at life histories as social research, shows that many began as 'qualitative supplements to quantitative projects' but later gained validity in their own right 'particularly for the exploration of subjective reality'. He goes on to say that such life histories document 'the inner subjective reality as constructed by the individuals themselves showing how they interpret, understand and define the social world around them' (p. 8).

The position taken in this thesis and developed further in the next chapter suggests there are actually two kinds of subjectivity distinguishable in Armstrong's 'inner subjective reality', depending on whether the *experience* or the *person having the experience* is foregrounded. Both approaches generate different and complementary knowledge: one is about the moods, elation and fears of the subject having the experience; the other is about the 'whatness' of the experience itself.

The autobiographical dimensions of this research are linked to the method used in the installations of the Main Gallery. Here the texts of the panels are built on narratives and recollections of adult educational practice embedded in, and shaped by, the sociocultural environment which influenced the author's dispositions and consequent activities.

Many of the questions which have emerged in portraying adult education as a lived experience were influenced by the subjective experience of being an adult educator engaged in the various adult education practices, whose approach to being an educator of adults changed considerably for a range of reasons more hinted at than explored. Although the subjective dispositions of the educator as such are not the main focus of this study, there is still a strong autobiographical flavour that needs to be acknowledged and accommodated. When it is explicitly said that the focus is, in fact, not on the subject, it is important to know that such an emphasis is no more than an 'emphasis'. The experience that is being contemplated always has a subjective element that needs to be catered for in the attempt to portray adult education practice as comprehensively as possible.

Andresen (1993, p. 60) summarises many of the debates surrounding the use of autobiographical research in academia:

Autobiography remains in much conventional academic discourse, a disputed, even a suspect element. Its particularity, its (purportedly) unrepresentative and ungeneralisable nature as data, the temptation it offers for narcissistic indulgence or fantasy reconstuctions, are all familiar pitfalls. Brookfield argues persuasively in its favour, however, claiming that 'aspects of generic processes are evident in single acts';

how 'the phenomenological truth of an insight does not depend on the number of people who report its occurrence'; and how 'One person's formulation of a problem or exploration of a dilemma may contain many points of connection to other's experiences' (Brookfield 1990a, p. 39).

Brookfield's defence of autobiographical approaches in this quotation relates to its use in forms of explanatory research, where a problem solved by one may be offered as a solution for others.

This thesis offers distinctions that would identify three foundations of Brookfield's arguments and attempt to keep them distinct.

The statement: 'aspects of generic processes are evident in single acts', is located as explanatory knowledge, generated by locating individual events as instances of generic laws. This is particularly true in negative experiences, where one well-described instance of the adult learners not behaving as the andragogic literature suggested they would is enough to challenge the universality of the general theory. The truth here is 'explanatory truth', which can be tested for validity and reliability.

The second statement: 'the phenomenological truth of an insight does not depend on the number of people who report its occurrence', needs to be understood as having a claim to a different kind of truth which it shares with expressive forms of qualitative research like this thesis. This is the truth of verisimilitude, which has its own criteria different from those for explanatory research. This is explored below in the section on the criterion for the quality of this project.

The third statement: 'One person's formulation of a problem or exploration of a dilemma may contain many points of connection to other's experiences', is located, like the first quotation, in explanatory knowledge, and can receive similar verification.

What is required here particularly is the dimension of autobiography's contribution to expressive research.

Autobiography has had a relatively recent history as a valid method of qualitative research. In the interests of its use in this thesis, it can be conceived in a number of largely complementary ways.

It can be seen as *personal story telling* – the making explicit and placing in historical context a series of contextualised events. This story is not in response to an inquirer whose questioning tends to create another shape to be mapped onto the educator's reflected-upon reality, but in response to the writer's own interests, style and preoccupations. It can also be seen possibly more readily as a form of *recollection* (or 're-collection'): remembering, ordering, imagining lived experience. Finally, autobiography can be conceived as *performance* through which the person presents him or herself to the reader.

Personal story telling: telling it like it is

Autobiography can be conceived as story telling. As Mitroff (1978, in Reason 1988, p. 82) says:

> Stories can be used in a variety of ways: as amusement or as devices
> with which to peer into human desires, wishes, hopes and fears. In
> this sense, stories ... provide the hardest body of evidence and the best
> method of problem definition.

A story engages the imagination. It does not show individuals necessarily
as they were or even as they are. Rather, it expresses what they believe themselves to have been, and to be at the time of writing. Reflection at another time
may lead to other insights. Thus the self ultimately is not something to be
discovered through autobiography. It is, in fact, something to be imagined,
constructed and narrated through the autobiographical story.

Brookfield (1990a, p. xi) wrote about this form of writing in one of his
recent publications:

> My intention in writing it was to tell the real story of teaching. This
> story, which is full of unexpected twists and turns, unpredicted events,
> and unlooked for surprises, is one of complexities, uncertainties, and
> passions. I wanted to tell the story in a way that communicated these
> passions, so that teachers could recognise their own emotional selves
> in its pages. I wanted to convey the marvellous messiness of classroom
> life and to explore the ways in which teaching is a deeply emotional
> process.

What Brookfield seems to be doing, and what autobiographers seem to do
when they are 'telling their story', is to recount a selective interpretation of
lived experiences which were personally significant and which somehow correspond to the inner reality of the experience of teaching. Brookfield's claim that
somehow his account is '*the* real one' is not a claim for some absolute knowledge, but for a truth of verisimilitude. He signals that there is a real story in
teaching that can be discovered and that should be told: that this discovered
story has common characteristics independent of the individual story teller but
brought to life in different ways with different tellers and tellings. He is trying
to create a text that is a 'grounded' and real account of the lived experience of
his teaching – in other words, it is his version of the real story of his experience.
The accounts used in this study similarly attempt to provide an account of the
real story of the author's education practice.

According to the meanings here, 'telling the real story'/'telling it like it is' is
a useful way to describe the project of constructing a phenomenological
portrayal of the writer's lived experience as an adult educator. Such an account
strives to be *a* real one, which presents *the* truth of experienced practice to
which others may add dialogue in light of their own 'real' experience.

Story telling fits well with the phenomenological agenda being pursued in this
research. It enables past events (in this case episodes of adult education practice)
to be accepted and described as whole lived experiences, and allows revisiting
what was going on in them. It makes it possible to use a range of communicative
vehicles – written text, song, poetry – with a range of images, metaphors and allusions encompassing ideas and thoughts accompanying the experience, as well as
the non-rational and complementary 'feeling' parts of the psyche.

The story-telling dimension of autobiography as research has been high-lighted by feminist writers like Oakley (1981), who saw that social research seemed often to be something 'done to' people as research objects. Armstrong (1987, p. 14) quotes Hilary Graham's (1982, pp. 13, 14) approval of the life history method for feminism, using story telling as an inclusive method which she contrasts favourably with the reductionism and objectivism of survey research:

> Story telling rejects the individualism of survey research. Social surveys encourage respondents to reduce their experiences to frag-ments which can be captured in a question-and-answer format. Stories, by contrast, provide a vehicle through which individuals can build up and communicate the complexity of their lives. While surveys 'tear individuals from their social context', stories are pre-eminent ways of relating individuals and events to social contexts, ways of weaving personal experiences into the social fabric. Secondly, stories provide a vehicle through which the existence and experience of inequality can be explored ... Thirdly, stories do not demand that experiences and activities assume an object-form. Instead, stories illu-minate the dynamic quality of experience, being themselves a process by which individuals make sense of past events and present circumstances.

This capacity of autobiography to be a process by which individuals 'make sense of past events' and where 'stories do not demand that experiences and activities assume an object-form' highlights and honours its subjective dimen-sions. The project being pursued here wants to adopt a third way when exploring and safeguarding the subjectivity in first-person accounts. It suggests that, while not attempting to create a decontextualised or abstracted account purporting to carry a totally 'objective' truth, first-person accounts can be more or less objectivising or subjectivising depending on the subject's focus of attention. This is derived from classical phenomenological theory and is considered at length in the next chapter of this study.

Whereas there are cases where stories can project all kinds of subjectivity, in this case there is a need for the story to illuminate and focus on the practice of adult education; in other words, to stay with the adult education phenom-enon in all its concrete experience and to step back a little from too subjective a focus, while allowing elements of subjective response some space in the objec-tivising narrative.

Ordering experience: autobiography as 're-collection'

When various forms of adult education practice are described, they are explored as personal experiences in a series of settings over 20 years each, with particular assumptions about the educator and the world and the place of education within it. But because this is being carried out after the event for specific purposes, the narrative is not a bald chronicle of events. It is a 're-ordering' of the past, selectively 're-called' in the interests of the present.

Armstrong (1987, p. 48) refers to this as 'retrospective re-interpretation', or what Michael Brady (1990, p. 43) calls 're-collection'. In his study on autobiography, Brady writes that:

> Memory is more than a recollection of past events; it is a critical element in the search for and construction of meaning in human experience in that it provides 'conscious consciousness of experience'.

This second role of autobiography in learning is cosmological; it spells out the way a person sees the world and their place in it. Human beings are capable of building order in their present-day lives by way of the remembered past. Autobiography also engages the imagination. It does not show individuals necessarily as they were or even as they are. Rather, it expresses what they believe themselves to have been and to be. Thus the self ultimately is not something to be discovered through autobiography. It is in fact something to be imagined and constructed.

Of course, in this case the autobiographical project is a story about adult education. It is about the writer and his experiences as an adult education practitioner. The objective is to reflect on, and name carefully, activities of practice in these different circumstances. When such experiences of adult education practice are presented over these times by re-calling and analysing significant incidents in educational practice in each period, the understanding of the phenomenon of adult education as an experienced and practiced reality is also being ordered into a comprehensible whole.

Stimson (1976, p. 90, cited in Armstrong 1987, p. 48) draws attention to this pressure on autobiographical writing to be coherent to the reader:

> The problem with any story is that it must appear rational to the audience … the life history must fit with the present situation. This may be done by selecting items from the past which are in line with the present, and so the life course is shown as consistent; alternatively, the discrepancy between past and present can be magnified in order to show the disjunction between past and present. The past is either incorporated or written off. Such consistency or disjunction maintains the rationality of the teller.

This 'ordering' is characteristic of autobiography as written text, to be read and interpreted. It is one of the factors limiting and shaping the kind of knowledge contained in this kind of work.

But of course, Brady's text is a reminder that what happens when a person engages in autobiographical writing is much more than just the description of a series of events. There is also a search for, or construction of, personal meaning attached to that experience. And once aware of this it is possible to search for the 'communities of consciousness' to which the writer belonged in the past episodes of adult education practice being revisited: what values were supported and how such communities saw and described the world. The nature of these communities will again contribute to uncovering more of the embedded and contextualised nature of the adult education experience.

This perception is based on the suggestion from Berger and Luckman (1971) that people's ideas are influenced and often shaped by the assumptions and dynamics within their familiar group of associates, the so-called *interpretatative community*, with whom one spends social time, explores issues and forms opinions. This 'community' is highly fluid. It is permanently being constructed by ongoing conversation between its members. As well as being influenced by the group's opinions, prejudices and feelings, participants in the group can also shape that field by his or her reactions to, and critique of, those opinions, prejudices and feelings. Since the practice of adult education was always carried out amongst a group of people, and the adult educator was also usually affiliated with a group of educators, the nature of these 'communities' in which the adult education episode was located are of great significance.

Sharing experience: autobiography as performance

The act of writing autobiography for publication adds the third layer to autobiography as story and as recollection, this time focusing on its character as something designed to have a particular impact on those reading it. As an act of sharing experience with others, of presentation of self, it is performance. Current work by Miller and Morgan (1993) highlights this *presentational* dimension of autobiographical writing, pointing to the agenda of the autobiographer wishing to be heard by others and to be interpreted in a particular way. In a recent review, Michael Erben (1992, p. 194) quotes an anonymous saying, that 'the three pitfalls of autobiography are nostalgia, paranoia and a transparent craving to appear likeable'.

The performance dimension of autobiography can lead writers into desires to appear more than likeable; they can also wish to appear powerful, honest, valuable or possibly repentant.

Using Goffman's (1959) notions of 'elements of performance' in the construction and presentation of the self, Miller and Morgan show how much the end to which the writing is directed actually shapes the 'performance'. In the case of the proposed autobiography of professional practice, there is a dilemma in that, at one level, the writer will be 'talking to himself' about his educational practice in order to uncover what the experience was like, as if in the presence of a respectful, empathetic and interpretative listener. In this state of awareness it can easily be imagined that the need to defend oneself or justify one's actions would not be so strongly felt. At another level, since the writing is undertaken to be read, and for the author's experience and insight to be understood (respected?) by others, some reluctance to wash dirty linen in public can be expected – and if any linen is washed, it would probably be presumed to be somewhat pre-laundered.

The way the agenda has been shaped is that the project is one seeking illumination rather than absolution or justification. It is to focus on the forms of adult educational practice which were practised in different periods of the writer's practice, focusing not so much on the rights and wrongs of particular incidents (although this may well be a component) nor on the writer as educator, but on how the adult education agenda was played out in each

incident and what could be learned of this kind of educational activity in practice. This may be more difficult than was expected. A preliminary attempt at
reflective autobiography on one of these episodes of practice submitted to a
refereed journal in 1992 drew criticism from one of the reviewers for its 'self
congratulatory tone', a characteristic which efforts had been explicitly made to
avoid.

One of the other agendas of this method is to map a kind of development
of thought and practice so that it is possible, without loss of face, to describe
and criticise a certain stance in the light of having already, as it were, 'repented
of one's folly'. It has emerged, however, that this is not always as easy as had
been imagined. It can be envisaged that there will always be places where
weaknesses in the writer's engagement in adult education practice are minimised, lest he appear in too unacceptable a light even for a pre-conversion
condition.

Autobiography in the thesis

The personal story-telling dimension of the autobiographical approach sits well
with the anecdotal elements in the Sketching panel, but with one major
proviso. Autobiographical anecdotes and stories tend to foreground the author.
Here, adult educational practice pursued by the author is the anecdotal focus.
'The phenomenon' is the centre of attention rather than the author. This
considerable difference is highlighted by the second element in autobiography
described above: its function of 're-collection'.

The re-collection agenda receives considerable modification when used in
the thesis. This is not the place for autobiographical defences and arguments
against the author's critics. In this context, the re-collection, the ordering of
events within the autobiographical genre, is the ordering of reflective contemplation, focused on portraying the lived experience of adult education practice
rather than justifying the writer's part in its past and present. The performance
characteristic of autobiographical writing, its third characteristic discussed
above, is shared with the whole text-building enterprise of the thesis. The exhibition metaphor builds on and develops the performance agenda, except that
here too the foregrounded performer is adult education practice, with the practitioner placed a little less front stage.

One of the components of autobiography which does not obtain in all
cases is that for many it becomes a narrative of things learned from the experiences undergone, and the learning itself becomes one of the experiences
described. This process of reflection, which has received considerable attention
in recent adult education writing, forms the final qualifying element – its character as a reflective narrative about practice – in the empathetic expressive
research being pursued here.

The reflective practice element

Besides being seen as a form of autobiographical research, the research project
was identified in the first chapter as also being a form of reflection on the
writer's practice. As with autobiography, there has been considerable

theoretical and practical research into the nature and processes of reflection and reflective practice. This section explores ideas from this literature into the nature and types of reflection and reflective practice, and seeks to locate and illumine the proposed research processes in the light of this research.

The main question is: 'What kind of reflection is the research project attempting and in what way does its location as a category of reflection illumine and shape what is being attempted? To pursue this question, the inquiry begins with ideas about the nature of reflection and reflective practice and its various types, then attempts to locate the reflection and reflective practice being carried out in the installations of the Main Gallery within the proposed categories and as such, to point out ways in which such location might tend to shape and frame its processes.

Reflection

In general terms, reflection occurs when people turn their minds to themselves and their activities, feelings, thoughts and judgements and become attentive to them and the influences which shape them. It is the beginning of much learning. Boud, Keogh and Walker (1985, p. 19) write that:

> ... reflection in the context of learning is a generic term for those intellectual and affective activities in which individuals engage to explore their experiences in order to lead to new understandings and appreciations.

This description expands the notion of reflection, which tends to be commonly restricted to thoughts and reveries, to include attention to feelings as well. Boud *et al*, speaking of reflection as a lead-up to learning, describe it as a process (1985, p. 27) by which learners can get in touch with all the dimensions of their experiences in order to understand more clearly what happened to them at the time, and to assess and change ideas and behaviours as a result. In later writings, they begin to identify component processes within reflection. They speak (Boud *et al* 1993, p. 9) of reflection containing processes 'to recapture, notice and re-evaluate their experience, to work with their experience to turn it into learning'.

In addition, the processes contained in reflection engage the whole person with his or her history, prejudices and feelings which in their turn shape the process. Boud *et al* (1985, p. 21) noted in their study on learning from experience that, in reflection, people bring to their learning all the baggage of their previous life:

> ... the response of the learner to new experience is determined significantly by past experiences which have contributed to the ways in which the learner perceives the world.

Practical reflection

People engage in practical reflection when they turn their attention to a purposive activity in which they are involved, with a view to understanding and improving it. These activities are reflected on as human goal-directed activities, while at the same time they are contextualised, instrumental, ethical and political.

Practical reflection in any kind of educational practice, whether in the classroom or, as has been pointed out above, in the informal exchanges of a group linked to the school, focuses on the pedagogic action of educators and trainers of adults when they were actually engaged in facilitating adult learning as teachers, group leaders, trainers, instructors or facilitators. It is the store of their experiences as purposive learning facilitators which is reflected on in the search to uncover the approaches to facilitating learning which were employed, so that these can be critiqued and improved. Ross (1989, p. 30) says that 'the reflective (practitioner) engages in thoughtful reconsideration of all that happens (in practice) *with an eye towards improvement*'.

'Practical reflection', which refers to thinking about one's practice, is often linked to 'reflective practice' when practitioners, in this case educators and community members caught up in learning facilitation, attempt to pursue reflection as a permanent component of their educational work. The phrase *reflective practice* has been developed by Argyris and Schon (1974) and Schon (1983, 1987), and has been enriched by the work of Boud *et al* (1985), van Manen (1977, 1990, 1991), Grundy (1987) and Collins (1985).

Jarvis (1992, p. 177) writes that reflective practice begins 'where practitioners are problematising their practice and learning afresh about both the knowledge and the skills and attitudes that their practice demands'.

In this context, reflective practice is also professional practice. Jarvis (1992, p. 176) defines professional practice in these terms:

> Professional practice is about meaningful conscious action in a specific field and seeking to learn from practice and so improve it constantly, and so become experts.

Professional practice which is based on professional knowledge requires some exploration of what Schon (1987, p. 12) calls an 'epistemology of practice'. He also refers to skills and artistry in professional practice:

> In the terrain of professional practice, applied science and research-based technique occupy a critically important though limited territory, bounded on several sides by artistry. There is the art of problem framing, an art of implementation and an art of improvisation all necessary to mediate the use in practice of applied science and technique.

Schon saw that communicating ideas and skills to others was a multi-layered exercise. He was influenced by Dewey's idea (1974, p. 151, cited in Schon 1987, p. 17) that 'the student cannot be taught what he [sic] needs to know but he can be coached. He has to see on his own behalf'. The expert needs to develop a particular form of ethical artistry to generate learning in the student so that he or she will be ready to engage in learning. Such ethical artistry involves being aware of what one is doing on the one hand, with all that entails, while on the other being reflexively aware of oneself as the actor with attitudes, assumptions and the like shaping and pre-informing the ensuing practice.

Reflexivity

Schon (1989, p. 191) cites Schein's (1973, p. 43) three-fold division of professional knowledge into *basic science* – the 'what' knowledge; *human art* – ethics and human prudence, the 'why' knowledge; and *the ways of carrying it out* – the 'how' knowledge, which he saw as linked to craft. Achilles (1989, p. 4), while pointing out that professionals are responsible for the how, what and why of their practice, goes on to talk about the 'tacit' knowledge (Polanyi 1966) which comes from a 'feeling for' the action. He suggests that this kind of 'feeling knowledge' is generated by reflection so that the practitioner's professional practice becomes *reflective and reflexive.*

Practitioners thinking about the elements of their practice and attempting to improve it have thus entered into a reflective practice cycle. They can also become aware of themselves engaged in this activity almost as if looking at another person. When that occurs they become *reflexively* aware of the 'self' they are displaying in their practice with its prejudices, biases, aspirations and fears. They seek to uncover, and change for the better, the assumptions and unexamined areas of their life which might be shaping their professional practice.

A reflexive reflective practice cycle

Applying reflection to professional practice, according to writers such as Boud (1985), Carr and Kemmis (1983), Sparks-Langer and Colton (1991) and Olson (1989), is a way for practitioners to understand and modify their professional work and to integrate professional reflection with critical reflexivity. Practitioners think back on their practice and attempt to understand and critique their engagements and reactions to significant events they recount in their professional activity.

When practitioners turn their minds to various elements in their practice, the process can combine a desire to know what is being generated by the professional purposive action in an episode of practice – whether it meets expectations, what are its hidden assumptions and how it could be improved technically and ethically with becoming aware of the event's deeper significance and meaning. The various forms of reflection under consideration here can be placed in a sequential cycle which can be repeated over time as practitioners continually pursue action, reflect on the action and their accompanying dispositions, critique it and attempt to improve subsequent episodes of practice.

The sequence outlined below follows, with some modifications and expansion, the general reflective practice scripts suggested by Smyth (1989b, p. 486). The sequence of reflective processes begins with DESCRIBING, which has been expanded to include four related processes: *contextual* reflection, in which the practitioner uncovers the social and cultural forces exerting influence on the shape of the educational process; *dispositional* reflection, which takes the practitioner back to consider her or his attitudes and espoused ideals; *experiential reflection*, in which the practitioner contemplates events of practice as lived experiences; and *instrumental reflection*, in which the practitioner reflects on episodes as purposive learning facilitative action.

DESCRIBING is followed by INFORMING, which includes *interpretative reflection* – looking for typicality and significance in the events being reflected upon; and *critical reflection* – looking to see the power relations being played out in the event chosen for reflection. Smyth (1989b) then integrates these reflective sequences into a cycle by adding CONFRONTING, in which fellow practitioners assist her or him to face up to the evidence from practice of her or his 'theories in practice' and how they compare with her or his espoused theories. RECONSTRUCTING forms the last part of the cycle, and is a process through which practitioners devise new ways of proceeding, consequent on their analysis and evidence of practice. The following provides a brief elaboration.

Describing

Contextual reflection occurs when an episode of experience is looked back on in terms of it being influenced and shaped by contextual forces: its locations in time, place and social relationships. Contextual reflection looks at social and cultural forces emanating from *macro* forces such as race, class, ethnicity, gender; *meso* forces such as the particular policies and style of an institution sponsoring educational action; and *micro* forces such as the actual tasks, levels of expertise and personalities of educator and participants.

Dispositional reflection looks to identify the predispositions of the teacher and learners towards the teaching/learning project. Phillida Salmon (1989, p. 231) has provided an acute exploration of the notion of stance, that is, how a person places him or herself within any learning context. A person's orientation has an enormous influence on the purposive action being attempted. It is shaped by her or his preferences, aspirations, feelings and personal reactions to the proposed purposive activity (cf. Heimlich and Norland 1994).

Experiential reflection wants to bring attention to the lived experience of a learning facilitative episode, an event involving a challenge to learning experienced by the reflecting person. Reflecting on their educational activity, the educator tries to think back to *what the event was like as an experience*. This reflective process serves to allow what something was like to be made present and foregrounded in the reflecting person's attention.

As will be explored in considerable depth in the following chapter, experiential reflection has been shown to have two forms of overlapping subjectivity, one focusing on the person having the experience and the other on the so-called 'whatness' of the experience (cf. Willis 1998). These complementary forms of subjectivity foreground the lived experience, make it present again and bring it into sharp focus so that it demands attention. Such an unavoidable experience may challenge participants in some way.

People involved in educational practice, for example, when reflecting on incidents of which they were a part, may begin to notice that these lived experiences, of their nature, seemed always to demand a measure of self-revelation from the educator and some readiness to be influenced by them. The realisation that this has been revealed as a necessary dimension of the lived experience (rather than just the incidental feelings of the educator at the time) may threaten certain people involved in learning facilitation, while being a source of great interest, even consolation, for others. Giving people the opportunity to go back over an experience, to *taste what something is like*, is generated by experiential reflection.

The descriptions of practice can then be correlated with educational theory, seeking to disclose and to elaborate on the practitioner's *theory of practice*. One of the most well known approaches to this form of practical reflection involves practitioners looking back at what they *did*, rather than what they *said they did*, in search of their educational *theory in use* rather than their *espoused theory* (Argyris and Schon 1974). It answers the question, 'What educational theories are expressed in the practice being reflected on?' The possible summing-up sentence seems to display the agenda well in these words: 'If this kind of thing is usually done during a teaching/learning session, then it looks like this practice is underpinned by this or that educational theory.'

Instrumental and interpretative theories of practice constitute major categories. The instrumental approach is located in the describing phase of the reflective practice cycle immediately below. The interpretative approaches appear below in the informing stage. Many reflective practitioners adopt complementary approaches in which their practice is at least in part informed by functional approaches, particularly when contracted to teach a specific form of skilling, like teaching a newcomer to an organisation the way the accounting is managed. Practitioners can also be encouraged to inform their practice with interpretative theories that make space for equity and inter-cultural understanding.

Instrumental reflection builds on the vivid portrayal of the lived experience of a typical episode. It begins by checking the typicality of the event as an example of how the educator usually engaged in educational practice. The reflector can ask him or herself if the way or he or she acted in the significant event was how he or she usually acted in professional practice.

Instrumental reflection then carries out a kind of 'efficiency audit' by which the practitioner reflects on the appropriateness and efficiency of the choice of particular means to achieve a set end. An educator may query whether the film chosen to illustrate the point being explored or the overhead transparencies used, or the group activity scheduled, were the best means under the circumstances to generate the desired learning or, in more technicist terms, achieve the instructional objectives. This seems to be the main emphasis used by Heimlich and Norland (1994, p. 4) on teaching style in adult education where they write that:

> ... the aim of reflection is to offer the opportunity to compare theory
> to practice, belief to behaviour, understanding to doing. Reflection
> can provide a bridge from an educator's technical knowledge to
> professional competence.

Practical reflection in this instrumental sense looks at the 'means ends' correlation in its various forms. Practitioners assess the congruence between strategies used and results achieved. They examine the level of preparation, the presentation of ideas, the materials or handouts used, etc., and how well these were received.

When the practitioner who has been engaged in these levels of descriptive reflection becomes interpretative and reflexive, he or she will be inclined to investigate the interpersonal understandings in the episodes, and the morality and equity of the educational activities carried out. At the same time he or she also looks back to reflect on how he or she was in the course of that episode of practice – what emerged about his or her interests and prejudices. When this occurs the reflective cycle moves into INFORMING, the next major stage seeking meaning and significance.

Informing

Interpretative or socio-practical reflection seeks to understand the meanings, interests and morality embedded in various forms of practice. Usher and Bryant (1989, p. 183) suggest that the agenda of interpretative reflection, when applied to the world of adult education, links with the Aristotelian notion of practical knowledge or 'phronesis' (cf. Dunne 1993) which they prefer to call 'socio-practical' to distinguish it from the 'technical practical'. They outline it in this way:

> ... the socio-practical with its emphasis on solving problems (acting appropriately) and its concern for human welfare (acting rightly) is in the realm of practical knowledge and located in the mode of hermeneutic understanding (Usher and Bryant 1989, p. 183).

Thus the eye of the reflective adult educator looks to the meanings, morals and ethics of the actions carried out in the name of adult education. Such meanings are generated by the frames of reference through which educators, equipped with their way of seeing the world and shaped by the values and priorities of the context in which they are working, name and place value upon the educational action they are pursuing. When practitioners reflect on the origins and foundations of the assumptions embedded in their judgements of value and appropriateness, and the influence of oppressive and unequal societal structures on the very culture and language with which they are naming the world, they are moving into critical reflection.

There is an investigative element, particularly in socio-practical reflection when it seeks to uncover the meanings that people attach to their actions as professionals. Carr and Kemmis (1983), in their critical stance, argue further that such meanings embedded in educational practice, often seemingly hidden, may also be distorted and influenced by a range of interests constructed from inequitable social forces like racism, sexism, ageism and the like which become enshrined in culture through language and relatively permanent inequitable distribution of status and opportunity. The action to improve educational practice consequent on realised meanings mentioned above may then become action to overcome existing unjust or prejudicial action.

Such an attempt at linking generalised practice to established general theory (like behaviourism, humanistic education, forms of critical theory) serves to uncover possible contradictions between actors' theories in use and their espoused theories. This delicate process builds on previous work to generate confident acceptance and hope for improvement. It leads to confrontation, the next step in the reflective practice process.

Confronting

Confronting asks the questions: 'How did I come to be this way? What are the causes of my theory in practice, my values, assumptions, beliefs?' When reflection seeks to discover whose interests are being served the practical reflection becomes critical.

Critical reflection (cf. Habermas 1972; Carr and Kemmis 1983) is linked to this level of reflection according to Habermas' notions of 'knowledge constitutive interests'. This is a kind of reflection through which learners seek to understand the ways in which inequitable social relationships shape their consciousness (their assumptions about themselves and the world), and seek to develop alternative ways of acting through which they can work to discern and free themselves from the dominance of false consciousness.

Reconstructing

The final phase, which may or may not arise, is the *reconstructing and seeking congruence phase*. It puts the questions: 'How might I change? What would I do differently? What do I consider to be important pedagogically? What do I have to work on to effect these changes?' (Smyth 1989b, p. 486; Heimlich *et al* 1994, p. 206). These are the questions leading to praxis – to implementing change, reflecting on what happened when different activities were attempted, critiquing the results and if necessary trying something else.

This description of this elaborated form of reflective practice is incorporated into this part of the Gallery of Method as a qualifying force, exercising influence on the applications of the empathetic expressive method employed particularly in the first three panels of each installation in the Main Gallery. One of the significant forces which often comes from reflective practice is an appraising, normative tendency. Although this study is avowedly concerned with portraying the experience of adult education practice, rather than overtly trying to improve it, its reflective professional character may be expected, at least implicitly, to generate a tendency to appraise, critique and improve performance; to offer excuses for evidence of failure, and to hunt for ways to improve. It will thus be necessary in the expressive research agenda to consciously resist such tendency and stick to the project of portrayal.

Of course expressive research of this kind, in the application of its empathetic and intuitive expressive methods, will provide a useful grounding for subsequent reflective projects aimed at appraising and improving adult education practice. I have also to confess that the portrayal of the practice I continue to pursue at the university, an episode of which was represented and intuited in the seventh installation in the Main Gallery, has, particularly in subsequent re-readings, generated in me a stance of appraisal, and I have ended up assessing what I have been doing in the classroom and thinking of ways to improve my educational practice at the university. I have thus ended up, as I suspect other readers will, continuing the reflective practice cycle which the expressive installations of the Main Gallery have so vividly begun.

Having reviewed the four potentially qualifying elements in this project, with their capacity to influence the empathetic expressive research processes under consideration here, the study turns to the challenge of representation. There is a real challenge to generate appropriate ways to present the fruits and modalities of the research inquiry so they will be understood and received according to their expressive agenda and the kind of knowledge being offered.

Representing expressive research

One of the major challenges in the construction of this study was the anomalous discovery that the phenomenological approach which seemed to illumine the inquiry I was pursuing was not easily presented in approachable texts. In a recent workshop where graduate students were addressing classical phenomenological texts, there were several comments on the prosiness and impenetrability of several of them and their tendency to engage in endless refinements of the naming of an experience, weighing down on the reader's stamina and interest and unwittingly creating yet another barrier between the knowers and the 'things themselves'.

The texts of the Main Gallery, which readers have already visited, were designed to be forms of expressive explication, in both the empathetic and intuiting senses. The writer, contemplating the phenomenon, tries to achieve the best fit between the experience as lived and contemplated and the experience being accounted for in text. The link between these does not complete the publishing process since writers write to be read by others and not purely for their private scrapbooks. In a similar way, the script in this thesis seeks to be a text to portray the experience of adult education practice and at the same time exhilarate, even 'inspire' the readers. Such writing re-experiences the tension of adhering to verisimilitude between the text and the actual lived experience on the one hand and vibrancy and interest on the other.

The Janus experience of facing the phenomenon and facing one's readers at the same time raises the additional requirement of readability in this expressive 'portrayal' text and with readability comes the question of the kind of writing chosen to be the vehicle of illumination. What is of interest here is how the contributions of the various textual forms have been integrated into the expressive project of the thesis.

The research project was thus challenged to develop an appropriate text to serve the qualitative approach outlined above. This attempt to articulate and explore lived experience has also had to respond to the requirements of producing an academic text and, for the same reason, the expressive texts in the panels have received some immediate modification by the act of academic writing, since the writing is initially for, and within, the community of scholars – and hopefully practitioners concerned with adult education.

Although such a cohort of readers can be expected to have developed literacy agility and a considerable knowledge of similar experiences to the ones portrayed in the installations, there is no guarantee that, even within this group, the adult education experiences will be able to be recognised with all their individualised messiness and charm. Boud *et al* (1993, p. 85) suggest that:

> … our lived experience can never be fully transmitted to another
> person, even when we go to great lengths to describe that experience
> … some will resonate more with the reader than others as they touch
> their sensibilities and have meaning for them.

This nature of the human mind to shift attention in an experience challenges the phenomenological researcher to contemplate, reflect upon, a lived experience in many ways in order to generate a more comprehensive awareness of the experience while safeguarding its wholeness and freshness as a 'lived' and 'immediate' experience. It is this sense of shifting awareness and attention which has generated the method pursued in this project through which a phenomenon is revisited several times from the different vantage point of each panel in the sequence of installations in the exhibition.

This attempt at naming, communicating and interpreting the adult education activities I experienced over time in the academic community has to be carried out through particular and recognisable personalised and professionalised language, or what Eisner calls 'representation'. He defines this (1993, p. 6) as:

> … the process of transforming the content of consciousness into a
> public form so they can be stabilised, inspected, edited, and shared
> with others.

He then suggests that, since forms of representation differ, the kinds of experiences they make possible also differ. Different kinds of experiences lead to different meanings, which, in turn, make different forms of understanding possible.

Thus the panels in the installations were developed in response to the challenge for the researcher to find appropriate tools of representation; to generate a knowing experience congruent with the attempt to highlight the 'livedness' and 'whatness' of adult education practice. This overlaying of different kinds of writing, each as it were opening a different window onto the lived experience, corresponds with the creative ability of the mind to link similar things, with at least partially similar messages, into meaningful wholes.

George Willis (1995, p. 173) has this to say about the active role of consciousness:

> The representation of the intuited reality may be more by holistic
> approximations which over time are refined and more refined. These
> seem to be more readily carried in meditative aesthetic genres of
> writing such as philosophical reflection, anecdotes and poetry.

The goal here is the construction of such a discourse applied to adult education. The texts for this project need to avoid the pitfalls of scientism or objectivism on the one hand (where the research texts have the style of a scientific report), and narcissism (where the texts would be too self preoccupied and self-referencing) on the other. This project has attempted to tread a fine line which somehow brings together the objective and subjective dimensions of the lived experience.

The agenda of this project is thus to portray the lived reality of professional adult education practice using meaningful language and complementary textual genres so that the phenomenon – that which presents itself to experience – can be portrayed to others and something of its lived 'whatness' can be evoked. Van Manen (1990, p. 10) has a clear statement of the outcome of this kind of research:

> The essence or nature of an experience has been adequately described
> in language if the description reawakens or shows the lived quality
> and significance of the experience in a fuller or deeper manner.

The complementary expressive method, the empathetic, seeks to portray the meanings an experience has for someone who has experienced it by, as it were, 'getting into the person's skin' and attempting to see and feel the world from that perspective. The texts carrying this method need to be able to account for the experience as subjectively processed and personally interpreted. The first three panels in the installations, Backgrounding, Sketching and Poetised reflection, have this method as their overlaid tasks. Their presentational contributions are explored below in the section entitled 'Calling to mind'. The intuiting expressive method requires poetic, metaphoric language in order to create texts that can carry the direct contemplation of the phenomenon. The presentations of the Intuiting and Distilling panels that carry the texts constructed by this method are considered briefly in the next chapter.

Calling to mind: representing empathetic expressive research

Following the introductory notes on the task of appropriate representation early in this chapter, three vehicles were chosen again, largely by trial and error, to carry the expressive work of the thesis. Backgrounding was a form of contextualising, Sketching was a form of story telling and Poetised reflection was a form of poetised soliloquy. The following explores how these three forms were chosen to carry the empathetic expressive task of the thesis.

Contextualising

In the empathetic expressive method, the contextualising process is used to locate the episodes and experiences within a historical and 'lived' framework. The process of 'getting into someone's shoes' is expedited by knowing something of where the shoes were and what the environment was like. Its agenda is to ground various narratives of experience so they are located in the historical, so-called 'real' world. In this thesis the contextualising process is necessarily incomplete, but it attempts to map the various social conditions and forces at work surrounding each episode of practice. It does not attempt to provide a foundation for a social analysis, but to ground, or 'anchor', the images and representations of the installations in real time and space.

This section in the empathetic expressive method draws on the work of Rowan (1981) who in his turn drew on earlier work by Kockelmans (1975) on finding ways to develop hermeneutic understanding. Rowan refers to the importance of developing ways of knowing which acknowledge, but are not overwhelmed by, the embeddedness of human knowledge and understanding in the social and cultural environment. His approach enriches and grounds the expressive project being pursued in this thesis by validating the contextualising element in the installations of the Main Gallery, which locate research understandings and portrayals in the lived historical world. As he writes:

> ... the complexity and historical roots of the phenomenon must be explored and articulated ... the interpreter must achieve the greatest possible familiarity with the phenomenon in all its complexity and historical connectedness and the interpreter must also show the meaning of the phenomenon for his [sic] own situation (Rowan 1981, p. 132).

The contextualising process, as was pointed out briefly in the first chapter, needs to give some account of significant contextual forces that were at work during the episodes of practice chosen for exploration. These include the culture and values of the stakeholders – educator and learners – and the situation in terms of issues, conflicts and the learning facilitative strategies employed.

Stories

As has been pointed out in the exploration of the narrative dimension of autobiography, story telling has emerged as a primary vehicle of interpretative research. It brings the freedom to highlight the dramatic and visual dimensions of an experience and to engage the reader in a kind of transference which highlights engagement in the ideas and values carried in the narrative, and of course takes the reader into the movement and finale of the plot. The main character in the story, even if somewhat flawed, calls the reader to sympathy and even forgiveness so that stories can make something or someone stronger or weaker, or else can show that certain depths and valuable elements of a person were actually there all the time. Stories can 'put' verbal passages describing what the hero is thinking and feeling; can bring out her or his doubts, passions, fears and especially the logic being used – the basic premises about what is important and what can or cannot be tolerated. Stories can present versions of the soliloquy in which the hero is given front stage to think aloud, to bring out thoughts and feelings so that the audience is given a key to characters' actions and reactions; not just as information but as communicable feeling and thinking.

In addition, as has also been mentioned, story limits by the demands of the kind of thing it is. As a story it has to have some kind of plot and dramatic movement and a denouement which doesn't always occur in real life, so that the story is always (although often unnoticeably) a 'gloss' on life – an interpretation of the meaning of an event or experience. As with life stories in autobiography, to tell a story is not to narrate something as if one was playing back a video recording of a sequence of happenings at a time and place: it is to frame and colour it anew, to make sense of the episode being examined, to turn it into a significant event and to convey this interpretation to listeners and readers.

In this study, sketching is all of the above. The author/researcher ranges over an episode looking for a significant and typical happening – a critical incident – in which the meanings of the experience can be seen and communicated. As the story unfolds there is a tension in the narrator's mind between meeting the dramatic and plot needs of the story as story, and the recollections of the actual happenings. And of course, even before the narration, the actual happenings have already been blurred by time and by the trawling process that has unearthed the incident to be pictured in the first place.

There is thus a living tension in the sketches. On the one hand is a desire to keep the stories as 'yarns of practice' where the actual circumstance of the event are retained and as much as possible portrayed. The stories need to have the smell of the coffee and the darkness of the coffee lounge, the heat, dust and flies of outback Australian life. They need to carry the feel of cotton clothing, leather boots, the heavy steering wheel of the Toyota and then the green carpet at the university and the strange potentiality of the neutral space of the classroom with its cleaned blackboard, its noticeboards with out-of-date notices. On the other hand there is the storyteller's desire to tighten the story line: to bring out the impact of the experience and its significance to the adult educator.

Although, as was mentioned in Chapter 1, the Sketching panel used here illuminates episodes of practice while attempting to root them in actual historical circumstances, there is some borrowing from the more classical phenomenological approaches in that the grounded 'realistic' stories contain elements of typification. The sketches are not only accounts of a specific event of practice. They also contain typical elements of the kind of practice pursued in the educational events of that episode. As such they have something in common with a typifying form of story telling which van Manen named 'the phenomenological anecdote'. His comment (1990, p. 119) that anecdote (understood in his phenomenological sense) is rather like 'a poetic narrative which describes a universal truth', provides a perfect transition to the third genre – the poetised text – which moves between the sketching just described, phenomenological anecdote as espoused by van Manen, and poetry.

Poetising

The task of this section is to look at characteristics of the poetic medium and how they might serve to advance or impede the research agenda. The question seems to be: 'What is it about poetry and poetic discourse that gives it such power to engage and to provide "immediate portrayal" at the same time?'

Poetising in the installations

Poetised reflections in the installations of the Main Gallery use a poetic discourse to enrich a personalised expressive reflection on each event of practice. The poetising texts use much of the freedom and distillation of the poetic genre while focusing on the lived experience called to mind and portrayed with some historicity in the backgrounding and sketching genres. It aims to evoke an immediacy and vividness in the represented experience for the reader. In so doing, it purports to serve empathetic as well as intuiting expressive research by making room for the practitioner's feelings, emotions, fears and joys as well as allowing the experience to 'declare itself'.

This is well expressed by van Manen (1990, p. 13) who, while following the general approach of Merleau-Ponty, refers to phenomenology which underpins the expressive method used in this thesis, as a:

> poetising project; it tries an incantative, evocative speaking, a primal telling, wherein we aim to involve the voice in an original singing of the world.

Before exploring the contributions and restrictions of the poetic medium, there is a brief account of how the poetising process came to be included in the installations of the Main Gallery.

The road to poetising

As a so-called folk singer in the early days of ministry, I had become aware of and endeavoured to employ the communicative strategies of the troubadour singer and poet. The troubadour wrote and performed songs and poems to inform and move the heart. The idea was close to the aims being pursued in youth ministry and its related adult education. I later expanded this approach to include recitation of poems of my own making, written for religious and community occasions.

In the course of research in adult education and acutely conscious of the difficulty of the insights of expressive research being effectively presented, I wanted to use a change of medium to make the ideas and approaches of the research I was reporting more approachable. To this end, I endeavoured to incorporate something of my 'troubadour' past by experimenting with writing poetry into the research text and reciting poems as part of research presentations. Two of the poems in the installations of this project began in this way.

Reading a poetic reflection as a component of a research presentation seemed to generate surprise and intensified attention from the audience. Their enhanced engagement seemed, at the same time, of shorter duration, as if listening to poetry called for greater energy than listening to a report. In conversations with members of the audience after these presentations I discovered as well that their heightened engagement was often accompanied by a stronger critical reaction (ranging from exaltation to irritation) towards poetic reflections than was accorded to the prose parts of the presentation. The conclusion seemed to be that one took the poetising path at one's peril, but since it seemed to make such a considerable difference I decided to risk incorporating a poetic reflection as a panel in each installation in the Main Gallery.

Assessing the risks and benefits

Given that there is an element of risk in including poetical reflections, the question then emerges: 'Is it worth doing something laudable and useful in itself and risking that the finished product will be judged harshly and serve more to irritate than enlighten? Will such risk-taking jeopardise the impact of the other panels in the installations?' To use poetry seemed to increase the degree of difficulty (as they say in diving competitions) and the risks and rewards that accompany this. This was something of a concern. It was one thing to be warned that poetical reflections do not belong in scientific research and to rebut such a suggestion along the lines pursued in this study by using the distinctions between expressive and explanatory knowledge. It was quite another to be warned that the idea is defensible but the level of risk is high, since the quality of the poetised texts would have somehow to match the quality of the academic prose in the thesis.

It was caution that had suggested that the approach be trialled and tested. The affirming response to two pilot presentations had encouraged the continuance of the approach. At the same time there has been more time spent on tightening and working and reworking the poetic reflection than on any other part of this thesis.

This section now needs to look briefly at some ideas of the nature of poetry and the criteria of its quality.

The nature of poetry

Poetry is a term like adult education, which resists definition while retaining continuing currency in ordinary parlance as a 'family resemblance' concept. According to the Encyclopaedia Britannica (1990, p. 542), poetry refers to:

> ... literature that evokes a concentrated imaginative awareness of experience or a specific emotional response through language chosen and arranged for its meaning, sound and rhythm.

According to this text, one of the most basic things that distinguishes poetry is that it looks like poetry. Poetry is built from the *line* rather than the paragraph or block of text, and this creates in the reader a different feeling according to the 'balance and shift of the line'.

What is useful to the agenda of this thesis is the poet's gift – to objectify and somehow make communicable experiences which he or she has had intensely and concretely. T S Eliot (1963a, p. 57) said that the poet:

> ... out of intense and personal experience, is able to express a general truth; retaining all the particularity of his [sic] experience, to make of it a general symbol.

Poetic writing is often in the first person so that it is clear from whose soul the words, with their images and cadence, have issued. This is true, even though at the same time it might seem for those to whom the poet's words 'speak' that in the act of reading they can get inside the body and voice of the poet and somehow feel that the words have taken on their own soul; and that in the making of the magic words of the poem, a dictating force of more than the personal, individuated, named and located poet might somehow have been at work.

The poetised reflections can thus be seen to have, to a greater or lesser extent, two voices: one a personal contextualised voice, owning, naming a concrete subjective experience; the other a second objectifying 'whatness-seeking' voice, harmonising with the first, trying to name and disclose the structures of experiences from where the poem has sprung.

Dimensions of poetry

In his now classic text on the discovery of poetry, Sanders (1966, p. 326) suggests several elements of poetry that can be examined: language, prosody, structure, and reason for the poem being written. These can serve as headings for readers to analyse their responses and see the constitutive elements of the poem more clearly – but of course that will not indicate whether what has been constructed has worth.

Poetry is also judged on the expressive ability and elegance of every line, every cadence, every punctuation mark. This was born out by Barry Oakley's experience as a student (Oakley 1996, p. x). He was commended by his tutor when, commenting on the position of a comma in W B Yeats' poem, *The wild swans of Coole*, he suggested that the punctuation mark breasted the line of words like the swans the water of the river. One might be able to 'get away' with a story that was a little lame in view of the brightness of the characters or the insightfulness of its punchline. Poetry, with all its flexibility and distillation, tends to require that nothing be admitted that is not deliberately and meticulously crafted.

Rosenthal (1974, p. 4) suggests that poetry is a heightened example of what people do, more than perhaps they realise. He writes that:

... when people say they do not 'get' poetry, it is because they think of language as factual description and the explanation of ideas. They forget the other ways in which they themselves use it – for social cordiality, for cold rejection or irritation, for outcries of pain and excitement, for joking or 'manly' obscenities or 'feminine' hyperbole ... These stimuli, active in every mind create in all of us a hunger to express ourselves accurately and vividly. Words like 'humorous', 'racy', 'dramatic', 'poignant', reveal that we want our speech to have a life of its own, something more than flat statement. So the poet is not working out of mere private eccentricity. The poetic process goes on incessantly in the minds of people who would never believe it, who are sure they have neither an interest in poetry nor the ability to grasp it.

Celebrating the concrete and the personal

The simplicity and directness and 'here-and-nowness' of the poetic genre, its concern with the 'whatness' of things (Nelson 1996), are summarised in Dinah Livingstone's paraphrasing of Ernesto Cardinale's guidelines for writing poems:

> The guidelines caution against thumping rhymes and metres; they recommend the use of particular rather than general terms: 'iguana' rather than just 'animal', 'flame tree' rather than just 'tree'. Poetry has an added appeal if it includes proper names of people, rivers, towns, etc. Rather than being based on ideas, poetry should be based on things which reach us through the senses. We should write as we speak with the natural plainness of the spoken language, not the written language. Avoid clichés or hackneyed expressions. Try to condense the language as much as possible; all words that are not absolutely necessary should be left out (1993, p. 117).

This represents in many ways the rules that have governed the poetic reflections attempted throughout this project.

The philosopher Walter Kaufmann (1960) celebrated poetry's intuiting and new-making functions; its search for the essence of experiences. For him it seemed important to acknowledge that the insights of the poets came, in fact, from the experience and feelings of concrete men (and presumably women) reacting to, and as part of, real worlds. He talks of:

> He [sic] is not bound by any man's thoughts; he records experience with its emotionally coloured thoughts and his thoughts about emotions ... he gives us the experience of a man who is unusually sensitive and thoughtful (1960, p. 257).

Illuminating and distilling everyday 'lived' experience

The poetic medium takes reader and poet into a depth of insight and representation. Poetry is able *to illuminate and crystallise* experience. As van Doren (1967, p. xii) said, paraphrasing the poet Thomas Merton:

> Poetry at its best is contemplation of things and of what they signify, not what they can be made to signify, but what they actually do signify, even when nobody knows it. Their meaning is not something we impose upon them, but a mystery which we can discover in them, if we have the eyes to look with.

It is this evocative power of poetry that inspires the intensifying and distilling of ordinary human emotions. Kaufmann (1960, p. 260), speaking of Rilke, suggests that:

> ... he realises that in our everyday world is not merely a brute reality but also a human creation that is no longer recognised as such, because the mass of men [sic] have lost the perception of those more poetic, more creative, more childlike men who originally fashioned words and values as a mirror of the mysteries they felt.

Poetry has a significant function in that it names and distils human experience. It does this through vivid language and prosody. Hogins (1974, p. 5) puts it succinctly: 'if we learn to read a poem well, like the poet, we learn to see things in a fresh way'.

Making familiar things strange so they can be seen anew

As was mentioned above in the quotation from Kaufmann, beside the intensifying agenda of poetry lies its more complex other side which was also highlighted by Crotty (1996a, p. 155). This is the power of poetry to make familiar things strange so as to create them anew in consciousness. This view is shared by Cardinal (1981, pp. 85, 86) in his book on the poetic imagination, when he talks of poets' unusual use of words and phrases:

> ... what he wants from a word which rocks the literary boat by 'sounding wrong' is not just that it should alarm the reader and make him [sic] feel uneasy. Rather, it is that it should awaken him to meanings to which ordinary prose and ordinary thinking have tended to make him impervious ... Making words 'sound wrong' is simply a means to revive their latent energies, to lend them an intensity which will allow them to mediate the new ideas, the 'right ideas'.

In this context Cardinal gives a strong case for the depth and integrity of the poetic vision, suggesting that the poet's preoccupation with naming the received phenomenon without shifting gaze from it could lead to words being press-ganged into service in new roles and new ways. The unusual uses of language in Blake's 'tiger tiger burning bright in the forests of the night' has been readily understood and valued, and serves as a common example of what poets might do to make the 'realness' of the experienced world visible. Blake's reference to the tiger and the use of oblique metaphors which work not by direct correlation, but by resonation, draw attention to the evocative power of poetry. By resonance and not direct instruction or experience, it can somehow call up feelings in the reader, similar to those possessed by the poet.

Commanding direct attention

Poetry can command direct attention and the intensity of its confrontation can generate a reciprocal intensity of response which is not always according to the agenda of the poem but may be in resistance or irritation. Poetry tends to be more 'in your face', more risky and perhaps less seductive than stories which take longer but are more inexorable in securing compliance from readers to accept the ideas and feelings desired to be produced. But of course, poems, perhaps more than stories, are written to be recited. They are written for performance.

Poetry slows and pulses: you 'tell' a story but you 'recite' a poem. A significant point in the experience is that the person reciting the poem 'disappears' into the poem so that the voice that is heard is the 'poetic voice'. By contrast, when a storyteller tells a story, there is the action of the story and there is its narrator who can be complicit in the action but not engulfed by it. When a storyteller tells a story to children, for example, there is often considerable eye contact between the person telling the story and the listening or fidgeting children. When a poem is recited, however, there is no provision for little asides or breaking off to call the audience to attention; the poem has taken over and bids the reciter be silent unless she or he is its voice.

Having looked at key elements in poetry that serve to shape the poetising text and give it its particular character, the text needs to explore how, and by what gauge, can the quality of such poetised texts be known or measured.

Criteria of quality

The criterion of the 'goodness' of poetry seems to hinge more on its expressive ability than its adherence to canons of genre. Even the most avant-garde story needs to follow some of the guidelines of plot, characterisation and integrity. Poetry is the medium with the most flexiblity and power to portray. Poetry is valued as good and useful when it opens up an insightful space that is shared between poet and reader.

Hogins (1974, p. 6) again:

When you feel a poem is 'right', it is not because you have been swayed by the poet's logic or the evidence marshalled to support his opinion. Rather you have been able to identify with him [sic] and find a common area between his view of experience and your own.

With these brief notes, the exploration turns to the contribution poetry, or more properly poetised reflections, can make to the thesis.

Poetry in the thesis

The extract from 'poetry' in the Encyclopaedia Britannica (1990, p. 542) has a brief mention of the Authorised Version of the Bible, referring to:

… its appearance in print, identifiable neither with verse nor with prose in English but rather with a cadence owing something to both.

In the service of the thesis, the poetised reflections seek a cadence which in its own way owes something to prose and to poetry as well. Only a small amount of the huge transformative power of poetry is used, but even then it is hoped that, in dipping even one toe into its lake of mystery, a change of stance might be evoked in the reader/listener whose imagination should already have been pressed into service from the Backgrounding and the Sketching panels.

It is the contribution of poetic discourse to human articulated reflection on life that makes it so useful and so demanding, and leaves the writer with the dilemma about its implementation, where there may be assurances that there will be a higher impact but with it, a heightened risk.

In attempting to use the poetic medium, since it has so much to offer, there has been considerable strain to finish and polish the poetised reflections. What has emerged has been the development of meditative reflections written in verse, almost soliloquies, which are prose poems in their general genre but are not as distilled as would ordinarily be expected. The challenge is to produce a vivid reflection that is strong and evocative, even if, as a poem, it is as yet not as distilled or as perfect as it could conceivably become. There is a sense that in the spiral of hermeneutic exploration, the thesis will always have a 'work in progress' feel to it, as do the poetised reflections.

At the same time this line of reflection takes the matter of representation back to media other than poetry, and challenges research writers to think not only about being true to their discoveries and revelations, but to their readers. Again perhaps, it is that poetry is an extreme example of the importance of knowing how to handle one's chosen expressive media, which should not remove the obligation for writers of prose to think equally of respecting their audience and attempting to write so they can reach them.

Poetry tends to lay claim to being words written for recital in a way that perhaps not all prose does. In a way, the exhibition metaphor of this thesis would be embellished or given more opportunity for verisimilitude if the reader could actually hear the poetic reflections being recited. But, seeing that the exhibition is a textual metaphor, the sound of the poems, like the installations and the panels, is also left to the reader's imagination.

This concludes the first chapter in the Gallery of Method. It has introduced the notion of expressive research as contrasted with forms of explanation and analysis. It has explored the expressive method's two versions: the empathetic and the intuiting. It has then gone on to show how the empathetic approach sustains the first three panels in the installations of the Main Gallery. These portray adult education experience and meanings in all their immediate, concrete, contextualised reality. The alternate, intuiting version of this expressive method that provides the foundation for the Intuiting and Distilling panels looks to the more classical, so-called 'objectifying' form of phenomenology. This, with the allied question of the overlap between them, is taken up in the following chapter, together with questions of establishing criteria and pursuing quality in this kind of qualitative research.

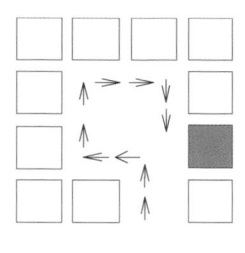

Chapter 10

Phenomenology and the expressive method

Introduction

This chapter has two parts. The first concerns phenomenology, its meanings, foundations, processes and knowledge outcomes. The second looks at its application in the installations of the Main Gallery, with a final section on criteria of quality in expressive research.

Introducing phenomenology

Meanings

The phenomenological approach has been chosen to underpin the expressive interpretative research pursued in this thesis. The task of this chapter is to develop the argument for its suitability and validity, beginning with its meanings and their application to human science research, looking briefly at its dual heritage in European philosophy and American pragmatism, then exploring its relevance in the project.

Definitions

Phenomenology is not so much a particular method as a particular approach which was adopted and subsequently modified by writers, beginning with Husserl, who wanted to reaffirm and describe their 'being in the world' as an alternative way to human knowledge, rather than objectification of so-called positivist science. Paul Ricoeur (1978, p. 1214) referred to phenomenological research as 'the descriptive study of the essential features of experience taken as a whole' and a little later, stated that it 'has always been an investigation into the structures of experience which precede connected expression in language'. Valle and Halling (1989, p. 6) described phenomenology as:

> ... the rigorous and unbiased study of things as they appear so that one might come to an essential understanding of human consciousness and experience ...

Phenomenology does not hold that the world 'out there' can be known in the way a photographic plate takes in an image of the world. All knowing is at one level subjective since it is always related to, and constructed by, the person engaged in knowing. As Spiegelberg, one of the authorities on the phenomenological movement, wrote (1959, p. 75):

> All phenomenology takes its start from the phenomena. A phenomenon is essentially what appears to someone, that is to a subject.

Some of this subjectivity focuses on the things being experienced, while some focuses on the person experiencing the thing. Spiegelberg (1959, p. 78) lists a range of meanings of subjectivity in order to explore the nature of more-than-purely-subjective subjective knowledge which is generated in phenomenological approaches. He writes:

> I conclude that all phenomenology as a study of the phenomena, is subjective in the sense that its objects are subject-related but not in the sense that it makes them completely subject-dependent.

Research of this kind into adult education practice aims to make the phenomenon of adult education a meaningful named reality. Meaningful refers in the first place to the person who experienced it, but then through that person's vivid portrayal – vivid it should be pointed out, initially to the eyes of the person experiencing it – to generate some echoes in others, particularly those with similar experiences. The goal here is the construction of such a discourse applied to adult education.

Adult educators returning to their experience can ask themselves what the experience, for example teaching adults in a literacy class, was like as a lived experience (identifying their objectivised subjective feelings). They can also ask how they felt while in such an experience (identifying their subjectivised subjective feelings). Answers to the first question would tell something of what *teaching literacy is like* in a way that would make it possible for others to imagine it could potentially be their experience. Answers to the second question tell more of what *the person having the experience is like*. This is the difference denoted between the two questions 'What was it like?' and 'How did you feel?' Both of these have a place in this study and are discussed at length below.

The distinction between the two questions relates also to a distinction between what Crotty (1996a) has called 'new' phenomenology and classical phenomenology, and which are called 'empathetic' and 'intuiting' forms in this thesis. This is explored below in the general background to phenomenology.

Background

Phenomenological research was originally developed by Husserl (1931 etc.), Heidegger (1962 etc.) and Merleau-Ponty (1962 etc.) and received elaboration by their great apologist, Spiegelberg (1975). It has become a major source of illumination for psychology (cf. Colaizzi 1973; Valle and Halling 1989) and nursing research (cf. Crotty 1996a). It has also been applied with great effect to school education by van Manen (1977, 1990), and to adult education, as has been pointed out in the first chapter of this thesis, by Stanage (1987), Collins (1984, 1987) and to a lesser extent, Brookfield (1990a, b). Phenomenology wants to slow the researcher down and hold his or her gaze on the phenomenon itself – the lived experience of some activity – seeking not to locate it in an abstract matrix by saying how its abstracted structure might be similar to others, but rather to illumine its specific quality as an experience.

In its historical origins, phenomenology rose out of a reaction to positivism through which the discourses of the physical sciences were applied to all forms of human inquiry. Husserl (1964) and his followers created a counter move, attending to the part humans play in the actual construction of the world as it is experienced. There is a tension between objectifying views that posit that the world, as we know it, exists 'out there' independently of human consciousness; and mentalist views that think the world is purely a construction of the mind. Phenomenology was to steer a middle path.

The great quest of phenomenological researchers was thus to 'go back to the things themselves'. But what are these 'things'? What kind of objectivity is meant here? One of the basic points of the phenomenological approach is that when we refer to 'things out there', we are in fact providing a name to 'things' constructed and named in the mind, without which they could not be thought. As Davis (1991, p. 5) put it, summarising the thought of Swingewood (1984):

> the meaning of things is not inherent in objects, but is actually located in the individual's inner life ... The researcher's task is to understand reality as it is, actively and consciously created by subjects, not as a pure entity that exists 'out there'.

Having said this, it seems that 'things' are not simply things but rather become 'things' in the act of perception and naming. This basic naming is always being further shaped and distorted by all kinds of cultural influences on the knowing subject. The phenomenological agenda is an attempt to get back to the first naming: 'to understand and describe phenomena exactly as they appear in an individual's consciousness' (Phillipson 1972). The leading idea is that humans need to be aware of the power of the human mind to distort basic ideas of reality according to culturally pre-set prejudices and ways of thinking. The phenomenological stance does not immediately attend to, or name, the source of distortion, but rather attempts to bypass it. This process, referred to as 'epoché' or 'bracketing', is discussed in detail below. It wants to bring the inquirer's eye and mind back to the thing itself and ask: 'What is it like?' The 'phenomenological eye' seeks to 'bracket out' later interpretative constructions and reconstructions. As Crotty (1996a, p. 38) puts it, 'the focus should lie with what manifests itself in experience rather than what the subject has made of it'.

A researcher in a particular field of human practice or endeavour (such as nursing, teaching, hairdressing, flying an aeroplane) pursuing this methodology, attempts to portray his or her lived experience, focusing specifically on what gives the experience its unique nameable qualities as a particular phenomenon impinging on her or his experience. As was pointed out in Chapter 1, phenomenology is not concerned with generating abstractions, concepts, hypotheses or theories, nor with identifying causes. The texts for this project need to avoid the pitfalls of scientism or objectivism (by creating a text in the style of a scientific report) on the one hand, and narcissism (by creating a self-preoccupied and self-referencing text) on the other. They need to tread a fine line which somehow brings together the objective and subjective dimensions of the lived experience.

This is the contribution which, it is claimed, the phenomenological approach makes. Within the expressive agenda pursued here, it also needs to produce a text that retains some vitality that, like Reason and Rowan (1981, p. xiii), will be an approach to inquiry 'which is a systematic, rigorous search for truth, but which does not kill off all it touches'.

As will emerge, the expressive method developed in this thesis to combine insight with vitality uses the two complementary approaches of phenomenology to enrich its general approach. Phenomenology can be co-opted for various approaches. Even in adult education research, as will be explained later in this chapter, there is considerable variety in the way phenomenology is used.

Foundations

This section concerns some of the foundational insights of phenomenology. It explores the meaning and significance of 'intentionality', one of the pivotal notions of phenomenology. This is followed by a brief exploration of the knowing process, looking firstly at stances in knowing, then different forms of interpretation and finally questions of objectivity and subjectivity.

Intentionality

Husserl's view was that all human thinking was, in fact, linked to something – that when one thought, one always had something as an end-point to the act of thinking. 'Thinking' is always 'thinking something'. This basic premise, called 'intentionality', meant that, in fact, the very act of thinking is an act that affirms the union that exists between the thinking subject and the object of thinking. As Merleau-Ponty says, paraphrasing Kant (1974, p. 201): 'We can only think the world because we have already experienced it'.

There is, in this view of human knowing, an assumption that since we are permanently in the life world, we have always somehow a sense of being engaged in the world. The expression 'life world', used in phenomenological writings, is defined by A. Schutz (1975, p. 15) as:

... the whole sphere of everyday experiences, orientations, and actions through which individuals pursue their interests and affairs by manipulating objects, dealing with people, conceiving plans and carrying them out.

Valle and Halling (1989, p. 9) refer to the life world as:

... the world as lived by the person and not the hypothetical external entity separate from or independent from him or her.

This idea of life world refers to the actual experienced world of a person corresponding to that person's intentional awareness.

In the act of knowing where language is used (and it is suggested there are certain kinds of knowings which do not use language), there is a presumption that everything which is known has some objective existence and that, at the same time, in the act of knowing, has been subjected to a hermeneutic through which it is named. In other words, the act of naming stands between the knower and the 'things themselves'. It is never possible to use the kind of thinking and knowing which is linked to language to get behind language to a direct intuiting of the world outside the mind.

The phenomenological perspective then goes on to suggest that abstract knowledge and forms of positivist scientific knowledge create a cleavage when people begin to imagine themselves as one thing and the world as another, rather than the whole world with people in it being the life world which is the only experienced reality people really possess. It is this experienced reality that phenomenological research wants to uncover and attend to. That desire to attend to the life world – the experienced world – requires knowledge which, as Heidegger (1982, p. 276) points out, is 'not cognition in the mere spectator sense'. It also requires appropriate language which is not built upon the separation between the world and the knowing person, but rather a language of attention and contemplation which allows the world to be.

Since all articulated human knowing is locked in language, the project to attend upon 'the things themselves' cannot expect to find a way of knowing that somehow goes behind language. It is rather in the way human knowers position themselves towards the world that may at least contribute to a way of knowing that minimises the amount of what might be called 'secondary processing' occurring in and around the acts of knowing and naming the world. This introduces the notions of stances and modes of knowing.

Knowing stances: proactive and reactive

Crotty (1996a, p. 38) speaks of the active role of consciousness:

... the mind reaches out to the object and into the object and draws it into itself, at once shaping the object and being shaped by it.

Allowing that consciousness has necessarily an active role in every act of knowing, it is useful to make a second distinction between active/reductive and intuitive/receptive forms of thinking. Thinking, the act of engaging in thought, does not always carry an active connotation in its use although, of course, in many cases it is imagined as a strongly active, almost transitive, process. One thinks when one 'puts one's mind to something'; when one 'gets a grip on' an idea; when one analyses, categorises, generalises, discriminates between things, or groups of things. The mind, when engaged in these proactive pursuits, can be imagined as a kind of sheepdog grouping ideas, separating, challenging ...

There are, however, other times when the mind is 'struck by', 'seized by', 'gripped by' something known. At these times, the mind seems more like a receptor, receiving ideas and images and feeling and being moved by them.

Thus, the more one reflects upon one's thinking, the more one is confronted with a proactive and a contemplative modality. The proactive way is imagined as a series of processes variously interpreted, in which a thinker moves from taking in and naming experiences in some fashion, to ordering them and locating them into the more generalised categories of one's language and ways of seeing the world.

The intuitive/contemplative way refers to more receptive and aesthetic forms of thinking and focusing attention. The thinking human positions him or herself *vis-à-vis* an object with a receptive stance and holds back discriminatory analytic thinking in favour of a more contemplative process. In this form of thinking the object of thought is less robustly dealt with. The mind does not 'seize upon' the object to analyse and subdue it but attempts to behold it, to allow its reality, its beauty and its texture to become more and more present. Even here consciousness is still active, but the act of thinking is different: it is an act of reception which holds the thinking mind back from closure and returns again and again to behold the object, allowing words and images to emerge from the contemplative engagement.

Heron (1992, p. 14) suggested that human consciousness could be viewed as being in four modes – affective, imaginal, conceptual and praxis – each, as it were, placed on top of the next in what he called an 'up-hierarchy', so that the lower one energised the one above it. In the *imaginal* mode, which is similar to the receptive, contemplative stance mentioned here, the psyche turns presences, brought inchoately into consciousness through experience, into images 'through the creative role of primary imagination in perceiving the world as a whole'. Heron says that this mode is evoked in knowing actions such as 'intuitive grasp' or 'metaphorical insight'.

While stressing its intuitive, receptive modality, it is important not to over-emphasise the receptive nature of this kind of direct knowing. The human knower does not open the shutters of the mind and an image of some object or experience does not physically imprint itself on the psyche. All kinds of knowing require work by the knower. Ihde (1973, p. 67), in his interpretation of Merleau-Ponty's work, refers to 'a world which is always pregnant with significance, but whose meaning must be re-won through an interrogation of its presence'.

Forms of interpretation

The outcomes of phenomenological reflection, like that of any other inquiry, are thoughts, discourses and written texts. As such, the person engaged in phenomenological reflection is trying to engage with the lived experience, which, as has been pointed out above, is in fact a processed experience. The person has engaged with the things in the world in so far as they are phenomena, that is, in so far as they are presented to consciousness. As we have seen, the 'thing itself' is not presented to consciousness. What is presented is only a named and therefore somewhat 'experienced thing'. Such an experienced thing is named from within the lexicon of the experiencing person.

The acts of naming and saying things about the phenomenon, even while consciously 'bracketing out' culturally generated abstracting interpretations, are still forms of interpretative action. For example, when a child learns the name of an object – the thing to which it has been pointing or touching and which it knows in an inchoate way is named, in that moment is known as named. Merleau-Ponty (1962, p. 177) writes:

> ... for the child the thing is not known until it is named, the name is the essence of the thing and resides in it on the same footing as its colour and its form.

But of course before the thing was named, it had some kind of existence in consciousness, which was evoked in the process of giving it its name. That existence was itself already a kind of interpreted existence through the way the thing-to-be-named was already used and referred to in the exchanges of the life world. Heidegger calls this 'primordial interpretation', which, as Cooper (1996, p. 428) writes:

> ... is carried out 'not in a theoretical statement but in an action' (Heidegger 1980: 200), as when one 'interprets something as a hammer by using it as such ... In basic interpretation, we do not 'throw a "signification" over some naked thing' (ibid: 190) for nothing is encountered in the raw but always as a door, house or whatever. Heidegger accordingly describes *Dasein's* [being in the world] relation to its world as 'hermeneutic', a term designating the business of interpreting. Since phenomenology, whose aim is the 'disclosedness of Being', can only proceed by uncovering *Dasein's* own implicit understanding, it follows that phenomenology itself is hermeneutics (1996, p. 61f).

The challenge is to think (and write) focused consciously on the phenomenon. When speech, language and thought patterns generated from experience in the world are used, they always involve an interpretative process: but the aim here is to try to disclose the most naive and basic interpretation that is already there but as yet is unelaborated in the life world experience.

The hermeneutic process refers to the way people interpret and make sense of experiences, usually by naming them according to their pre-existing values and ways of seeing the world. The question is, can we develop an as it were pre-interpretative interpretation by which we hold the phenomenon in our gaze and drink it in, waiting for it almost to name itself in our consciousness while resisting the temptation to locate it on conceptual grids and grand theories.

Admitting that this process is still an interpretation, after Reason (1988, p. 79) it can be called an 'expressive' or 'immediate' interpretation so that more elaborated interpretations can be referred to as explanatory interpretative processes, as was pointed out in the previous chapter of this Gallery of Method. The important construction of abstracting interpretations within, or consequent to, an experience can then be grounded in reality and enriched by building on the intuitive, expressive interpretation of the experience. This is the phenomenological project by which the meanings things have in our life world experience are brought into view.

This initial hermeneutic still calls upon one's store of language and values generated from our ways of being in our culture. The difference will be in our stance, which will be consciously trying to avoid analytic or generalising language, and letting the phenomenon declare itself. As van Manen (1987, p. 19) says:

> The aim is to construct an animating, evocative description (text) of human actions, behaviours, intentions and experiences as we meet them in the life world.

Given that the life world is what is there all the time – the lived world as it is experienced – the consciousness generated by this phenomenological exploration – contemplation – does not create new knowledge of the phenomenon; it creates a space in which phenomena manifest themselves. In the previous chapter mention was made of the distinction between what was called conceptualising and perceiving, and Merleau-Ponty's speaking about 'perception' (his word for the ummediated awareness of the life world) 'not giving truth like geometry, but presences' (1974, p. 198). 'Presences' refers to a kind of unveiling of something that was there all the time but not explicitly present in consciousness. Stanage (1987) has coined the phrase 'consciousing' to refer to that permanent, implicit awareness of being in the life world of which one is a part:

> ... it means knowing-together, or knowing in such intimate, and logically primitive, form that all knowing and all cognitive activities or persons are constituted partly through it (Stanage 1987, p. 327).

Related to questions of perceptual and conceptualising knowing, and to their related modes of knowing, is the question of the subjectivity and/or objectivity of such knowing experiences, particularly when pursued under a research rubric when they are represented in language and various verbal and textual forms.

Objectivity and subjectivity

As was pointed out in the opening chapter of this study, research requiring 'objectivity' has become associated with the positivist approach to research. Alternative approaches have sought to admit forms of human subjectivity into academic writing and to portray the personal as political and socially relevant. Neither of these positions has quite met the phenomenological project with its interest in, and focus on, 'the experience' that human subjects have, rather than the human subjects having the experience. The phenomenological question was to find a way to name and portray human experience which would be both somewhat subjective and at the same time somewhat objective. To meet this challenge, I have coined the phrases 'subjectivised subjective' experience and 'objectivised subjective' experience, which seem similar to Spiegelberg's 'subject dependent' and 'subject related' categories.

The phenomenological project seeks what can be called objectivising subjectivity – focusing on the thing being experienced but still as experienced *by me* – as apart from subjectivising subjectivity. Human language carries this distinction easily when a person is asked what something was like (for example, a childhood visit to the dentist). The person might say: 'It was terrifying. I felt as if my heart would break, my palms were sweating, and I wondered if I would ever get out of it.' The listener might interrupt saying, 'I can understand what *you* felt like, but can you tell me what *it* was like?' The speaker might then talk about the shiny instruments, the white coat, the strange smells and sounds; the cold or the heat, the contoured chair, being recumbent; the pink hands of the surgeon and the grinding noise of the drill.

The phenomenological project seems to need both dimensions of the account. There is a sense that the objectivities that are highlighted in an experience are those which generated a strong subjective response. In a way, elements of an experience that do not impact upon the awareness of the person narrating it may not, in fact, be part of the phenomenon. The definition of a phenomenon – 'what manifests itself in experience' – suggests this, although in the process of reflection a person may become aware of many dimensions of an experience that were, in fact, manifested but somewhat not attuned to, or at least not foregrounded in, awareness.

Variations

The distinction between these forms of subjectivity has had considerable ramifications in approaches to phenomenological research. Crotty's research (1996a) into phenomenological approaches in nursing research was to point out what he called 'new' and what is called here 'empathetic phenomenology' in contrast to classical phenomenology, and to show how whole traditions of research have been built on different construals of this approach.

The explorations of phenomenology to this point in this chapter have largely been brief outlines of the classical approach beginning with Husserl. According to Crotty's exposition, the alternative approach does not focus so much on the phenomenon as it becomes visible, but on the subjective experiences and meanings that are generated in or are generated by its beholders. It is this more interpretative approach which, as has been pointed out in the previous chapter, informs the first three panels in the installations of the Main Gallery.

This 'new' phenomenology focuses on the meanings and significances given to an experience by those experiencing it. Crotty writes that (1996a, p. 3):

The new phenomenology works hard at gathering people's subjective meanings, the sense they make of things ('What does giving post-mortem nursing care mean to those nurses?').

Such knowledge is of great interest in many explorations of social science. It shows that different people participating in an event in their lives may give it radically different meanings. Thus a patient and a health professional, an adult educator and an adult learner, may engage in a shared activity but have quite radically different experiences of it. It is then possible to inquire about the nature of the experience and how it presented itself as a phenomenon as in classical phenomenology or to follow the alternative empathetic phenomenology by inquiring what the subject made of that experience: what was its significance. This latter pursuit, with interviews, thematic analysis and clustering of interview transcripts looking for the common meanings an experience had for a group of subjects, represents a major way of working in qualitative social science research. Its contribution is that it brings to view the subjective states and interpretations of people who have engaged in a common experience like school, university, hospital, church and the like, and which may have been overlooked or repressed by powerful interests in society. The focus is on the subject; it protects and values the contributions of various subjects engaged in life experiences.

In the discussion on autobiography as one of the streams influencing and enriching the method of this thesis, there was mention of the considerable research around autobiography pursued particularly by feminist scholars. Their project was to make space in the academy for the full range of human subjectivities, and to include women's voices (and by the same reason the voices of other more or less silenced groups) reporting on their own personal, individual and subjective experiences in society. It was pointed out in that section that the radical subjectivist agenda was not the main concern of this thesis; and that the voice of the writer, while requiring to be acknowledged and located, as it were, in the inquiry, was not the focus point of the study. It was, in short, not the story of the author's life as such, although it was based on elements of his life as an adult educator. It was, in reality, the story of adult education practice experienced in the seven episodes of his practice, presented in the Main Gallery.

The interpretative or empathetic approach to phenomenological research has made a contribution by showing the socially embedded nature of human consciousness. It may not have advanced the cause of classical phenomenology, but it has defended and made known what groups of people – teachers, nurses, soldiers – have felt when involved in a shared experience, and what sense they made of it. The experience is then named in terms of the subjectivity it evokes in those who experienced it.

Much of the earlier considerations of autobiography and reflection in this study draw heavily on the interpretative approach. In fact, as has been pointed out in the previous chapter, it informs much of the first three panels of the installations of the exhibition concerned with 'bringing to mind' the experience of adult education practice in each of the episodes. As will be explained in more detail below, these three 'bringing to mind' exercises – Backgrounding, Sketching and Poetised reflection – move to a greater or lesser extent between an objectivising subjectivity and a more subjectivising one. There is, however, a price to be paid for attending to the significance something has. The research focus then remains with the subject and it is easy to imagine that the structure of the experience itself may tend to become shadowy, and to be drowned in the subject's self-awareness, self preoccupation and self-talk. That is why the expressive project in this study, while welcoming and wanting to find a place for some subjectivity (particularly since phenomena in human awareness always have elements of subjectivity), wants as well to move back to the phenomenon – to the lived experience – which generates the subjective feelings and meanings. It wants to bracket out these feelings and thoughts for a moment and let the experience present itself for contemplation. This is pursued directly in the Intuiting and Distilling panels in the installations. It is not difficult to see why classical phenomenology, pursued in these latter panels, is more than a little about desisting from things (arguing, analysing, debating) rather than doing things.

Having once more looked at the two versions of phenomenological research in the course of clarifying the nature of 'classical' phenomenological research, the study considers three major processes of classical phenomenological research in the quest for 'the things themselves'.

The processes of classical phenomenological research

Classical phenomenology when pursued in research projects tends to use three essential processes in a variety of ways and styles: description, reduction and naming essential themes. These are discussed briefly in general before moving to consider their application in the method of this thesis.

Description

Description is the essential task for classical phenomenology. Seamus Heaney, the poet (1990, p. 89), referred to description as 'revelation', which literally means removing veils which obscure or disguise the realities of the world. It is significant that in some contexts social scientists were warned to avoid 'mere' description. Of course there is nothing mere about generating phenomenological description: attempting to get back to 'the things themselves' and to set aside preconceptions and tendencies to analyse or generalise, and at the same time to unveil the lived reality of an experience. As Crotty (1996a, p. 280) puts it:

> The difficulty does not lie merely in seeing 'what lies before our eyes' (which Husserl saw as a 'hard demand'), or knowing 'precisely what we see' (Merleau-Ponty said there was nothing more difficult to know than that). We will also experience great difficulty in actually describing what we have succeeded in seeing and knowing. When we attempt to describe what we have never had to describe before, language fails us. We find our descriptions incoherent, fragmentary,

and not a little 'mysterious'. We find ourselves lost for words, forced to invent words and bend existing words to bear the meanings we need them to carry for us. This has always been characteristic of phenomenological description. We may have to be quite inventive and creative in this respect.

This significant quotation succinctly points to the project of classical phenomenological writing and its challenges to build adequate, or perhaps better, 'less inadequate' texts. It points to the challenge of inventiveness, of ways to 'get past oneself'. The project has a kind of infinite end-point in that it can never be absolutely achieved; that there will always be some kind of 'hermeneutic' – some kind of processing – involved in the choice of intuitive words and language in the very act of rejecting intermediate interpretative processes. The significant thing in the argument of phenomenology is that to take steps to bracket everyday understandings, even when the task can never be perfectly achieved, is to perform a service to human science by going back attentively, receptively to the experience itself – to the phenomenon.

Of course in a way the proof of the pudding remains in the eating. Readers of this text will already have had the opportunity to address texts attempting to provide directly phenomenological descriptions in the intuitions of the Main Gallery. They would have had the opportunity to reflect whether such a portrayal provided a way to the thing itself – to a revisiting of the experience – to let the experience tell its own story.

The way phenomenological description is attempted here has been by using various texts from various perspectives to generate a 'layered picture' of a phenomenon – almost a series of transparencies – overlaid on an overhead projector. These are then explored for common elements that recur not in the idea of the thing but in its experience narrated from different points of view. This creates a multi-perspective text, as was done in the installations in the Main Gallery. Valle and Halling (1989, p. 13) suggest that:

> Phenomena as they present to us, seem to reveal themselves in
> different ways depending on how we look at them or 'take them up'
> in our many, varied perspectives and life situations... The perceived
> phenomenon is analogous to a mineral crystal that appears to have
> many different sizes and shapes depending on the intensity, angle and
> colour of the light that strikes its surface. Only after seeing these
> different reflections and varied appearances on repeated occasions
> does the constant, unchanging crystalline structure become known to
> us.

Of course there is a presumption here that phenomena have a 'constant unchanging structure', whereas it seems that some phenomena, like adult education practice or religion, as was shown in the first chapter, do not seem to have a strictly univocal structure, but appear to be grouped under a common name due to a 'family resemblance'. What is suggested, however, is that even gaining insight into elements that mostly, but not always, occur in a less bounded phenomenon is still to be provided with considerable illumination.

Bracketing

'Bracketing' refers to the process of standing apart from one's usual ways of conceiving the world and the things in it, and attempting to intuit 'the thing', the object of interest, the phenomenon, directly in an unmediated way. Van Manen (1990, p. 175) defines it as 'suspending one's various beliefs in the reality of the natural world in order to study the essential structures of the world'.

The term 'essential structures' of the world has a hard and substantifying feel to it, as if 'the world' was understood as something 'out there', whose structures – another term implying reification – could somehow be discovered. This is not van Manen's intention at all. The 'world' in this phenomenological discourse is the 'experienced life world', understood as a fluid overlaying of which the person finds her or himself as a part of all the familiar and recurrent experiences of body, time, space and social relations which make up a person's felt world. The 'structures' of such a 'world' refer more to recurrent central themes within the experience: 'what' makes the experience what it is, and the 'world' in this sense 'what' *it* is. The concept of themes or essences is explored further below. To turn one's mind back to these experiences in their raw unclassified or unanalysed state requires developing a way to bypass rather than extinguish the ordinary, habitual ways people develop to interpret and name their world. This is the function of bracketing.

Husserl (1973, p. 53) suggested that there is, in ordinary consciousness, a pre-existent bracketing (or what he calls universal 'epoché'), which shuts out the unmediated perception of the world and replaces it with overlays of perception, judgement and the like:

> The universal epoché of the world as it becomes conscious (the 'putting it in brackets') shuts out from the phenomenological field the world as it simply exists; its place however is taken by the world as given in consciousness (perceived, remembered, judged, thought, valued etc.).

Husserl then suggested that people have to take on a transcendent attitude to avoid being imprisoned by one's everyday awareness and judgements of the world. He suggested that people should make their pre-judgements explicit so that they could be laid aside.

Heron (1996, p. 120) explains that a person seeking to pursue the phenomenological task needs to:

> ... bring these implicit everyday epistemic frameworks into clear relief and become fully aware of them. Then we can become relatively independent of them, peer over the edge of them and regenerate our vision.

The research of Heron and his colleague has been enriched by their explorations of psychotherapy and forms of human transpersonal and spiritual activity. Their writings have no difficulty with this notion of 'peering over the edge of one's everyday epistemic frameworks'. It bears the stamp of practice, where this thesis is also based, and it is common enough in the experience of people attempting to learn or re-frame their way of seeing the world by developing skills in 'standing apart from' or 'aside from' their habitual ideas, feelings, convictions, etc., so as not to allow them to cloud the whole of their awareness. Heron (1996, p.122) cites Reason (1994, p. 34), who puts it thus:

> Behind the attachment of the everyday mind to its constricting perspectives, there is a 'mind which is able to see through this attachment and is open to the ways in which we create ourselves and our world moment to moment' and which is available through meditation.

Bracketing can thus be seen as an implied activity when researchers want to focus their eyes on a phenomenon in itself, and resist taking on alternative analytic or generalising agendas. As such, the process amounts to nothing more than focusing on the phenomenon and allowing it to declare itself.

The third process in the applications of phenomenology to human science research – naming essential themes or thematic analysis – must now be considered.

Naming essential themes

Phenomenological research brings the mind to a phenomenon as it presents itself through different windows of experience and different times. Phenomenology wants to discover the essential elements of a particular phenomenon. In other words, as Spiegelberg (1975, p. 64) wrote, to seek 'what is essential and what is merely accidental or contingent' in the phenomenon. Valle and Halling (1989, p. 13) put it this way:

> Regardless of which of the phenomenon's particular variations is revealed at any given time, this phenomenon is seen as having the same essential meaning when it is perceived over time in many different situations.

Thematic analysis suffers the difficulty of being mistaken for a conceptual rather than phenomenological exercise. When one looks for phenomenological themes one's eyes are held on the phenomenon as it is experienced in a range of settings and episodes, looking for recurrent themes in its lived experience. The act of separating accidental elements from necessary or substantial ones in a recurrent *experience* is very different from looking for accidental or contingent elements, in contrast to substantial or necessary elements in an *idea*, which is characteristic of forms of conceptual analysis. The reducing or distilling process, applied as it is to such different entities, ends up quite different in its notion and its practice. In practice, searching for themes in phenomenological research means to resist the tendency to leave the phenomenon behind in the reducing process. Van Manen has made some strong points here about the drawing out of themes and phenomenology needing to keep its attentive and contemplative stance. He writes (1990, p. 88) that theme analysis is the process of insightful invention, discovery and disclosure:

As I arrive at certain thematic insights, it may seem that insight is a product of all of these; *invention* (my interpretative product), *discovery* (the interpretative product of my dialogue with the text of life) and *disclosure of meaning* (the interpretative product 'given' to me by the text of life itself).

These quotations highlight the importance of ensuring that this process, subsequent to description, keeps with the phenomenon – the lived experience. It needs to tread a middle way between two extremes. One is succumbing to too much subjectivity, where themes would end up being linked to a person's recurring feelings and not elements of the experience itself. The other is being caught up in too much analysis, by which the experience would be located in an explanatory category and the characteristics of the category imputed to it.

There is a holographic perspective in searching for phenomenological themes, in that the whole of the experience is represented in each theme, which presents more like different windows on the whole experience. This correlates with Valle and Halling's (1989) notion of the phenomenon as crystalline (quoted above), with many facets each presenting the whole. The structure of experiences, by which they are accorded some commonality, are the recurring elements that are most meaningful to us. Thematic analysis is a way of uncovering those elements that constitute the phenomenon as experienced.

Having developed the elaborated view of the two complementary forms of phenomenological research over the last two chapters, the study can now explore in greater depth the contributions of the three major adult education researchers mentioned in the previous chapter, who used phenomenological approaches and located their contributions within the categories that have now been established.

Phenomenological researchers in adult education

Stanage

Sherman Stanage, who could lay claim to being the founding father of phenomenology in adult education research, published his major text *Adult education and phenomenological research* in 1987. His aim was to build a phenomenology of adult education from the ground up. He sought to 'bracket out' received explanations of adult education and brought his gaze to bear on the phenomenon in the broadest sense as it presented itself to him.

He distinguishes (1987, p. 36) between two kinds of terms: generic concepts which overlap each other as in Plato's ideas of goodness, truth and beauty; and class concepts which are mutually exclusive as the circle and triangle are mutually exclusive in mathematics.

This distinction forms the foundation of his choice to set aside the existing classifications of the different philosophical foundations made under an analytical agenda: liberal, functional, progressive, radical, analytical and critical, as pursued by Elias and Merriam (1980). As he sees them, these are class concepts with little direct links to lived reality. He wants to 'take on a phenomenological investigation of the phenomena presented by the thoughts and actions (with thoughts and action overlapping as generic concepts) of persons' (1987, p. 37).

His subsequent provisional definition of adult education on the same page has it as:

> ... the enactment of, and systematic investigation of the phenomena constituting the adult eductions of *person*, specifically of persons' free and deliberate motives for acting.

'Eduction' in this definition is defined earlier (1987, p. 5) as 'genuine education'; *person* is distinct from 'person'. It is 'what is drawn forth, pulled out, or what flows forth from persons in their lifeworlds' (1987, p. 333). This definition seems to define adult education by its objectives which, in his personalist vision, he takes to mean deepening the 'person-being' of adults.

Stanage, with his high level of abstraction and idiosyncratic, philosophical style, has constructed what would be called in this thesis an explanatory text in which he has attempted to bring a Husserlian philosophical approach to the task of constructing a phenomenology of adult education. In the course of this task he has generated a lexicon of terms and phrases which constitute his insights into the phenomenon of adult education.

In many ways the project of this thesis, which uses phenomenology to portray adult education practice in the seven chosen episodes in the Main Gallery, is encouraged and to some extent daunted by the huge elaborations of Stanage's text. In its general phenomenological agenda, the methodology of this thesis has many parallels to his work and draws on many of the same theoretical texts.

A major difference emerges in the thesis' related aim of producing an expressive portrayal of adult education practice. In this regard, except for the friendly stance of Stanage's interactions with the reader, the aim and method are radically different. Stanage's writing style and stance is that of the academic explanatory scholar. He quotes philosophers liberally and develops groups and clusters of terms I found both useful and obfuscatory. The brilliance and difficulty (almost impenetrability in places) of Stanage's text created a crisis in my own desire to use the phenomenological approach as a 'grounding' component of my expressive project. I was committed to keeping my text 'in the street' and yet I wanted the illumination and distillation that the method promised.

At one level it is not surprising that Stanage's phenomenological text should prove such hard going, since he is avowedly cutting a new track, avoiding the comfortable usual roads. As such, the reader seeking explanation and analysis cannot expect to cruise on familiar paths. A different path was pursued in this study with a different aim. Phenomenology was used to further its empathetic and intuiting approaches in an expressive rather than explanatory way. As has been pointed out, the aim was portrayal rather than explanation. This approach has hopefully avoided a too prosaic, scholastic kind of discourse which, while being true to the structure of the phenomenon, might have killed its sense of colour and life.

Collins

The phenomenological approach was also used to great effect in Collins' monograph on competency-based adult education (1987). In the study, he uses the phenomenological theory of 'relevance', taking into account the 'stock of knowledge' people possess from their life experiences to critique the assumptions about adult education built into the competency movement in adult education. Collins' elaborated phenomenology was then applied in a major analysis of education policy and practice texts relating to the implementations of competency-based adult education.

A major difference between the approach of this thesis and that of Michael Collins in the use of phenomenology is that Collins, similarly to Stanage, uses the classical intuiting form of phenomenology in a strongly analytic and explanatory way to explore educational policy and its relationship to educational practice and learning. The phenomenological approach of this thesis, outlined in this and the previous chapter, has sought to complement that of Collins and before him Stanage, by using an expressive approach to present 'empathically' and 'intuitingly' the experience of adult education practice in various episodes of practice. This puts it in a complementary but very different space.

Brookfield

Brookfield explored phenomenological and expressive approaches informally in his introduction to his text *The Skillful Teacher* (1990a) and more formally in a chapter he wrote on the experience of learning (1990b).

He had said in *The Skillful Teacher* that as an adult educator/researcher, his first aim had been 'to present a picture of teaching that seems truthful to readers' (1990a, p. xii). His other aims of inspiring adult educators in training and providing them with advice and suggestions on all aspects of teaching were to be based on this first aim which, in another place, he refers to as telling 'the real story of teaching' (1990a, p. xi).

His interpretative approach to 'telling the story' of educational practice (Brookfield 1990a) has been discussed in the previous chapter in this Gallery of Method in the section on personal story telling and its part in autobiography. It seems to have a hermeneutic stance looking for the meanings that the actual experiences of adult education can generate, which is similar to the one adopted here with significant differences. In his introduction, where he outlines the practical goals of his book, he says that 'it would be easy to write a book long on experience and inspiration but short on practicalities' (1990a, p. xiv). The agenda of this thesis has been to create a text which is *deliberately* long on experience. Its aim has been to develop a focused hermeneutic exploration of experience expressively and phenomenologically. It did not and has not seemed an easy task, but it is one which seeks to complement Brookfield's more practical works and the work of a later writer, Jane Vella (1994).

In the chapter which appeared in the same year as his book, Brookfield (1990b) is more explicit in his use and understanding of the phenomenological approach. For him the phenomenologist:

... investigates the meanings of events or actions to the people experiencing these and seeks to apprehend or intuit these event and actions in a way their subjects do (1990b, p. 330).

He points out, on the same page, that phenomenology uses a strategy called 'reduction' which is carried out by 'intuiting' one's experiences, that is, by 'reflecting on the essence of people's subjective experiences'. He then suggests that phenomenological approaches are especially useful in two particular cases. One is in studies 'which are trying to enter people's interpretative frames of reference and explore their structures of understanding' (1990b, p. 331). The other is in what he calls 'scene-setting' studies where researchers are investigating unexplored territory for which there are as yet no detailed and replicable methods that have been tested for reliability and validity.

Following the argument of this and the previous chapter, Brookfield's version of phenomenology would be typified as 'empathetic' because it seeks to get into the subject's shoes and to map the meanings and subjectivities she or he may have around an experience. Although he quotes Stanage and locates his inquiry in that stable, his empathetic approach seems different from, and complementary to, the more classical and intuiting approach Stanage has followed, particularly in the latter's strong links to the objectifying tendencies of Husserl, which are a long way from the subjectivising focus of the empathetic interpretative. In addition, the liveliness and narrative style of his writing place it more in the expressive camp as complementary, rather than belonging to Stanage's more analytical and explanatory approach.

This completes the brief review of the contributions of existing phenomenological research in adult education. The study now returns to the application of phenomenology in the Main Gallery. The contribution of the first three panels has already been examined in the previous chapter, since they used a more empathising form of phenomenology. What follows now concerns the Intuiting and Distilling panels, which were informed by the more classical or intuiting form of phenomenology.

Classical phenomenology in the Main Gallery

The representing or naming process of the whole exhibition in the Main Gallery takes place, as it were, with the lived experience of adult education practice in its texture and grubbiness and reality held before the mind. Frederick Franck, in his book *The Zen of seeing* (1973), encourages his students at one point to attempt to draw the object of their choice without looking away from it, letting the sketching hand with the pencil take care of itself. There is some similarity here with the phenomenological project as one seeks to know and to 'image' the known by holding it within one's gaze and bringing that immediate intuit onto text, without in the first instance seeking to analyse it or compare it with other things.

The phenomenological researcher attempts then to 'image' the intuited experience by seeking to contemplate – reflect upon – a lived experience in many ways in order to generate a more comprehensive awareness of it while safeguarding its wholeness and freshness as a lived and immediate experience. It is this sense of shifting awareness and attention which has generated the method pursued in this project through which a phenomenon is revisited several times from slightly different vantage points.

Intuiting

The intuiting process was described briefly in the first chapter of the thesis. It needs to be pointed out that it is not just intuiting in the sense of contemplating the phenomenon. It is *turning that intuiting into text* while safeguarding its immediacy and making sure not to analyse or explain but just represent, portray. After considerable exploration, the two related activities introduced in the first chapter, the 'existential coordinates' of Merleau-Ponty and Crotty's 'sentence stems', were chosen to provide a catalyst for the intuiting text building.

The first was to dwell upon the phenomenon and then to describe what presented itself in so far as it was an experience in four existential coordinates: a *bodily experience*, an experience in *time*, a *spatial* experience and *a socially embedded* experience. The text-building involved in describing the phenomenon as a lived experience means using a kind of illuminating scaffold. By using the existential co-ordinates, the phenomenon comes into view made visible and illumined as it were by its temporal, spatial, bodily or social windows. The text describing the phenomenon was somehow triggered by the four windows.

The rationale for this approach to intuiting the phenomenon is that one way to discover the nature of a phenomenon is to explore what it was like as a bodily, spatial, temporal and social experience. This was following the work of Merleau-Ponty who, among early classical phenomenologists, highlighted the importance of the body as a dimension of intentionality; that just as humans are never just conscious but always conscious 'of something', so that consciousness is always experienced either directly or in an implied way, as bodily. Merleau-Ponty refers to the body as 'the system of all my holds on the world' (1974, p. 202).

A major exponent of the use of these co-ordinates in contemporary research was Max van Manen. When for example, he speaks of the co-ordinate of *lived space*, he reminds readers (1990, p. 103) that:

> ... to understand [a phenomenon], it is helpful to inquire into the nature of the lived space that renders that particular experience its quality of meaning ... Phenomenologically it appears that the structure of an experience asks for a certain space experience. In other words a phenomenon has its own modality of lived space and may be understood by exploring the various qualities and aspects of lived space ... Lived space is a category for inquiring into the ways we experience the affairs of our day to day existence.

The phenomenon can also be intuited as a *lived bodily experience*. There was an additional challenge to avoid too much subjectivism. The challenge was to set the question: 'What was it like as a bodily experience?' rather than 'What did you feel like?' The difference can be seen in subjective reactive sentences like 'I felt as if my heart would break'; 'I was sweating and trembling', as against texts reporting direct bodily experience, for example: 'The experience involved my body being immobile and becoming numb during the long hours of waiting.' This is the body *in* the experience rather than the body in the meaningful interpreted reaction to the experience.

In this case the 'bodily me' having the experience is not me resonating with the emotions and feelings generated as a result or in view of what the experience is construed to be by the subject. The bodily reaction is the 'bodily dimension' of the actual experience.

Again *lived time* is a dimension of the lived experience as it is intuited as a series of events following one another slowly or quickly, lingeringly or tensely. The temporal axis of an experience is a revealing window through which its moment, its importance and the way it is experienced are revealed. The temporal dimension of experiences discussed in the installations was often a first indicator of its value and significance and a trigger for later more considered assessment of it.

Lived relationship is the social dimension of an experience in so far as it is experienced as being various forms of interaction with other humans. This social window points to the co-ordinates of the closeness to or distance from others, not physically but interpersonally. A powerful experience, for example, later to be concluded to be emotionally challenging or conflict ridden, will be intuited initially in terms of its interpersonal warmth or coldness, the threatening or friendly interactions and interpersonal stances mixed in with space and body and time.

It is important to point out that not every experience may render up meaningful insights from every co-ordinate or window. One could imagine certain experiences like looking at the stars, which would not have a strong social window. Adult education practice in the episodes explored in the installations of the Main Gallery was significant since its very identity as an experience was spatial, bodily, temporal and social, so that the four windows did in fact yield a harvest.

Van Manen (1990, p. 105) concludes:

> These four existentials of lived body, lived space, lived time and lived relation to the other can be differentiated but not separated. They all form an intricate unity which we call the life world – our lived world. But in a research study we can temporarily study the existentials in their differentiated aspects, while realizing that one existential always calls forth the other aspects.

In practice, Merleau-Ponty's co-ordinates as expounded by van Manen were invaluable and served to bring the lived experience to foreground and to text.

Crotty's complementary approach invited the researcher to complete what he called 'sentence stems', each carrying ingenious variations to the basic phenomenological questions: 'What is "x" like as a lived experience'? Crotty's process involved identifying the phenomenon, bracketing any received interpretations and bringing the mind to bear on it directly as has been described earlier in this chapter. The following phrases are listed since they were used in the intuiting panel of each installation. The underlying agenda is to generate a stance of receptive contemplation in which the phenomenon is placed in front of one's gaze and one allows the pen to generate the word in a manner analogous to the free drawing described by Frederick Frank in the *Zen of Seeing* mentioned above.

Below is a chart showing the sentence stems from the second part of the intuiting process (Crotty 1996b, p. 279), with the words 'adult education practice' written in as the phenomenon in question.

When these generative sentence stems were used in the Intuiting panels of the installations in the Main Gallery of the exhibition, the texts generated from them varied according to the episode being considered. The challenge was to keep attention on the phenomenon itself and not to turn the focus of attention onto the subject. This proved challenging since the experiences had been vividly brought to mind by the earlier processes of backgrounding, sketching and poetised reflection, but in the process of bringing the experience to mind, the subjective feelings, fears, regrets and elation were also, as it were, stirred up and the bracketing process had to be implemented strongly. The actual experience of creating the intuiting text is explored more fully in the Epilogue of the thesis.

Adult education practice is like …	Adult education practice sounds to me like …	Adult education practice strikes me as being …
What I discover in adult education practice is …	What I see in adult education practice is …	What shows up when I think of adult education practice is …
Adult education practice can be described as …	Adult education practice looks to me like …	Adult education practice presents itself to me as …
I picture adult education practice as …	What I detect in adult education practice is …	I recognise adult education practice as being …
Adult education practice feels like …	Adult education practice seems to be …	I depict adult education practice in graphic form as …
What comes to light when I focus on adult education practice is …	What is uncovered when I focus on adult education practice is …	What unfolds for me as I dwell on adult education practice is …
When I gaze at adult education practice I see …	I depict adult education practice in poetic terms as …	The metaphor(s) that best convey adult education practice is (are) …

Distilling

The distilling process searches for phenomenological themes as mentioned in the introduction above. This process of discerning recurrent themes in the experience requires a mixture of insight and lateral grouping. The advantage of the Crotty sentence stems is that the phenomenological 'eye' makes a series of passes over the lived experience, letting it present itself in the variety of windows created by the different stems. It is then possible to collate these sentences so that insights about the phenomenon can be grouped or clustered around recurrent perceptions named in the various textual representations. Again the agenda is a matter of discernment, since one eventually wants to ask the question as to how central a particular theme is to the phenomenon and whether an experience such as adult education practice, for example, could retain its integrity if a particular theme was absent.

It should be pointed out that the distillation process in this study is in the service of the expressive project which has a broader agenda to portray adult education practice in as vivid and insightful a way as possible. This agenda is realised through the distillation process together with the other expressive processes in the 'calling to mind' section of the exhibition.

There is a significant point about the distillation process in which themes have been identified and reduced into thematic statements which ring true of the adult education process as experienced. There is a difficulty when one attempts to separate the necessary from the contingent themes, which, in the light of the expressive project of the whole thesis, are not seen to be central, since the expressive process is not analytical and is often satisfied, even enriched, by overlays of recurrent themes. It was easier in this expressive agenda to group recurring themes in a kind of collage rather than have to decode which were contingent and which necessary. It is also worth raising the question about the assumptions, which draw on Husserl, that experiences always have necessary themes and contingent ones. In the traditional areas of interest of classical phenomenologists, the topics chosen were elemental and largely univocal – the gaze, the sick bed, the hotel room, the handshake. Adult education practice is not such a univocal idea but, to refer back to Wittgenstein's contribution in Chapter 1, a family resemblance concept where phenomena having a number of elements, some of which were the same in each case, are grouped under the one name.

In the expressive agenda the distilled elements, arrayed and clustered according to their recurrence and commonality, provide a dense and living collage which seems to give a density and crystallised feel to the phenomenon vividly made present in the first three panels.

The distillation process serves to ground and objectify the structures of the experience of adult education practice and, as such, has contributed significantly to the overall project.

In demonstrating his approach to phenomenological writing, van Manen gives an example taken from his research into children's experience of being left by their parents in the care of others (1990, p. 86). In his research, he collected anecdotes from various people concerning their childhood experience of this phenomenon. He explores these experiences initially under the heading 'situations'. He then begins the laborious task of what he calls 'seeking meaning', in which he builds a thematic account of the structure of this childhood experience.

In the text being constructed here, 'distilling' represents what 'seeking meaning' does in van Manen's text. As he writes (1990, p. 86):

> We try to unearth something 'telling', something 'meaningful', some-
> thing thematic in the various experiential accounts – we work at
> mining meaning from them.

Whereas in the account of van Manen's research there is provision for a summary of the experiences of a range of contributors, in this project there is provision, under the heading 'distilling', for a summary of the major elements in the one intuited experience. These intuitions are thus first represented comprehensively in the Intuiting panel and then reduced in the summarising processes of the Distilling panel. In many cases themes named in the Intuiting panel are listed in the Distilling panel by similar, if not identical, language. This is again due to the representative agenda of these complementary panels where the Distilling panel, which has the task of bringing together recurring elements from the intuiting process, tries not to change the language which emerged in portraying the direct experience of the phenomenon.

Value and relevance

In the first chapter it was asserted that the thesis is attempting to portray adult educational practice rather than analyse or explain it. This expressive interpretative research project needed an appropriate vehicle to carry out its agenda and the one chosen, in the course of much time of contemplation and reflection, is, as the reader has seen, an exhibition constructed as a group of installations in a large gallery which the reader has been invited to enter.

Besides the academic defence and explanation of the expressive approach, the Gallery of Method has to explore the value and usefulness of such a portrayal. How does it contribute to the store of critically evaluated knowledge, purported to be safeguarded and built up by the academy? And secondly, does it contribute to improved educational practice? There is also a sense in which despite all the academic arguments mounted in its defence, the proof of the pudding of expressive research, as this purports to be, is in its eating – its acceptance by and impact on its readers. And so it is useful in the first instance for readers to ask themselves whether, in addressing the installations in the Main Gallery, they were illuminated by the evocations of lived practice and whether as a result of their contemplations, their knowledge of adult education practice has been somehow enriched.

In addition to this reflective appraisal of how the Main Gallery was received, the thesis needs to look more analytically at the kind of knowledge being produced in research of this kind and the criteria of its quality.

Knowledge outcomes from phenomenological research

The meanings attached to a lived experience relate to the activity itself as a human activity, rather than to the incidental subjective moods that might affect the actor while engaged in the activity. As has been pointed out already, it is the difference between exploring what adult education is like as a lived experience, and how an adult educator might feel while engaged in adult education practice. It is the former question which is the phenomenological one. This distinction between asking what something is like, rather than asking how one feels when engaged in it, has also already been raised and linked to work by Crotty (1996a). The concern at this point in this thesis is with the knowledge outcomes of each approach. Crotty suggests that the latter question generates narratives of subjective experience, interpreted according to ideas of engagement and self-actualisation developed by Carl Rogers (1961, 1983). While of importance to the study of professional development, they are not products of classical or 'intuiting' phenomenology, since they do not focus on the experience as a lived entity, but rather on themselves within the experience. Texts issuing from such research are an exploration and analysis of the range of meanings and feelings accompanying a certain experience. As Crotty points out, this significant contribution to knowledge amounts to a new kind of phenomenology. The 'new' phenomenology has been called empathetic in this text and applied in the first three panels of the installations. It was then complemented by the more classical intuiting approach used in next two panels. Crotty's point is that where new phenomenology is used without an awareness that it actually is quite a major departure from the old, the academy will lose the very different contribution that classical phenomenological research can contribute. This thesis thus combines the two approaches in the service of the expressive agenda. What follows is a brief exploration of the type of knowledge produced by such methods and the criteria of its quality.

Knowledge and validation

The phenomenological method used in this expressive project is not another road to the knowledge attained through abstracted and quantitative analysis. Its truth is the truth of verisimilitude rather than the truth of categorical statement. Questions of verisimilitude have been summarised by Denzin and Lincoln (1994, pp. 577), who define it as 'the ability to reproduce (simulate) and map the real'. They are concerned with the kind of possible relationships that can exist between what they call 'the real' and the text (which always appears within a particular genre, for example a letter, lecture, news report, poem) that purports to represent it. They point out that there are, in one sense, many verisimilitudes: those concerning whether the text is true to its genre – a question posed briefly in the considerations of the sketching and poetising panels; or whether the text is true to the world it purports to represent. It is the second which is of consideration here and the criterion of its quality seems to have been found in what Heron (1992, p. 164) refers to as 'true likeness'; as 'declarative' proof:

... declarative proof is in the palate, on the pulse, in the embrace, in the gaze. It is what Perkins crudely called 'what-like understanding' which is 'that understanding of an experience that consists in knowing what an experience is like, and we know what an experience is like by virtue of having that experience' (Perkins 1971). Declarative proof is transactional or interactive: it is the function of my interpenetration with whatever it is that declares itself.

Thus a phenomenological portrayal may generate the moment of insight – intuition in the reader who has had a similar experience but may not have penetrated beyond its everyday interpretations: 'Yes, that is how it is for you. My experience of it may be somewhat different but I can recognise it in yours'.

This truth is not the same as the truth claimed in a generalised statement such as 'all adult learners are volunteers'. It is not possible to oppose the two views in a direct line. It seems rather that both have their place in contributing to human knowledge of a phenomenon that exists as a concept in commentators' minds, but as a lived experience when actually engaged in.

If the researcher seeks to clarify and sharpen his or her conceptual edifice relating to adult education, this is a laudable enterprise requiring logic and precision. Work along these lines has been useful in the development of the discipline relating to adult education. But where it seems to me there has been a lack has been in a focus on the lived experience of adult education.

If, as Usher and Bryant (1989) suggest, adult education is a socio-practical enterprise and research relating to it is equally a socio-practical enterprise, then we need the kind of research which generates data about lived experience to enrich and ground theoretical knowledge.

Heron (1992, pp. 164, 165) gives an illuminating insight into the symbiosis between rational and phenomenological attention. He points out that phenomena need to be identified and bounded by a:

> ... concept definition that points to the presence that is disclosing itself. This definition is a necessary signpost to the presence which, however, has fundamental imaginal and affective parameters which go beyond it.

Heron's insights have been of assistance in this study since the two modes of thinking – the explanatory and expressive or representative – purport to refer to the same thing. What is planned here is an enrichment of rational accounts rather than a denial of them. He writes:

> There is a dialectical tension here between the bracketed concepts and the declaration. If you suspend the concepts absolutely and utterly out of the way, then there is no determinate experience that you can pick out and ask to declare itself. If you don't bracket them off at all, the declaration is repressed by the conceptual imposition (1992, pp. 164, 165).

Criteria of quality

Garman and Piantanida (1994, p. 7), in their summary of criteria for qualitative research, list eight criteria which are listed and elaborated below. It is important to see these as linked to the exploration of expressive rather than explanatory knowledge, with its associated subjective/objective tension. The criteria are: verité, integrity, rigor, utility, vitality, aesthetics, ethics, verisimilitude.

Verisimilitude, last on the list but perhaps key to a quality test of this kind of inquiry, refers to what has been called the 'phenomenological aha'; the moment of 'that's it'; 'yes, that is what it is really like'. As has been pointed out above, verisimilitude is a significant criterion for inquiries in qualitative research using, or at least influenced by, phenomenological approaches. The arts-based research approach of Barone and Eisner (1997), explored in the previous chapter of this Gallery of Method, points out that one of the features of research of this expressive kind is that its texts are presented to the reader as 'virtual realities', seeking to provide a recognisable representation of the real world. The quality of such texts is to be found in the strength of their 'virtuality'. They write (1997, p. 74) that:

> In a text with verisimilitude, the reader recognises some of the
> portrayed qualities from his or her own experiences and is thereby
> able to believe in the possibility – the credibility – of the virtual world
> [presented in the expressive text] as an analogue to the 'real' one.

By *verité*, the authors mention the work's consistency with accepted knowledge; as they say, a phrase or sentence 'rings true'. *Integrity* is the measure of the study's structure and cohesion, and the strength of the rationale advanced for the use of this method in the particular study under question. *Rigor* questions the sufficiency of the intellectual work in it and the soundness of the portrayals. *Utility* tests the usefulness and professional relevance of the work and its contribution to the field.

The criterion of *vitality* is a significant expressive category. The authors invoking this criterion ask:

> Is it important, meaningful... non-trivial? Does it have a sense of
> vibrancy, intensity, excitement of discovery? Is the proper personae
> (or voice) used for the author(s) and other participants? Do meta-
> phors, images, visuals communicate powerfully?

Aesthetics is used by the writers to measure the research work's ability to enrich and illumine its readers. As they say:

> Does it give me insight into some universal part of my educational
> self? Does it touch my spirit in some way?

Under the criterion of *ethics*, the research work is interrogated as to its protection of confidentiality and respect for participants, as well whether the research work has what they call an 'ethical sensibility' – a general tone of respect for the rights and feelings of those mentioned in the research.

Fulfilling the criteria

The installations of the Main Gallery attempt, through the expressive and phenomenological processes, to present a recognisable portrayal of the lived experience of adult education practice. The question can still be put about how does or will one know if such presentations are 'good or useful'? All that one can do in the expressive medium is to ensure that the foundations of accurate and vivid presentation have been followed and that processes have been put in place to meet the criteria for 'good' expressive research, like those explored above.

At the same time it has been good to be able to report that at least to some extent, some of the installations have already had an airing and have attracted a kind of desirable response. On three occasions when components of the installations from the Main Gallery were presented at conferences, a number of adult educator members of the audience validated the portrayal, saying that the juxtaposed texts 'brought the experience to life', and that that 'made alive' experience resonated with experiences of their own.

These comments responded to my concern, as author, for the design and execution of the method of the project, and they validated its claim to *verisimilitude, verité* and *vitality*.

The claim to *utility* is argued particularly through the work on reflection, and the contribution of phenomenological portrayal to the reflective process. The claim to *expressive rigor* is linked to the careful dovetailing of expressive and phenomenological hermeneutic approaches to construct the deep and vivid portrayal of the Main Gallery, defended and elaborated in the Gallery of Method.

The criterion of *aesthetics* has been met by the conscious attempt in the expressive processes to strive for beauty and elegance of expression. How this is realised or received remains of course something of a mystery, but at least the pursuit of beauty and the receiving soul were acknowledged and written for.

This completes the Gallery of Method. The two chapters have traversed the method employed in the Main Gallery, exploring the foundations of expressive research in its complementary empathetic and intuiting approaches. The thesis now returns to the work of portrayal presented in the Main Gallery. It seeks to generate a kind of coming together of ideas and images encountered therein: to revisit and, as it were, distil its various processes to focus the impact of the exhibition within its expressive agenda.

Visitors to the Gallery of Method move now with their curator to the Exit Foyer.

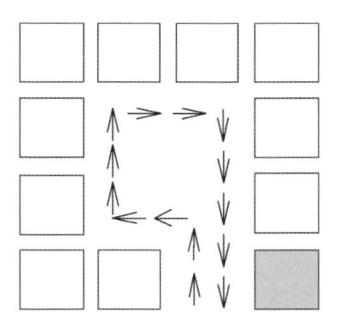

PART IV
THE EXIT FOYER

Orientation

The group with the curator has now traversed the entrance foyer, the Main Gallery and the Gallery of Method and is imagined to have arrived at the Exit Foyer and to have been offered a drink.

The visitors are imagined to be seated comfortably in a reflective mood, with the installations of the Main Gallery and their theoretical justifications in the Gallery of Method fresh in mind. The Exit Foyer is provided to make a space where the experiences of the exhibition can be pulled together and where some, at least, of their implications brought to mind. Whereas the mood in the Gallery of Method was contemplative and that of the method gallery dialogic, the mood aimed for here is reflective, moving between the experiences of the exhibition and the implications they may have for the professional and personal world of each visitor outside the gallery.

There is a challenge in the design of the exhibition metaphor in the thesis which places the Gallery of Method between the Main Gallery and this Exit Foyer. On the one hand this is useful, since readers will have had a clearer idea of the expressive agenda and its foundations in research theory. On the other hand, and it is a considerable other hand, the Exit Foyer is directly linked to, and builds on, the experiences of the Main Gallery. The stance and cultural expectations of the reader need to re-adopt the expressive approach used in the Main Gallery and with the analytic and explanatory mode to one side, attempt to return to the more contemplative stance.

As we move into the foyer, we are taking with us the images and stories and poems and their intuitings and distillations, and there is possibly almost an air of repletion, of stimulus overload. The gallery visitor wants time to digest and reflect and to allow the intuited sense of the implications of some of these revelations time to take shape and settle. There may even be some element of nervousness as reflecting adult educators may find themselves reviewing their own practice and comparing parallel experiences. They may be wondering whether some of the dimensions of the experience revealed or made plain in the installations of the Main gallery are also present, possibly unnoticed, in their own practice with similar implications.

The mood of this chapter wants to be reflective and retrospective. It wants to hold its gaze to the phenomenon and to deepen the intuition of recurrent themes in its experienced structure. It wants to retain and deepen the expressive stance and so bring the circle of expressive inquiry to a close within its own style and genre.

Whereas the Exit Foyer has the task of bringing the exhibition to a close, the thesis itself, in which the exhibition is embedded, is concluded through a brief commentary appended as an epilogue. This is linked in the first place to the Prologue which prefaced the whole thesis and introduced the project of the thesis and the exhibition metaphor with its expressive and phenomenological approach, through which this was to be pursued. In the Epilogue the whole exhibition enterprise and its contribution are briefly reviewed and its strengths and weaknesses commented upon without detracting from the main agenda of the thesis, which is the portrayal of the phenomenon of adult education practice as lived experience.

Without further ado, let us enter the Exit Foyer.

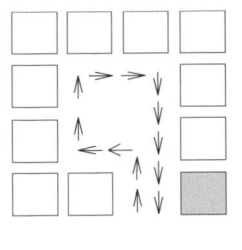

Chapter 11

Final reflections

This final chapter consists of three parts which constitute the Exit Foyer. The first is a brief overview of what is in this chapter. The second is a collage of the phenomenon of adult education practice built by overlaying themes taken from the distilling panels of the installations in the Main Gallery. The third part seeks to explore the significance and implications of these distilled elements of the phenomenon of adult education practice which are presented in the collage.

Bringing to closure

The question that immediately arises is how does one bring to closure a dissertation concerned with portrayal, where the main agenda has been to bring an experienced entity into close view as what it is/was *as lived* and not *as-hoped-to-be* or *intended-to-be*? Although conclusions are not drawn from such a process as they are from a proven hypothesis, a deep realisation of the lived nature of a pursuit like adult education practice can lead to an awareness of its significance and the implications embedded in it. The classical line: 'Well, if that's what it's really like (for example marriage, childbirth, war, living in a commune, and of course engaging in adult education), then it will require more time or resources, space, appreciation, community gratitude.' Thus, close on this realisation of what the 'livedness' of a phenomenon is like can come a perception of some of the real implications built into it, including requirements to be met and certain dispositions to be cultivated.

The collage-building and exploration of significance and implications are pursued by a continuance of the reflective processes used in the Main Gallery. There is a revisiting of the Main Gallery installations and in the process of highlighting recurrent themes, the phenomenon in the installations is once more foregrounded, this time in the quest for recurrent elements to enrich the collage.

This condensing process pursues the reflective agenda outlined in the first chapter of the thesis and expounded further in the first chapter of the Gallery of Method. The suggestion made in the chapter in the Gallery of Method is that when one deliberately restricts one's inquiry to the descriptive phase of reflection, people reading will almost instinctively wish to take things further and explore the implications of such experience and the interests behind it. In this final chapter the building of the collage of the phenomenon is again confined to deep and vivid portrayal. However, the third part of the chapter, on its way toward closure of the exhibition, when it revisits themes from the collage, does seek, albeit briefly, to point to their significance and to implications flowing from them. The reflections on the significance and implications of the revealed face of adult education practice, as experienced, are linked briefly to relevant writings of researchers and practitioners who have already addressed some of the themes which emerged in the collage.

At the completion of the exploration of significances and implications, there is a brief summary and farewell from the curator who recalls the aim and invitational theme of the exhibition, and retraces the steps of the visitors through its galleries. He then suggests in his farewell that others might wish to build their own gallery and look at ways in which they, in their turn, experienced their own invitations to learning.

The collage: picturing the phenomenon of adult education practice

The following overlays several pictures of the experience to build a composite collage. The highlighted text represents the major themes, which have been elaborated in the various chapters of the main gallery.

- As an educator, the experience of the phenomenon of adult education practice is: **challenging and rewarding: dark-making and healing**. It is like: being blessed and valued; being caught in one's own whirlpool. The experience: has a dimension of rawness; is sometimes entropic. Adult education practice appears as: darkness and frustration mixed with unexpected healing and achievement.
- The phenomenon of adult education practice appears as: **a feast of madness and exuberance**. It is like a maelstrom of: good humour; debate; anger; political contestation.
- The phenomenon of adult education practice is also referred to as: **dealing and dancing and being left with the washing up**. It presents itself as: diplomatic negotiation; dealing and counter dealing; reassurance collaboration; being caught with the washing up.
- Another theme of the phenomenon of adult education practice is referred to as: **grabbing and dancing: pushing and laughing**. Inviting people to learn is experienced as: joined with an invitation to friendship; trying to convert the energy in anger into energy for learning; sparring to convert distractions to learning.

- Adult education practice presents as a precarious experience of: **'being with' and 'staying with' learners in ambiguity.** It is experienced as: 'staying with' the learners; connection; accepting helplessness and precariousness; flying a hang glider.
- Elements of the phenomenon of adult education practice appear as: **seating and showing the learning menu to a respected but volatile 'restaurant' group.** It is like: an orchestrated group experience and subsequent debriefing; being on trial for the quality of the learning offerings and processes, being judged; a mixture of all kinds of interpersonal exchanges; unlimited contestation.
- A significant theme recurring often is: **'siren singing for learning': a form of enchantment.** Practising adult education manifests itself as: introducing a friend to another friend; an educator on the make; kidding to learn; kidding the trainees along.
- The phenomenon of adult education practice appears here as: **amplifying and integrating learners' responding voices.**
- Adult education is experienced as an: **instructing, drilling and testing experience.**
- The phenomenon of adult education practice has a theme of: **a utopian space being built and defended.** The experience is one of: listening, attention-pursuing; cranking a heavy flywheel; making spaces; standing back; becoming silent; working to become invisible; opening-out, closing-in.
- The phenomenon of adult education practice has a theme of: **brokering a cease-fire: bandaging and healing.**
- From another window, the phenomenon of adult education practice sounds like: **feeling to learn.** It is like: winnowing for the learning agenda; trying but not knowing; sailing a boat in the dark; colluding in a fantasy of learning adoption.
- The phenomenon of adult education practice has a theme of: **being caught between inspiration and assessment.**

The collage now has a range of clustered images and representations of the experience of adult education practice, ordered to some extent by juxtaposing them with the different activities listed in the sequence of learning facilitative processes laid out in the list above. The following explores some of the implications of the junctions and disjunctions between planned activity and experience, and their implications for current theories and practices of adult education.

Messages from the collage: significance and implications

The element of personal challenge and the call for selflessness

The experiences of engaging adult learners in adult education have been revealed as personally challenging for the educator, and thus to require him or her to develop a respectful, even virtuous disposition. This manifestation of the lived experience of adult education practice confronts policy makers, administrators, practitioners and educators of practitioners with the need to be aware that they will be challenged – their personal values, knowledge and skills will be often under scrutiny. This view counters an 'instrumental' and 'outcomes referenced' view of learning facilitation as 'information or skills transfer'. Such language does not account for the experience of being scrutinised and challenged by willing learners, who may wish to take knowledge or skill without acknowledging or appreciating its source or the skill and tact that often goes into creating the learning facilitative processes. Practising and would-be adult educators, reflecting on the Main Gallery (and no doubt reflecting on their own experience or future), would be in no doubt that the experience of being an adult educator can mean personal challenge involving darkness, rawness, entropy and healing.

Adult educators, in reaction to the fraught nature of the adult education experience, can, on occasion, feel used and abused by learners so that they may need to acknowledge this theme in their preparation for, and engagement in, adult education practice. To some extent it is analogous to the mentorship experience of a person who 'shows' or 'tells' another, basically out of care and affection for the learner. Of course, the learners may not look at, or appreciate, the facilitator. Their eyes may be fixed on the new knowledge and skill and how that takes them into the future, rather than on the at least partially hidden hand and voice of the adult educator trying to help the learner to see and hear.

Would-be policy writers, programme managers, adult educators and educators of adult educators can, in the course of this exhibition, become aware of, and cater for, the personal challenges embedded in learning facilitation. There is an additional dimension to the experience of adult education practice in the personally exuberant, enraging, frustrating and stressful experience that adult education practice can also be for the learners, whose manifestation of feelings in the presence of the educator contributes to the lived experience of adult education practice. The significance of learning facilitation being experienced in practice, as witnessing deep upheavals in the minds and hearts of the learners, carries an implied call for compassion and protection of confidentiality on the part of the educator.

Adult education practice unmasked, at least in the episodes of practice portrayed in the exhibition, needs to be understood and treated as a stress and illumination generating experience. Adult education practice needs to be aware of deep internal reactions of the learners, and needs also to develop appropriate predispositions to cater for peaks and troughs and occasional difficult times generated by the interpersonal encounters and challenges which present as common themes in adult education practice.

Respectful mobilising for learning and the requirement of respect

The adult educational experience was also described above as respectful mobilising for learning. This catalytic process was experienced as fragile and unpredictable; and that the educator, in attempting to create the chemistry for learning, often experiences peaks and troughs and drudgery and little guaranteed success. Little, McAllister and Priebe (1991, p. 52) refer to the importance of not impeding 'latent learning', which is the learning humans pursue independently of, and often in the course of, being instructed. This has some resonance here since it reminds the educators that the experience of being 'out of control' may in fact be appropriate, since humans retain control over their learning and that education action needs to factor in time and space to allow and encourage learners to orient themselves towards the learning on offer.

The significance of this experience is also the importance of planning learning facilitation with attention to the complexity of its processes. As an experience, adult education practice in this cluster of themes has elements of needing to be planned and embarked upon with as many different access and engagement points as possible.

The implications of needing to monitor and serve the learning group – the call to be 'safeguarding'

Another element concerns the *group dimension* of learning facilitation – the lived experience presents as an interactive tension between the educator and the learners and among the learners themselves. One of the significant points in the themes clustered here was the unpredictable nature of learning groups. Just because a group is involved in an educational process does not mean that the social dynamics of interpersonal and group relationships are suspended. The adult education experience pursued in groups is pursued in, and within, various kinds of group behaviour which need to be acknowledged and catered for. This point was well made by Tennant (1988, p.133) when he wrote:

> Paradoxically, one of the greatest dangers of group work comes from the power of the group to shape and maintain the behaviour and beliefs of its members. In this context a knowledge of group dynamics can best be used to ward off oppressive aspects of the group.

Certainly, it is a salutary reminder of the interpersonal and group exchanges that need to be catered for in learning facilitative processes.

The implications of the mentoring element: the call to engage, challenge and nurture

'Siren singing for learning' refers to learning facilitative experience surrounding various *activities to generate a learning response* in the learners-to-be. In highly structured and examined courses, this experience may not stand out as much as it does in less structured and linear forms of adult education such as group projects, workplace training and the like. Even in structured programmes there may be some doubt as to whether the students have, in truth, decided to 'take on' the learning and admit new knowledge to their inner self. There may well be a question about whether it will be retained in a kind of ante-room to be used in exams and then disregarded as an unappealing end to an educational but not learning project.

The siren and the mentor

The significance of themes within siren singing – 'enchantment', 'kidding to learn' – point to a form of kindly interaction which draws little from the rational and objectives-focused agenda of the instructor. It points to a complementary role: that of a mentor. The mentor has a mixture of loving collusion with the learner, seeking her or his enrichment through the proposed internalising of the learning under question, together with some rough, bracing challenge calling forth strength, courage and dormant potentiality. Laurent Daloz, in his book *Effective teaching and mentoring* (1986), in some ways a precursor to this study, gives insight into this mentor role with its challenge to give respectful care and concern and some self-forgetting in the process of 'siren singing' for learning.

A mentor is someone engaged in a supportive relationship with people attempting to learn/become something. A mentor is usually a person who has already achieved a measure of success in the matter to be learned. Apart from offering support to aspiring learners, a mentor provides encouragement by providing living proof that the learning tasks being attempted can be achieved. Daloz (1986, p. 30) speaks of Virgil, Dante's mentor:

> Mentor supreme alternatively protecting his charge from threat,
> urging him on, explaining the mysteries, pointing the way, leaving
> him alone, translating arcane codes, calming marauding beasts,
> clearing away obstacles and encouraging – always encouraging. A
> mentor begins by engendering trust, issuing a challenge, providing
> encouragement and offering a vision for the journey.

Mentoring moves teaching from any exclusive concentration on detached 'information transfer' to a much more demanding interpersonal relationship. People may 'map themselves onto' the mentor. They will say: 'See, they can do it and they are just like me; it must be possible.'

From another perspective, the teacher mentor has a kind of *licence to challenge* which comes from the inner experience of having overcome a particular learning challenge on the one hand, and of a strong feeling of oneness with the learner being taught on the other. The mentor has this sense of being 'one' and 'other' at the same time. In a similar vein, women have always been able to challenge their sisters to acts of self-liberation, particularly in matters relating to gender, in a way that men cannot do so readily. Similarly, blacks have been able to challenge and comfort each other in a way that whites cannot do so readily, and people who have negotiated a particular life transition can challenge and comfort those people about to enter it, in this same mentoring way. For Daloz (1986, pp. 17, 18), mentors have a strong metaphoric dimension. They are:

> ... creations of our imagination, designed to fill a psychic space some-
> where between lover and parent. Not surprisingly, they are suffused

with magic ... Their purpose is to remind us that we can indeed
survive the terror of the coming journey and undergo the transformation by moving through, not around, our fear ... What distinguishes
(mentors) is their willingness to care – about what they teach and
when. They know they exist as teachers only because of their
students.

The phrase 'siren singing', which emerged in the intuiting and distilling
processes, carries a notion of attraction mixed in with challenge, but highlights
its encouragement dimensions. When it is seen as overlaid with instructing,
grabbing and dancing, it points to a composite picture expressed in the term
'mentoring'. Even here, more brusque 'challenge to learn' elements which characterise some forms of mentoring are not strongly present. 'Invitation' seems a
better way to describe the experience of adult education practice portrayed in
the episodes of practice displayed in the Main Gallery.

The implications of listening, hearing and responding: the call to attend and be present

The experience of adult education practice in the installations presented has
also been portrayed as *an amplification of the student's voice*, responding to
the educator's proactive engagement. The significance of this is that it points to
elements of *adult exchange* in adult education. The most significant point
seems to be that making provision for adult learners to respond to the
educator's learning facilitative initiative amplifies the voice of the learner as she
or he responds to the adult educator. The learner's response becomes a major
element in the learning which is supposed to follow, and which needs to be
factored into the ongoing learning facilitative process.

This is not the same as a commonly used technique that engages the
learner in a kind of pseudo-openness at the beginning of a course. Questions
are asked and participants' wishes are sought, but only in order to gain their
attention. The facilitator then proceeds with a pre-set teaching programme,
with the quickened interest and engagement of the learners put to one side. In
the article cited earlier, Tennant also draws attention to the 'illusion of
freedom', since 'most adult learning groups function within non-negotiable
parameters and constraints' (1988, p. 138).

In this case it is not just the question of learners' wishes being followed but
a related question of their voices being heard – the 'learning' voice as well as
the 'suggesting' voice. The 'amplifying the learners' voices' theme of the lived
experience of adult education practice highlights to adult educators the
dialogue/dialectic characteristics of the phenomenon of facilitated adult
learning in these episodes. This 'adult' element in the phenomenon highlights
the challenge educators and trainers of adults face when they have to follow a
set curriculum. The set curriculum has an implied contract of an advertised
course, while at the same time needing to make space for, and somehow 'factor
in', students' responses and contributions to the overall learning facilitative
processes.

The implications of rendering things to be learned, learnable: the call to didactic clarity

The *instructing/drilling* words were used to portray the experience of adult education practice particularly when it involved teaching basic knowledge (which had to be memorised) and necessary skills (which had to be mastered). The instructing/drilling experience reminded the educator that the so-called 'content' or 'things-to-be-learned' must be *rendered learnable*. This experience of struggling to clarify the learning to be facilitated has great significance for the practice of adult education, where a broad learning agenda is being pursued. It is one thing to think about ways of communicating information like the names of botanical species in horticulture (although even here teachers may struggle to find ways to facilitate memorising work), or skills in using tools. It is quite another to think about communicating a value such as empathy or tolerance, or a particular perspective. To seek to make such things learnable requires different approaches.

Considerable work has been done by academics following Habermas' idea of what he called 'knowledge constitutive interests' and their influence on the kind of knowledge being pursued. Michael Collins (1985, p. 104) cites Habermas' (1984, p. 77) idea of three worlds, each with its own way of being and of being known: the world of physical states; the world of conscious states; and the world of scientific and poetic thoughts – culture. It is not the aim of this study to enter into a searching exploration of these notions except to point out that the kind of learning that an adult educator may want to promote requires careful consideration as to its nature and how it may appropriately be fostered.

Jack Mezirow, a pioneering exponent of adult education practice, used Habermas' idea of the three knowledge constitutive interests: instrumental, communicative and critical, which are linked to the three worlds just mentioned. He stressed the importance of knowing what kind of knowledge is embedded in the learning that is being facilitated, and what approach can be used to facilitate that kind of learning.

It is this insightful approach which has challenged the technicism and instrumentalism in approaches that use language like 'knowledge and skills transfer', without attending to the kind of knowledge under consideration. As Mezirow writes (1991b, p. 80):

> ... the distinction between instrumental and communicative learning
> is extremely important to point out because instrumental learning has
> been too commonly taken as the model of all learning.

The implications of making friendly spaces and silences for learning: the call to let go, to relinquish control

Building a utopian space, the next element in the collage of the phenomenon of adult education practice portrayed in the exhibition, resonates with the writings of Mechtild Hart and Deborah Horton (1993, p. 238). When referring to transformative education, they said that it has to 'allow for a creation of spaces where positive future-oriented, utopian possibilities can take shape in people's imagination'.

This central theme in the experience of inviting learning has apparent similarities with some current discourses on learning environments and self-directed learning. There is a clear portrayal of invitational practice as 'making spaces' and 'becoming invisible', that are linked to the importance of safeguarding and supporting adult autonomy in learning. This theme in the experience resonates with the humanistic psychology of Carl Rogers.

Like the Rogerian approach, it is essentially a 'warm' rather than 'cool' experience. The learner is not placed in a detached disengaged space to fend for her or himself. Such a notion, which may have some support in current rationalistic discourse, is not meant here. The 'space' that is opened up, the 'becoming silent,' 'becoming invisible', is not initially the same as being absent. The adult educator must still be present, but present in a way analogous to the woman supporting her friend learning to use a computer for the first time. She lets her friend hold her autonomy and move into a more independent space, but a space that is still within her friend's approving, supporting ambience. It would be true that in such emerging utopian spaces, the educator's initiatory and 'siren singing' roles would eventually diminish as the learner gains confidence and skills in managing the required learning. There is a fragility in adult learning that requires tactful and often silent presence, particularly if not pursued regularly. The tension between being present but invisible represents elements of the experience when the adult educator was consciously supporting and making spaces at the same time.

The utopian space experience includes an element of 'disposability': of being able to be disposed of. Such an element of the experience has resonances with non-directive community development practice, where the activist consciously allows for his or her rejection, or for the would-be learners to withdraw from whatever relationship may have been established between facilitator and learners-to-be. Implicit in this space-making exercise is that the educator will desist as soon as possible from initiatives, but will stay around as supportive but non-directive friend. Also implicit is that the learners-to-be may dismiss or reject or move away from her or him according to their choice. This notably 'self-less' stance – 'to do ourselves out of a job', needs to be acknowledged and factored into the adult educator's personal standing orders. It is not comfortable to be rejected even when, from one perspective, such an outcome is desirable as an indicator of the learners' choice for self-reliance.

The implications of cranking the flywheel and allowing time for healing: the call for patience, care, commitment

The *bandaging and healing* theme in the adult education experience was linked to the experience of engaged learners who, often having overcome serious obstacles to take on the learning project, run into difficulties of all kinds. This happens when they attempt to continue the ongoing processes that led to learning: reading, writing, discussing, becoming skilled, attempting a skill, accepting feedback and trying again. Others are linked to disagreements and conflict between learners or between learners and the educator. These are also the same difficulties, arising from her or his personal and social environment, that beset the continuing learner. The 'bandaging' and 'brokering a cease-fire' themes in the lived experience of adult education practice again highlight the nurturing and encouraging dimension of adult education, and call for tolerance and forbearance. What is significant in this theme in the phenomenon of adult education practice is the ease with which delicately nurtured confidence and willingness to try can be destroyed and negativity returns.

There is consequently some usefulness in adult education practice of spending time on 'cranking up the flywheel of enthusiasm and confidence'. This can be done by direct and indirect encouragement, and by integrating into the spin of the flywheel a kind of being 'forewarned' that difficulties can be expected and hopes may be dashed, at least temporarily, in the course of learning.

The implications of the 'feeling to learn', and the 'invitation' experience: the call for tact

The *feeling to learn* theme represents the initiatory and invitational way that the 'challenge to learn' activity in the learning facilitative sequence was actually experienced in the described episodes of practice. This is in marked contrast to stories of confronting or even dismissive and hostile teachers, where a learning challenge is issued accompanied by elements of disdain. Where the learning facilitator appears reluctant to accept or recognise the learning power and response of the learners, there would be an unspoken text saying something like: 'You probably aren't bright enough for this, but I suppose I must at least go through the motions of trying to teach you.' Successful, resistant learners, who overcome hostile challenges implicit in dismissive teaching, draw on their own resources and self-esteem. Many adult learners-to-be in the episodes of practice of the exhibition referred to earlier experiences of being taught as an experience of disdain, against which they felt powerless.

In the episodes of practice explored here, the invitatory agenda was implemented from an espoused stance of respect and encouragement. As experienced, the educational practices were largely without assurance that the learners-to-be (many of whom spoke of being wounded in earlier experiences of being taught) had taken up a positive, predisposing stance towards this. Many were unsure whether they would confidently accept invitations to engage in learning facilitative exercises: think, concentrate, read, reflect, discuss, explore alternatives, critique ideas and their premises.

The inconclusive evidence of students' application and engagement in various episodes of practice gives no firm foundation upon which to build a challenge to reluctant learners to embrace the knowledge: to seize upon it and so move it from surface or rote learning to a deeper space.

The reality of lived experience showed a much less linear phenomenon. The adult education experience is manifested as complex and as constantly looping back almost to the beginning of the educator/learner encounter in an ongoing attempt to 'call out' a learning commitment from hesitant participants-to-be.

The metaphors of this theme, in portraying the phenomenon, have a strong minimalist feel. It is as if for the adult educator in this arena of poverty and resistance, something is better than nothing; and that an ambiguous and intermittent engagement is better than no engagement at all. The experience of this kind of adult education practice seems to present a kind of doggedness: that it is preferable to attempt to build on whatever ambiguous engagement can be secured, than to do nothing in the face of high need and alienation.

The implication of being transparent to inspire and assess: the call to vision, consistency and clarity

The intuited experience of adult education practice revealed an ongoing tension between an opening of boundaries and possibilities through inspiration – a kind of growth of confidence – and a shrinking and 'bottom line' feeling in the process of learning appraisal. The experience of appraisal in this context seemed to have been one of disjunction and anomaly, as if the process was unexpected and a kind of affront.

This manifested some of the ambiguities in the real-life experience of attempting to involve reluctant or unknowing learners-to-be in the learning facilitative processes. It was an achievement to get such learners to engage in the processes, and to see a small spark – at least for some of them – a beginning of interest in the reflections, explorations, discussions, self-tests and the like. It was as if one could feel the flywheel begin to turn and the educator, when attuned enough to that process, would begin to load the accelerating process with more interesting and challenging activities, to get the learners to have some small wins in their experience of learning as adults. The energy was so strongly focused on the learner and the educator's attention so concentrated on signs of growth in the learner's interest and energy for learning that there seemed little energy or call for appraisal or quantification of the learning itself. That would come for some, but in most of the experiences which formed the installations of the exhibition, appraisal of learning took oblique and muted forms. One experience mentioned in the collage was the discovery and celebration of learning already achieved. In others, appraisal was performed through ongoing interviews with learners, where the question was not put of the learning but of the learner taking on learning. When in the final installation, appraisal was placed in naked relief, the experience seemed to change the whole process and, I suspect, usher in a tighter and possibly more detached contractual process in which the learner begins to focus and to measure his or her application and retention of specific learning. This appears to represent a particular progression or transition in formal education, but of course it may also represent a kind of loss of innocence of exploration and questioning, and the tyranny of objectifying appraisal which at another level, particularly in formal education, is experienced as necessary.

It is the challenge of the 'learning inviter' to 'invite learners' to take up and sustain the love of learning that may have initially been aroused in the early exchanges of the teaching/learning exchange, and to keep something of a young spirit in the measured and processed learner who may emerge.

The curator's farewell

With these words, the journey through this *Inviting learning* exhibition is completed. From the initial welcome and briefing in the Entrance Foyer, readers have traversed the seven installations of the Main Gallery and contemplated portrayals of experience of adult education practice before engaging in the debates and discussions surrounding the method employed, and its claim to academic status. This Exit Foyer has begun by building a collage of the experience of adult education practice, bringing together recurrent themes from the distillations in the installations of the Main Gallery. A consideration of the significance and implications of these experiences has then followed.

It is hoped that as they leave this foyer, adult education practitioners and phenomenological researchers will continue on their own reflective way, and possibly construct their own exhibition in turn, about their experiences of inviting learning.

This completes the exhibition metaphor but, as was pointed out in the orientation of this section, there is still the need to conclude the thesis itself in which the exhibition has been embedded, by providing a space to reflect on the use of the exhibition literary device and its contribution to the expressive aims of the thesis. This is the task of the Epilogue.

EPILOGUE

Looking back at the thesis and its use of the exhibition metaphor, there are two questions that need attention, the exploration of which forms a brief epilogue to this study. The first concerns the actual experience of carrying out the phenomenological exercises of the Main Gallery. It is put to the author/curator: What was it like to reflect back on those episodes of your adult education practice and attempt to bring them to the present through the backgrounding, sketching, poetising, intuiting and distilling processes? Did the experience confirm your stated agenda of bringing the lived experience to the present as vividly as possible?

The second question concerns the contribution of the expressive method to research: What kind of knowledge was generated and in what way did it complement other forms of social inquiry?

Doing phenomenology

As has been outlined in the first chapter, the aim of creating and juxtaposing the six panels in the installations in the Main Gallery was to highlight and give weight to different aspects of the phenomenon of adult education practice. Writing the lengthy backgrounding was to provide a focus on contextual elements of the phenomenon, some of which were manifested as a dimension of the phenomenon itself. The writing process was like building a detailed reproduction of the dramatic stage, on which significant adult education events were played out, taking into consideration the terrain, the personal characteristics of the main actor, the educator, and the geographic, cultural and situational contexts.

Some of the components of the context, for example the cultural preoccupations of the players, seemed in fact more a component of the phenomenon, since at least to some extent the lived experience of adult education practice did of course include the feelings and dispositions of the adult-educator himself and his learners. There were, however, other elements that were experienced more truly as a frame: a background against which the phenomenon manifested itself, in accounting for these elements, it seemed that, the more the backgrounding text developed, the more the actual lineaments of the lived experience began to blur. As attention became centred on the background, the sharp lineaments of the phenomenon moved slightly out of the foreground. By focusing on myself in detailed narrative of the context and background of my adult educational action in each episode of practice, I felt like I was writing about a stage set in which a whole range of possible action could take place – a general sense of *possibility* rather than actuality. The backgrounding tended to highlight the power such contextual forces were capable of generating, rather than highlighting what they were actually doing. There was less emphasis on the actual peaks and troughs of the contextualised experience itself.

As I moved from the backgrounding to write the sketch – an anecdote of a significant moment in my engagement in adult education practice in each episode – there was another influence on the immediacy (the direct and unpolluted narrative). This time it was shaped by the movement and critical momentum of the sketch, in giving it point and structure, I included events prior to and post the incident in the narrative, to serve the dramatic agenda, to serve the punch line, to get the reader in. I then wondered how such editing might have corrupted my direct phenomenological gaze. I then remembered that the tension and resolution described in the narrative actually came from the actual experience in the staff meetings at that coffee shop. The story style had actually jogged my memory about an aspect of the lived experience that I had not hitherto noticed as strongly.

The story genre was also selective in its foregrounding of various contextual dimensions of the event, in a very real sense, the background story became a first positioning chapter for the action where the lived experience was actually sited. As I read the story after having read the background, its flickers and shadows, reflected from the detailing of the context, added richness and vividness to the story. I was still a little concerned that the story, 'as story', had its own dynamic which threatened to shape or colour the actual experience, in reply to this feeling of being a little reduced by the story genre into 'killing more than showing', I realised that of course the phenomenon I was attempting to portray had to be presented as 'my experience' and not some imagined generic experience, in a way the story of the experience had to be both 'its' story and 'my story of it'.

Besides the tensions and complementarity between the two forms of writing, there was also the more crucial dialectic in each writing experience between trying to represent the lived experience as accurately and immediately as possible while obeying the rules and requirements of the literary form being used. The background account had to provide a comprehensive picture of the context of the event: the sketch needed to be a story with its dramatic tension and punch line, in the backgrounding, this tension was experienced between the possible and the actual, in the story narrative, it was between the messy reality of the actual event and its becoming organised into a largely linear, dramatic and selective account of actions leading to the point – the punch line of the sketch.

Thus, a phenomenologist of my own research, I also noticed that, in writing the backgrounding and the sketch more or less at the same time, the two forms fed each other – my attention to the background would precipitate recollection of a moment in the sketch and the thrust of the story would take my attentive eye into a component of the context of the action which had escaped description. Responding to such complementary clues helped me move progressively to focus on every visible element of the lived experience of my adult education practice, and to clarify parts which might have remained vague or undeveloped. This, combined with the ongoing concern to transcend the demands of form for the reality carried within it, seemed to contribute to removal of successive 'gauze veils', thus creating a progressively more vivid and living portrayal of the phenomenon. This was then to receive further clarification in the third process: the act of poetising the experience.

The poetic experience was the strangest. If the story had brought my attention to the movement, issues, resolution and thrust of the educational experience, the act of writing poetically seemed to take me to a more holistic place in my awareness. The act of poetising seemed to take a theme more than an event, and to let it percolate up into consciousness as one experience. The conjunction and juxtaposition of ideas and images I experienced in writing the poem emerged, while in focused contemplation on the experience, as something specially my own in its experienced 'whatness'. The poem seemed to grow from the other texts as a kind of crystal, precipitated when the solution of reflection had become supersaturated through the intense and careful preliminary backgrounding and sketching work.

Writing the poetised text was thus linked to the experience of writing the other two. There is even a hint that the first two ways of writing formed preliminary energisers and carriers for the deeper, more comprehensive experience manifested in the poem, as if, having completed their necessary functions, they could now be jettisoned. I am not sure of this. Perhaps this is the reader's experience who, having scaled the heights, feels no further need for the ladder, but leaves it for others coming after. Or perhaps the builder, having locked the keystone in the arch, knows it no longer needs the scaffold that was needed to hold it during its construction, but leaves the scaffold there to show how it was done.

The other question remains that if in fact the poem built upon the others, is there a sense in which it is to some extent a conceptual elaboration derived from earlier, more primitive forms of engagement with the phenomenon? This remains a possibility but it is not what I experienced. The poetising experience does seem to contain a crystallising, intense portrayal – a sharpening of the edge and awareness of the objective lived experience – but this is combined with an elaboration of its subjectivity.

As I read the three accounts, I experienced an ongoing tension. Each genre had two forces. The first was a *focusing* force to bring attention to, and engagement with, the lived experience. The second was a *distracting* force to move that attention away from the thing contemplated, to the form of its portrayal and the selectivity of its genre. I found I could, in the experience of this dialectic, come to a form of breakthrough by being aware of and bracketing out the distracting tendencies and by flowing with the immediacy of their aesthetic and direct attention.

In the course of writing the phenomenological accounts of adult education practice for this study, I have become more consciously aware of the experience of actually constructing such accounts. The experience has a link with Miles Horton's (1990) famous phrase: 'we make the road by walking'. Here the expressive researcher is 'making windows by looking'. This refers to being illumined and obfuscated variously by the three 'calling to mind' processes as described above. Each approach, each way of looking, seemed *create* as well as *open* a window, illuminating and enriching the awareness of the lived experience and hinting that all is not revealed: that other ways of looking might as well create other windows.

The subsequent more overtly phenomenological texts – intuiting and distilling – had a much 'cooler' feel, as if it was time to bring a kind of reduction – to seek a tight, even spare focus and to see what such a net would catch. There was a different but equally real sense of discovery: things emerged from what can be called 'unnoticed facets' of the diamond. The name of the thesis itself came from the revelatory power of the phenomenological approach, where 'inviting learning' was revealed as a recurrent metaphor carrying an essential element of the lived experience of adult education practice. It pointed up the initiatory element of so much adult education practice where the adult educator, in many non-formal and formal settings, has to begin and begin and begin again as an essential part of his or her work.

The intuiting and distilling texts are less agile and 'reader friendly' in their flow, partly because they are constructed as completions of various prompts, directly from Crotty and indirectly from van Manen and Merleau-Ponty, and partly because their style is more particular and focused, and less narrative. The preoccupation is on getting a picture of the phenomenon which complements the 'reaching out to the reader' that is an important part of the 'calling to mind' panels. The baldness and sparseness of intuiting and distilling texts are less literary but have had a great use in the overall project of the thesis.

Portrayal in research: the final word

A major element in this 'Phenomenology of doing Phenomenology' is the recurring sense that there is no last word, no grand theory, in what has been termed explanatory and analytic research, a tentative hypothesis can be explored, verified, replicated and considerable satisfaction achieved from having extruded and established a recurrent element; a general law. There has always been considerable satisfaction in this abstracting-generalising process, by which problematic experiences can be described, abstracted, correlated with laws linked to generalising theories of causality and some conclusion and recommended action prescribed.

The phenomenological project appears increasingly in a very different guise. There is less intellectual satisfaction in the achievement of a problem solved and another contribution made to the general theorems of the laws of the universe.

This research is noticeably different, but on reflection has made a complementary contribution to human knowledge in the care and rigour it expends on seeking to portray fully, immediately and accurately something which is an experience and not an objectivised entity. As an experience, the thing portrayed, in this case adult education practice, will not be represented univocally as the one abstracted entity, but will appear in the collage of images creating a dense picture with subjective and objective elements entwined.

Instead of having extracted recurrent and general laws that are concluded to be verified in each instance, the study has endeavoured to bring the experience as a whole to attention. The rational and logical mind which seeks to expose truth and avoid prejudice and unwarranted assumptions has this time sought to apply the same critical rigour to the perceiving rather than conceptualising process, in other words, the research in this study has attempted to represent rather than measure, to portray rather than analyse; to present the realities of experience not as some imaginary 'objects', separate from the human subject knowing and naming them, but in their experienced 'whatness'.

This has called out different genres of thinking and writing that are closer to the immediacy and particularity of aesthetic work than to abstracting scientific analysis.

This kind of research goes back to the notion of 'human science' which van Manen stressed. The major point outlined in the Gallery of Method can be revisited here. It is to draw a clear demarcation between those objectified elements of the world which humans know – like rocks or birds or water – and those subjectivised objective realities like love, fear, knowing and teaching, which through their existence are embedded in, and partake of, human subjectivity.

This reality of human experience has a significant challenge in the development of science as applied to human life and experience. The process of abstraction and construction of generalising laws extrapolated from data in, for example, chemistry or physics, is always going to need a major caveat causing investigators to interrogate their data gathering processes when applied to elements of human experience.

There has been widespread caution about so-called laboratory studies of human experience on the grounds that data gathered on human cultural behaviour would be of little use, since so many key variables linked to real-in-the-world experiences would be missing and replaced by the in-the-laboratory-under-observation experiences.

When attempts have been made to study humans 'in the wild', as it were, it is quickly realised that such investigations need the subjects to *tell* the investigator what is being experienced, since what is experienced is a mixture of something happening to a person and that person becoming aware of it, naming it, expressing it and even theorising about it. Once the person begins naming this experience, as has been pointed out in the Gallery of Method, all kinds of processes come into play by which the experience takes on its reality and significance for the person. The common phrase, 'oh, it's nothing', said for example by a parent to a child, is the result of a chain of appraisals: classification, critique, conclusion.

What the study had wanted to do in its quest to go back to the experience itself, was to see what methods could be pursued to allow the particularity and 'livedness' of the experience to be portrayed. This has meant experiencing the tension between an experience and the words that humans use to name it and a constant tendency to take another person's word for it; and not to give the experience itself enough space and attention.

As became apparent in the Exit Foyer of the exhibition, adult education practice emerged from its portrayals in the exhibition's Main Gallery as a far juicier, fraught and exhilarating process than might have been concluded from the instructional manuals setting out objectives, strategies and competencies, as well as the generalised information about the adult learner and what she or he was likely to be like.

One of the related differences in this study has been the use of artistic, aesthetic forms of writing with particular use of simile and metaphor. These literary devices, while having a certain immediacy, seem not to be addressing what a thing is – which is implied when one says adult education *is* a form of learning facilitation – but what it is *like*, for example 'siren singing for learning'.

Of course in neither case is the thing itself being presented, in the first it is assigned to a category; in the second it is grasped as an experience – as a whole, analogously similar to previous experiences of certain kinds, in the second, it is compared to a similar experience using the process of 'experience focused imagination', in which, while letting the experience speak to one's receptive self, the receiving person casts about for a way to represent the image as a whole. It is that imaginal process which emerges in metaphor and simile and the range of poetic ways of writing and using language discussed in the Gallery of Method.

It is probably this link between image and experience in the course of the study of adult education practice – a very human and 'messy' entity in comparison to a beautiful diamond or sunset – that drew the research to include empathetic as well as intuiting phenomenological approaches. When attempting to intuit a human cultural reality that includes considerable subjectivity woven into objectivising subjectivity of lived experience, the imaginal writing seemed to need both an empathetic and intuiting stance.

As Maxine Greene wrote (1991, p.116):

> The importance of imagination increased for me as I saw that it is a capacity not solely for reaching beyond to the 'as if' or the 'not yet' or to the 'might be'. Imagination ... breaks with the humdrum and the repetitive; it brings integral wholes into being in the midst of multiplicity. Not insignificantly, it makes metaphor possible.

She then goes on to value *the ability to take a fresh look at the taken for granted*. It is this imaginal work, made possible by metaphor and related expressive devices, that can serve to give people in the act of knowing another dimension to their lived world, and in its attempt to portray, provide a useful complement and enrichment to analytical processes which must also be pursued.

This study has portrayed the experience of engaging in education with adults as having many elements of invitation – the putting oneself on the line; the sense of risk; the exhilaration when learners and adult educators engage; and the challenge of a shared enterprise. It was probably these elements which seemed absent in the 'how to' and 'you should' books that prompted this project and may hopefully prompt further portrayals and further galleries. And as T S Eliot wrote in *Little Gidding* (1963b, p. 192),

> We shall not cease from exploration
> And the end of all our exploration
> Will be to arrive where we started
> And know the place for the first time.

But somehow we will be more awake and more aware of what happens when we are engaging in adult education practice. We can be more prepared to accept and, as it were, 'factor in' its actual lived and experienced reality, rather than what it was said to be or hoped to be like.

REFERENCES

Achilles C M (1989) *Challenging narcissus or reflecting on reflecting*, University of North Carolina.

Argyris C and Schon D A (1974) *Theory in practice: Increasing professional effectiveness*, Jossey Bass.

Ariyarante A (1985) 'Learning in Sarvodaya' in Thomas A and Ploman E W (eds), *Learning and development*, Ontario Institute for Studies in Education Press.

Armstrong P (1987) *Qualitative strategies in social and educational research: The life history method in theory and practice*, University of Hull, School of Adult and Continuing Education.

Andresen L (1993) 'On becoming a maker of teachers. Journey down a long hall of mirrors' in Boud D, Cohen R and Walker D (eds), *Using experience for learning*, Society for Research into Higher Education and Open University Press.

Aslanian C B and Bricknell H M (1980) *Americans in transition: Life changes as reasons for adult learning*, College Entrance Examination Board.

Barone T and Eisner E (1997) 'Arts-based educational research', in Jaeger R M (ed), *Complementary methods for research in education*, American Education Research Association.

Becker H S, Geer B, Hughes E C and Strauss A L (1961) *Boys in white: Student culture in medical school*, University of Chicago Press.

Benner P (1984) *From novice to expert: Excellence and power in clinical nursing practice*, Addison-Wesley.

Benner P (ed) (1994) *Interpretive phenomenology: Embodiment, caring and ethics in health and illness*, Sage.

Berger P and Luckman (1971) *The social construction of reality*, Penguin.

Biggs J B (1989) 'Approaches to the enhancement of tertiary teaching', *Higher education research and development*, Vol 8 No 1, pp 7–25.

Boud D (1992) 'In the midst of experience: Developing a model to aid learners and facilitators', in Harris R and Willis P (eds), *Striking a balance*, CHRS.

Boud D, Cohen R and Walker D (1993) *Using experience for learning*, Society for Research into Higher Education and Open University Press.

Boud D and Griffin V (eds) (1987) *Appreciating adults learning: From the learners' perspective*, Kogan Page.

Boud D and Miller N (eds) (1996) *Working with experience: Animating learning*, Routledge.

Boud D, Keogh R and Walker D (eds) (1985) *Reflection: Turning experience into learning*, Kogan Page.

Boud D, Keogh R and Walker D (eds) (1993) 'Introduction: Understanding learning from experience', in Boud D, Cohen R and Walker D (eds), *Using experience for learning*, Society for Research into Higher Education/Open University Press.

Bourdieu P and Passeron J (1990) *Reproduction in education, society and culture*, Sage.

Brady M B (1990) 'Redeemed from time: Learning through autobiography', *Adult education quarterly*, Vol 41 No 1, pp 43–52.

Bridges W (1980) *Transitions*, Addison-Wesley.

Brodkey L (1987) 'Writing critical ethnographic narratives', *Anthropology and education quarterly*, Vol 18 No 2, pp 67–76.

Brookfield S (1987) *Understanding and facilitating adult learning*, Jossey Bass.

Brookfield S (1990a) *The skillful teacher: On technique, trust and responsiveness in the classroom*, Jossey Bass.

Brookfield S (1990b) 'Expanding knowledge about how we learn', in Smith R M and Associates (eds), *Learning to learn across the life span*, Jossey Bass.

Brookfield S (1991) 'A critical definition of adult education', *Adult education quarterly*, Vol 36 No 1, pp 44–9. Cited in Watkins K, *Facilitating learning in the workplace*, Deakin University Press.

Brookfield S (1993) 'Review of a friendly rebel: A personal and social history of Eduard C. Lindeman', *Adult education quarterly*, Vol 43 No 2, pp 121–4.

Brookfield S (1995) *Becoming a critical reflective teacher*, Jossey Bass.

Brooks C and Warren R P (1960) *Understanding poetry*, Holt Rinehart and Winston.

Brundage D H and Mackeracher D (1980) *Adult learning principles and their application to program planning*, Ministry of Education.

Bruner J (1985) 'Narrative and paradigmatic modes of thought', in Eisner E (ed), *Learning and teaching the ways of knowing* (84th Yearbook of the National Society for the Study of Education, pp 97–115), University of Chicago Press.

Bruner J (1986) *Actual minds, possible worlds*, Harvard University Press.

Bruner J (1988) 'Research currents: Life as narrative', *Language arts*, Vol 65 No 6, pp 574–83.

Bruner J (1990) *Acts of meaning*, Harvard University Press.

Burbules N and Rice S (1991) 'Continuing the conversation', *Harvard educational review*, Vol 61 No 4, pp 393–416.

Candy P C (1989) 'Constructionism and the study of self-direction in adult learning', *Studies in the education of adults*, Vol 21, pp 95–116.

Cardinal R (1981) *Figure of reality: A perspective on the poetic imagination*, Croom Helm.

Carr W and Kemmis S (1983) *Becoming critical: Knowing through action research*, Deakin University Press.

Carter K (1993) 'The place of story in the study of teaching and teacher education', *Educational researcher*, Vol 22 No 1, pp 5–12, 18.

Casey K (1995/96) 'The new narrative research in education', in Apple M W (ed), *Review of research in education*, Vol 21, American Educational Research Association.

Charlesworth M (1989) *Life, death, genes and ethics: Biotechnology and bioethics*, The 1989 Boyer Lectures, Crows Nest: ABC Enterprises.

Charlesworth M (1993) *Bioethics in a liberal society*, Cambridge University Press.

Charlesworth M (1997) *Religious inventions*, Cambridge University Press.

Clandinin D J and Connelly F M (1994) 'Personal experience methods', in Denzin N and Lincoln Y (eds), *Handbook of qualitative research*, Sage.

Clark D (1987) 'The concept of community education', in Allen G, Bastiani J, Martin I and Richards K (eds), *Community education – an agenda for educational reform*, Open University Press, pp 50–69.

Clark M C and Wilson A L (1991) 'Context and rationality in Mezirow's Theory of transformational learning', *Adult education quarterly*, Vol 41 No 2, pp 75–91.

Clark R and Ivanic R (1991) 'Consciousness-raising about the writing process', in Garrett P and James C (eds), *Language awareness in the classroom*, Longman, pp 168–85.

Clarke M A (1990) 'Some cautionary observations on liberation education', *Language arts*, Vol 67 No 4, pp 388–98.

Colaizzi P (1973) 'Psychological research as the phenomenologist views it', in Valle R S and King M (eds), *Existential phenomenological alternatives for psychology*, Oxford University Press, pp 48–71.

Collins M (1984) 'Phenomenological perspectives: Some implications for adult education', in Merriam S (ed), *Selected writings on philosophy of adult education*, Krieger, pp 179–189.

Collins M (1985) 'Jurgen Habermas' concept of communicative action and its implications for the adult learning process', *Adult education research conference (AERC) proceedings*, Arizona State University.

Collins M (1987) *Competence in adult education: A new perspective*, University Press of America.

Collins M (1991) *Adult education as vocation: A critical role for the adult educator*, Routledge.

Connell R W, Ashenden D J, Kessler S and Dowsett G W (1982) *Making the difference: Schools, families and social division*, Allen and Unwin.

Coomb A (1991) 'Discovering me', in *The Independent* (Australian Newspaper), Dec. 14, pp 41–2.

Cooper D (1996) *World philosophies: An historical introduction*, Blackwell.

Cortazzi M (1993) *Narrative analysis*, Falmer Press.

Cox E (1995) *A truly civil society: 1995 Boyer lectures*, Australian Broadcasting Corporation (Radio National broadcasts of lectures 1–6, cassette tapes and ABC Books).

Cranton P (1992) *Working with adult learners*, Wall and Emerson.

Crotty M (1996a) *Phenomenology and nursing research*, Churchill Livingstone.

Crotty M (1996b) 'Doing Phenomenology', in Willis P and Neville B (eds), *Qualitative research practice in adult education*, David Lovell Publishing.

Culler J (1981) *The pursuit of signs: Semiotics, literature deconstruction*, Cornell University Press.

Culler J D (1975) *Structuralist poetics: Structualism, linguistics and the study of literature*, Routledge and Kegan Paul.

Daloz L (1986) *Effective teaching and mentoring: Realizing the transformative power of education*, Jossey Bass.

Davis K (1991) 'The phenomenology of research: The construction of meaning in data analysis', paper presented at the annual meeting of the conference on college composition and communication.

Davis M (1994) 'Adult education and life history: Self as the learning context', in *Life histories and learning: Language, the self and education*, papers from an Interdisciplinary Residential Conference at the University of Sussex, Brighton, UK, September.

Day D (1952) *The long loneliness*, Harper and Row.

de Chardin T (1965) *The divine milieu* (translated from the French Edition, originally published in 1957 by Editions du Seuil) Harper and Row.

Denzin N K (1989) *The Research Act* (3rd edn), Prentice Hall.

Denzin N and Lincoln Y (1994) *Handbook of qualitative research*, Thousand Oaks: Sage.

Deschler D (1992) 'The use of metaphor in adult education research', in Mezirow J (ed), *Fostering critical reflection in adulthood*, Jossey Bass.

Deschler D and Hagan D (1990) 'Adult education research: Issues and directions', in Merriam S and Cunningham P (eds), *Handbook of adult and continuing education*, Jossey Bass.

Dewey J (1934) *Arts as experience*, Capricorn.

Dewey J (1974) *John Dewey on education: Selected writings* (Archambault R D, ed), University of Chicago Press.

Diesing P (1972) *Patterns of discovery in the social sciences*, Routledge and Kegan Paul.

Dilthey W (1987) *Introduction to the human sciences*, Scholarly book services.

Dominice P F (1990) 'Composing education biographies: Group reflection through life histories', in Mezirow J (ed), *Fostering critical reflection in adulthood*, Jossey Bass, pp 194–212.

Dunne J (1993) *Back to the rough ground: Phronesis and Techne on modern philosophy and in Aristotle*, University of Notre Dame Press.

Eckartsberg R V (1981) 'Maps of the mind', in Valle R S and von Eckartsberg R (eds), *The metaphors of consciousness*, Plenum.

Edgar D (1987) *Focus on adults: Towards a productive learning culture*, Ministry for Education.

Egan G (1975) *The skilled helper and model for systematic helping and interpersonal relating*, Brooks Cole.

Ehrich L C (1996) 'The difficulties of using phenomenology', in Willis P and Neville B (eds), *Qualitative research practice in adult education*, David Lovell Publishing, pp 197–214.

Eisner E (1991) *The enlightened eye: Qualitative inquiry and the enhancement of educational practice*, Macmillan Publishing.

Eisner E (1993) 'Forms of understanding and the future of educational research', *Educational Researcher*, Vol 22 No 7, pp 5–11.

Eisner E and Peshkin A (eds) (1990) *Qualitative inquiry in education: The continuing debate*, Teachers College Press.

Elias J and Merriam S B (1980) *Philosophical foundations of adult education*, Krieger.

Eliot T S (1963a) 'Yeats', in Unterecker J (ed), *Yeats: A collection of critical essays*, Prentice Hall, pp 54–63.

Eliot T S (1963b) *Collected poems 1909–1962*, Faber and Faber.

Eliot T S (1970) *Collected works: 1909–1962*, Faber and Faber.

Ellis C (1991) 'Emotional sociology', in *Studies in symbolic interaction*, Vol 12, JAI.

Ellis C and Flaherty M G (eds) (1992) *Investigating subjectivity: Research on lived experience*, Sage Publications.

Ellsworth E (1989) 'Why doesn't this feel empowering? Working through the repressive myths of critical pedagogy', *Harvard education review*, Vol 59 No 3, pp 297–324.

Encyclopaedia Britannica (1990) *Micropaedia*.

Erben M (1992) 'Review of Lis Stanley's *The autobiographical I: The theory and practice of feminist auto/biography*', *Sociology*, Vol 27 No 1, pp 194–6.

Evans C S (1979) *Preserving the person: A look at the human sciences*, Intervarsity Press.

Fairclough N (1989) *Language and power*, Longman.

Fairclough N (1992) *Discourse and social change*, Polity Press.

Faraday A and Plummer K (1979) 'Doing life histories', *Sociological review*, Vol 27 No 4, pp 773–792.

Foley G (1991a) 'Radical adult education', in Tennant M (ed), *Adult and continuing education in Australia: Issues and practice*, Routledge.

Foley G (1991b) 'Terania Creek: Learning in a green campaign'. *Australian journal of adult and community education*, Vol 31 No 3, pp 160–76.

Foley G (1993a) 'The neighbourhood house: Site of struggle, site of learning', *British journal of sociology of education*, Vol 14 No 1, pp 21–37.

Foley G (1993b) 'Political education in the Chinese liberation struggle', *International journal of lifelong education*, Vol 13 No 1, pp 323–42.

Foley G (1993c) 'Progressive but not socialist: Political education in the Zimbabwe liberation struggle', *Convergence*, Vol XXVII No 4, pp 79–88.

Foley G (1994) 'Adult education and capitalist reorganisation', *Studies in the education of adults*, Vol 26 No 2, pp 121–43.

Foley G (1994) 'Dynamics and dilemmas of politically committed adult education research', in Neville B, Willis P and Edwards M (eds), *Qualitative research in adult education: A colloquium on theory, practice, supervision and assessment*, Centre for Research in Education and Work, University of South Australia.

Foley G (1995a) 'Domination and resistance in workers' political learning', paper presented at Annual Conference of the Canadian Association of Adult Education, Concordia University, Montreal, 1–3 June, 1995.

Foley G (1995b) *Understanding adult education and training*, Allen and Unwin.

Foucault M (1972) *The archaeology of knowledge* [trans by A Sheridan], Tavistock Publications.

Fowler J W (1987) *Stages of faith: The psychology of human development and the quest for meaning*, Collins Dove.

Franck F (1973) *The Zen of seeing: Seeing/drawing as meditation*, Vintage Books.

Freire P (1970) *Pedagogy of the oppressed*, Penguin.

Freire P (1972b) *Cultural action for freedom*, Penguin.

Freire P (1973) *Education: The practice of freedom*, Writers and Readers.

Gadamer H G (1975) *Truth and method*, Seabury.

Garman N (1996) 'Qualitative inquiry: Meaning and menace for educational researchers', in Willis P and Neville B (eds), *Qualitative research practice in adult education*, David Lovell Publishing.

Garman N and Piantanida M (1974) 'Criteria of quality for judging qualitative research', in Willis P and Neville B (eds), *Qualitative research practice in adult education*, David Lovell Publishing.

Giorgi A (1970) *Psychology as a human science: A Phenomenologically based approach*, Harper and Row.

Giorgi A (1971) 'Phenomenology and experimental psychology', in Giorgi A, Fischer W F and Von Eckartsberg R (eds), *Phenomenological psychology Vol 1*, Duquesne University Press, pp 6–16.

Giorgi A (1985a) 'Phenomenological psychology of learning and the verbal tradition', in Giorgi A (ed), *Phenomenology and psychological research*, Duquesne University Press, pp 23–85.

Giorgi A (1985b) 'Sketch of a psychological phenomenological method', in Giorgi A (ed), *Phenomenology and psychological research*, Duquesne University Press, pp 8–21.

Giorgi A (1989) 'One type of analysis of descriptive data: Procedures involved in following a phenomenological method', in *Methods: A journal of human science*, Annual edition.

Giorgi A, Fischer W F and Von Eckartsberg R (eds) (1971) *Duquesne studies in phenomenological psychology Vol 1*, Duquesne University Press.

Giroux H (1983) *Theory and resistance in education: A pedagogy for the opposition*, Bergin and Garvey.

Goffmann E (1959) *The presentation of self in everyday life*, Doubleday Anchor Books.

Goodson I F and Walker R (1991) *Biography, identity and schooling: Episodes in educational research*, Falmer Press.

Gore J (1993) *The struggle for pedagogies*, Routledge.

Graham H (1982) 'Surveying through stories', in Bell C and Roberts H (eds), *Social researching: Politics, problems, prospects*, Routledge and Kegan Paul.

Grant A N (1985) 'Learning from the life stories of adult students', in *Readings in adult basic education*, Australian Council for Adult Literacy.

Grant A (1988) 'Notes on doing case study research', in Beattie S (ed), *Moving from strength to strength*, Education, University of Technology.

Grant A (1993) 'Perspectives on literacy. Constructs and practices: An overview', in McConnell S and Treloar A (eds), *Voices of experience, Book 2: Positions on literacy theories and practices*, AGPS/DEET, pp 2–11.

Grant A, Treloar A, Muir R and Waterhouse P (forthcoming) *Adults learning literacy in groups: A national level research project funded by the national policy on languages adult literacy action campaign*, Unpublished draft of Initial Research Report Melbourne: La Trobe University.

Greene M (1972) *Teacher as stranger*, Wadsworth.

Greene M (1975) 'Curriculum and consciousness', in Pinar W (ed), *Curriculum theorizing*, McCutchan.

Greene M (1987a) 'A response to interpretive, normative theory of education', *Educational philosophy and theory*, Vol 19 No 1, pp 12–14.

Greene M (1987b) 'Toward wide-awakedness: Humanities in the lives of professionals', in Wear D, Kohn M and Stocker S (eds), *Literature and medicine: A claim for a discipline*, McLean, Society for Health and Human Values, p 7.

Greene M (1991) 'Blue guitars and the search for curriculum', in Willis G and Schubert WH (eds), *Reflections from the heart of educational inquiry*, State University of New York Press.

Gribble H and Grant A (forthcoming) *Life stories: Adult students take on literacy*, La Trobe University/DEET.

Griffin V R (1990) 'Holistic learning/teaching in adult education: Would you play a one string guitar?', in Draper J and Stein T (eds), *The craft of teaching adults*, Department of Adult Education, Ontario Institute for Studies in Education.

Gross H S (1990) 'Poetry', *Encyclopedia Britannica, Micropaedia*, p 542.

Grundy S (1987) *Curriculum, product or praxis*, Falmer Press.

Grundy S (1982) 'Three modes of action research', *Curriculum perspectives*, Vol 2, pp 23–34.

Guba E and Lincoln Y (1985) *Naturalistic inquiry*, Sage.

Guba E and Lincoln Y (1989) *Fourth generation evaluation*, Sage.

Guba E and Lincoln Y (1990) 'Can there be a human science? Constructivism as an alternative', *Person centred review*, Vol 5 No 2 (May).

Gusdorf G (1980) 'Conditions and limits of autobiography', in Olney J (ed), *Autobiography: Essays theoretical and critical,* Princeton University Press, pp 28–48.

Habermas J (1972) *Knowledge and human interests* [trans from German by J Shapiro], Heinemann Educational.

Habermas J (1984) *The theory of communicative action* (Two vols translated by Thomas McCarthy), Beacon Press.

Hart M and Horton D (1993) 'Beyond God the Father and the Mother: Adult education and spiritu-
ality', in Jarvis M and Walters N (eds), *Adult education and theological interpretations*, Kreiger.
Heaney S (1990) *New selected poems*, Faber and Faber.
Heeren J (1970) 'Alfred Schutz and the sociology of commonsense knowledge', in Douglas J (ed),
Understanding everyday life, Aldine.
Heidegger M (1949) 'Holderlin and the essence of poetry', in Brock W (ed), *Existence and being*,
Regenery, pp 270–91.
Heidegger M (1962) *Being and time*, Basil Blackwell.
Heidegger M (1968) *What is called thinking?* [trans by J Glennray], Harper and Row Inc.
Heidegger M (1975) *Poetry, language, thought*, Harper Colophon.
Heidegger M (1980) *Being and Time* (trans by J Macquarrie and E Robinson), Blackwells.
Heidegger M (1982) *The basic problems of phenomonology* [trans by A Hofstadter], Indiana
University.
Heimlich J E and Norland E (1994) *Developing teaching style in adult education*, Jossey Bass.
Heron J (1973) 'Re-evaluation counselling: Personal growth through mutual aid', *British Journal
of Guidance and Counselling*, Vol 1 No 2, pp 26–36.
Heron J (1975) *Six category intervention analysis*, Human Potential Research Project.
Heron J (1981a) 'Philosophical base for a new paradigm', in Reason P and Rowan J (eds), *Human
inquiry: A sourcebook of new paradigm research*, Wiley.
Heron J (1989) *The facilitator's handbook*, Kogan Page.
Heron J (1992) *Feeling and personhood*, Sage.
Heron J (1996) *Co-operative inquiry: Research into the human condition*, Sage Publications.
Hillman J (1978) *Further notes on image*, Spring Publications.
Hogins J B (1974) *Literature: Poetry*, Science Research Associates, Inc.
Horton M and Freire P (1990) *We make the road by walking*, Temple University Press.
Husserl E (1931) *Ideas: General introduction to pure phenomenology*, George Allen and Unwin.
Husserl E (1962) *Ideas: General introduction to pure phenomenology* [trans by W Boyce Simpson],
Collier.
Husserl E (1964) 'Introductory essay', in *The Paris Lectures* [trans by Peter Koestenbaum],
Martinus Nijhoff.
Husserl E (1964) *The idea of phenomenology*, Martinus Nijhoff.
Husserl E (1970) *Logical investigations*, Vols I–II, Routledge and Kegan Paul.
Husserl E (1971) 'Phenomenology', article for the Encyclopaedia Britannica 1927, [trans by R E
Palmer], *The British Society for Phenomenology*, Vol 2 No 2, pp 77–90.
Husserl E (1973) *Experience and judgment: Investigations in a genealogy of logis* [Langrebe L, ed],
Routledge and Kegan Paul.
Hyland D T and Ackerman A M (1988) 'Reminiscence and autobiographical memory in the study
of the personal past', *Journal of gerontology: Psychological sciences*, Vol 43 No 2, pp 35–9.
Ihde D (1973) 'Singing the world: Language and perception', in Gillan G (ed), *Horizons of the
flesh: Critical perspectives on the thought of Merleau-Ponty*, Illinois University Press.
Jacobsen R (1988) 'Linguistics and poetics', in Lodge D (ed), *Modern criticism and theory: A
reader*, Longmans.
Jarvis P (1992) 'Reflective practice and nursing', *Nurse education today*, Vol 12, pp 174–81.
Kaufmann W (1960) *From Shakespeare to existentialism*, Anchor Books.
Kazemak F and Rigg P (1995) *Enriching our lives: Poetry lessons for adult literacy teachers and
tutors*, International Reading Association.
Kemmis S and McTaggart R (1988) *The action research planner*, Deakin University.
Kemmis S (1984) 'Educational research is research for education', *Australian educational quar-
terly*, Vol 11 No 1, pp 28–38.
Knowles M (1970) *The modern practice of adult education: Andragogy versus pedagogy*, Associa-
tion Press.
Knowles M (1980) *The modern practice of adult education* (2nd edn), Follet.
Knowles M (1990) *The adult learner: A neglected species*, Gulf Publications.
Kockelmans J (1975) 'Towards and interpretative or hermeneutic social science', *Graduate Faculty
Philosophy Journal*, Vol 5 No 1, pp 73–96.
Lather P (1986a) 'Research as praxis', *Harvard Education Review*, Vol 56 No 3, pp 257–77.

Lather P (1986b) 'Issues of validity in openly ideological research: Between a rock and a soft place', *Interchange*, Vol 17 No 4, pp 63–84.

Lather P (1991a) *Feminist research in education: Within/against*, Deakin University.

Lather P (1991b) *Getting smart: Feminist research and pedagogy with/in the postmodern*, Routledge.

Lather P (1992) 'Critical frame in educational research : Feminist and post-structural perspectives'. *Theory into Practice*, Vol XXXI No 2 (Spring).

Lincoln Y and Guba E (1985) *Naturalistic inquiry*, Sage Publications.

Lincoln Y (1994) 'Discussant commentary in Session 48.01', in *Promise and controversy in qualitative inquiry: Different traditions and standards for rigor*, American Educational Research Association Annual Meeting, New Orleans, 4–8 April.

Little D, McAllister J and Priebe R (1991) *Adult learning in vocational education*, Deakin University Press.

Livingstone D (1993) *The poetry handbook for readers and writers*, Macmillan.

Lovat T and Smith D (1990) *Curriculum: Action on reflection*, Social Science Press.

Maclean M (1988) *Narrative as performance: The Baudelairean experiment*, Routledge.

Macquarrie J (1992) *Existentialism*, Penguin.

Mannheim K (1936) *Ideology and Utopia*, Routledge and Kegan Paul.

Marcel G (1964) *Creative fidelity* [trans from the French and with an introduction by Robert Rosthal], Noonday Press.

Marginson S (1995) 'Is competency based education a good enough framework for learning?', *Critical Forum*, Vol 3 Nos 2–3 (April), pp 103–13.

McCall R J (1983) *Phenomenological psychology: An introduction*, The University of Wisconsin Press.

McDuffie K (1988) *Phenomenology and Australian education*, Unpublished Masters Thesis Monash University.

McIntyre J (1993) 'Research paradigms and adult education', *Studies in continuing education*, Vol 15, No 2, pp 0–97.

McIntyre J (1994) 'Research understandings and qualitative methodology', in Neville B, Willis P and Edwards M (eds), *Qualitative research in adult education: A colloquium on theory, practice, supervision and assessment*, Centre for Research in Education and Work, University of South Australia.

McIntyre J (1995) 'Research in adult education and training', in Foley G (ed), *Understanding adult education and training*, Allen and Unwin.

McKelson Fr (1966) *Verbal instructions on starting the generator*, La Grange Mission.

Mead G H (1962) *Mind, self and society*, University of Chicago Press.

Merleau-Ponty M (1962) *Phenomenology of perception* [trans by Colin Smith], Routledge and Kegan Paul.

Merleau-Ponty M (1964) *Signs* [trans by Richard McLeary], Northwestern University Press.

Merleau-Ponty M (1974) 'The primacy of perception and its philosophical consequences' and 'Eye and Mind', in O'Neill J (ed), *Phenomenology, language and sociology*, Heinemann.

Merriam S B (1984) *Adult development: Implications for adult education*, ERIC Clearinghouse on Adult, Career and Vocational Education.

Merriam S B (1988) *Case study research in education: A qualitative approach*, Jossey-Bass.

Merriam S B (1991a) *Learning in adulthood: A comprehensive guide*, Jossey-Bass.

Merriam S B (1991b) 'How research produces knowledge', in John M, Jarvis P and Associates (eds), *Adult education*, Jossey-Bass, pp 42–65.

Merriam S and Simpson E (1989) (revised edn) *A guide to research for educators of adults and trainers*, Krieger.

Mezirow J (1977) 'Perspective transformation', *Studies in adult education*, Vol 9 No 2, pp 153–164.

Mezirow J (1985) 'A critical theory of self directed learning', in Brookfield S (ed), *Self-directed learning from theory to practice*, Jossey-Bass.

Mezirow J (1991a) 'A critical theory of adult learning and education', in Boud D and Walker D (eds), *Experience and learning: Reflection at work*, Deakin University Press, pp 61–82.

Mezirow J (1991b) *Transformative dimensions of adult learning*, Jossey Bass.

Mezirow J (1995) 'Emancipatory learning and social action', paper delivered at Social Action and Emancipatory Learning Seminar, University of Technology, Sydney, September.

Mezirow J and Associates (1990) *Fostering critical reflection in adulthood: A guide to transformative and emancipatory learning*, Jossey-Bass.

Miles M B and Huberman A M (1994) *Qualitative data analysis*, 2nd edn, Sage.

Miller N (1993) *Personal experience, adult learning and social research: Developing a sociological imagination in and beyond the T-group*, Centre for Research in Adult Education for Human Development, University of South Australia.

Miller N and Morgan D (1993) 'Called to account: the CV as an autobiographical practice', *Sociology*, Vol 27 No 1, pp 133–4.

Miller W D (1973) *A harsh and dreadful love: Dorothy Day and the Catholic Worker Movement*, Darton, Longman and Todd.

Mitchell J G (1990) *Revisioning educational leadership: A phenomenological approach*, Garland.

Mitroff N (1978) *The subjective side of science*, Elsemer.

Mott V W (undated) 'The role of intuition in the reflective practice of adult education', unpublished paper.

Moustakas C (1990) 'Heuristic research', *Person-centered review*, Vol 5 No 2 (May), pp 170–90.

Mulligan J and Griffin C (eds) (1992) *Empowerment through experiential learning*, Kogan Page.

Natanson M (1974) *Phenomenology, role and reason: Essays on the coherence and deformation of social reality*, Charles C Thomas.

Nelson A (1994) 'Researching adult transformation as autobiography', *International journal of lifelong education*, Vol 13 No 5 (September–October), pp 389–403.

Neruda P (1970) 'Ode to the Book {1}.' In Tarn N, (ed) *Selected poems: A bilingual edition*, Dell publishing.

Neugarten B L and Datan N (1973) 'Sociological perspectives on the life cycle', in Baaeds P B and Schaie KW (eds), *Life span development psychology*, Academic Press.

Neville B (1989) *Educating psyche: emotion, imagination and the unconscious in learning*, Collins Dove.

Neville B (1994) 'Researching good practice', in Neville B, Willis P and Edwards M (eds), *Qualitative research in adult education*, University of South Australia Centre for Research in Education and Work.

Neville B, Willis P and Edwards M (eds) (1994) *Qualitative research in adult education: A colloquium on theory, practice, supervision and assessment*, Centre for Research in Adult Education for Human Development, University of South Australia.

Newman M (1975) *Adult education and community action*, Writers and Readers Publishing Cooperative.

Newman M (1979) *The poor cousin*, George Allen and Unwin.

Newman M (1993) *The third contract: Theory and practice in trade union education*, Stewart Victor publishing.

Newman M (1994) *Defining the enemy: Adult education in social action*, Stewart Victor Publishing.

Oakley A (1981) 'Interviewing women: A contradiction in terms', in Roberts H (ed), *Doing feminist research*, Routledge and Kegan Paul.

Oakley B (1996) 'Good verses evil', *The Australian magazine*, April 20–21.

Oiler C (1986) 'Phenomenology: The method', in Munhall P L and Oiler C J (eds), *Nursing research: A qualitative perspective*, Appleton-Century-Crofts.

Olson L (1989) 'Surviving innovation: Reflection on the pitfalls of practice', *Journal of curriculum studies*, Vol 21 No 6, pp 503–8.

Olney J (ed) (1980) *Autobiography: Essays theoretical and critical*, Princeton University Press.

Ortega y Gasset J (1932) *The revolt of the masses*, Norton.

Ortega y Gasset J (1958) *Man and crisis*, Norton.

Ortega y Gasset J (1963) *Concord and liberty*, Norton.

Packwood A and Sykes P (1996) 'Adopting a postmodern approach to research', *International journal of qualitative studies in education*, Vol 9 No 3 (July–September), pp 335–45.

Perkins M (1971) 'Matter, sensation and understanding', *American philosophical quarterly*, Vol 8, pp 1–2.

Perry WG (1968) *Forms of intellectual and ethical development in the college years: A scheme,* Holt, Rinehart and Winston.

Phillipson M (1972) 'Phenomenological philosophy and sociology', in Filmer P, Phillipson D, Silverman D and Walsh D (eds), *New directions in sociological inquiry,* MIT Press, pp 119–64.

Polanyi M (1966) *The tacit dimension,* Doubleday.

Popkewitz T S (1984) *Paradigm and ideology in educational research: The social functions of the intellectual,* Falmer Press.

Psathas G (1973) 'Introduction', in Psathas G (ed), *Phenomenological sociology: Issues and applications,* Wiley, pp 1–21.

Reason P (ed) (1988) *Human inquiry in action: Developments in new paradigm research,* Sage Publications.

Reason P (ed) (1994) *Participation in human inquiry,* Sage Publications.

Reason P and Hawkins P (1988) 'Storytelling as inquiry', in Reason P (ed), *Human inquiry in action: Developments in new paradigm research,* Sage Publications.

Reason P and Heron J (1986) 'Research with people: The paradigm of co-operative experiential enquiry' (Working paper), Bath: Centre for the Study of Organisational Change and Development.

Reason P and Marshall J, (1987) 'Research as personal process', in Boud D and Griffin V (eds), *Appreciating adults learning: From the learners' perspective,* Kogan Page.

Reason P and Rowan J (eds) (1981) *Human inquiry: A sourcebook for new paradigm research.* J Wiley.

Richardson L (1990) 'Narrative and sociology', in *Journal of contemporary ethnography,* Vol 19 No 1, pp 116–35.

Ricoeur P (1967) *Husserl: An analysis of his phenomenology,* Northwestern University Press.

Ricoeur P (1978) 'Modes of thinking and the different classes of reality', in Havet J (ed), *Main trends of research in the social and human sciences,* Mouton Publishers, pp 1038–318.

Rogers C R (1961) *On becoming a person,* Houghton Miffin.

Rogers C R (1970) *Carl Rogers on encounter groups,* Harper and Row.

Rogers C R (1983) *Freedom to learn for the 1980s,* Charles Merrill.

Ronai C R (1992) 'The reflexive self through narrative', in Ellis C and Flaherty M G (eds), *Investigating subjectivity: Research on lived experience,* Sage Publications.

Rorty R (1993) 'Human rights, rationality, and sentimentality', in Shute S and Hurley S (eds), *On human rights: The Oxford amnesty lectures 1993,* Basic Books.

Rosen H (1986) 'The importance of story', *Language arts,* Vol 63 No 3, pp 226–237.

Rosenthal M L (1974) *Poetry and the common life,* Oxford University Press.

Ross D D (1989) 'First steps in developing a reflective approach', *Journal of teacher education,* Vol 40 No 2, pp 22–30.

Roth R A (1989) 'Preparing the reflective practitioner: Transforming the apprentice through the dialectic', *Journal of teacher education,* Vol 40 No 2, p 32.

Rowan J (1981) 'A dialectical paradigm for research', in Reason P and Rowan J (eds), *Human inquiry: A sourcebook of new paradigm research,* John Wiley and sons.

Rowland F (1995) Unpublished M Ed thesis (Honours), Faculty of Education, Murdoch University.

Salmon P (ed) (1980) *Coming to know,* Routledge and Kegan Paul.

Salmon P (1989) 'Personal stances in learning', in Warner-Weil S and McGill I (eds), *Making sense of experiential learning: Diversity in theory and practice,* Society for Research into Higher Education/Open University Press, pp 330–241.

Salmon P (1992) 'Old age and storytelling', in Kimberly K, Meek M and Miller J (eds), *New Readings,* A and C Black, pp 216–223.

Sandelowski M (1991) 'Telling stories: Narrative approaches in qualitative research'. *Image, Journal of Nursing Scholarship,* Vol 23 No 3, pp 161–6.

Sanders P (1981) *A phenomenological study of teaching role perceptions of college and university professors who are recipients of an outstanding teaching award,* PhD Dissertation University of Connecticut.

Sanders P (1982) 'Phenomenology: A new way of viewing organisational research', *Academy of Management Review,* Vol 7 No 3, pp 353–60.

Sanders T E (1966) *The discovery of poetry,* Scott, Foresman and company.

Sarton M (1980) *Of the muse: From 'Halfway to silence'*, WW Norton.

Schein E (1973) *Professional education*, McGraw Hill.

Schlossberg N K (1984) *Counselling adults in transition*, Springer.

Scholes R (1981) 'Language, narrative, and anti-narrative', in Mitchell W J T (ed), *On Narrative*, University of Chicago Press, pp 200–8.

Scholes R (1982) *Semiotics and interpretation*, Yale University Press.

Schon D (1983) *The reflective practitioner*, Basic Books.

Schon D (1987) *Educating the reflective practitioner: Towards a new design for teaching and learning in the professions*, Jossey Bass.

Schon D (1989) 'Professional knowledge and reflective practice', in Sergiovanni T and Moore J H (eds), *Schooling for tomorrow*, Alleyn and Bacon.

Schutz A (1967) *Phenomenology of the social world*, Heinemann Educational Books edition.

Schutz A (1975) *On phenomenology and social relations*, [trans by H Wagner], The University of Chicago Press.

Schutz W C (1975) *Elements of encounter*, Bantam.

Shaw B (1981) *My country of the pelican dreaming: The life of an Australian Aborigine of the Gadjerong, Grant Ngabidj, 1904–1977 as told to Bruce Shaw*, Australian Institute of Aboriginal Studies.

Shaw B (1983) *Banggaiyerri: The story of Jack Sullivan*, Australian Institute of Aboriginal Studies.

Skelton R (1957) *The poetic pattern*, Routledge and Kegan Paul.

Smith D (1991) 'Critical adult education: A response to contemporary social crisis', *Canadian journal for the study of adult education*, Winter, Vol V, Special issue, pp 1–20.

Smith F (1978) *Reading*, Cambridge University Press.

Smyth J (1989a) 'Developing and sustaining critical reflection in teacher education', *Journal of teacher education*, March/April, pp 2–9.

Smyth J (1989b) 'A critical pedagogy of classroom practice', *Journal of curriculum studies*, Vol 21 No 6, pp 483–502.

Soltis J (1984) 'On the nature of educational research', *Educational researcher*, December, Vol 13 No 10, pp 5–10.

Sparks-Langer G and Colton A B (1991) 'Synthesis of research on teachers' reflective thinking', *Educational leadership*, March, pp 37–44.

Spiegelberg H (1975) *Doing phenomenology: Essays on and in phenomenology*, Martinus Nijhoff.

Spiegelberg H (1959) *The phenomenological movement: A historical introduction*, Martinus Nijhoff.

Spinelli E (1989) *The interpreted world: An introduction to phenomenological psychology*, Sage.

Squires G (1993) 'Education for adults', in Thorpe M, Edwards R and Hanson A (eds), *Culture and processes of adult learning*, Routledge.

Stanage S M (1986) 'Learning how to learn: A phenomenological analysis of adult educative learning', *Adult education research conference proceedings*, Syracuse University Press.

Stanage S M (1987) *Adult Education and phenomenological research: New directions for theory, practice, and research*, Robert E Krieger.

Stephen J F (1967) *Liberty, equality, fraternity*, Cambridge University Press.

Stevens W (1964) 'The man with the blue guitar', in *Collected poems*, Alfred A Knopf.

Stimson G (1976) 'Biography and retrospect: Some problems in the study of life history'. Paper presented at the Annual Conference of the British Sociological Association, Owens Park, Manchester, United Kingdom.

Swicegood M L (1980) 'Adult education for home and family life', in Boone E, Shearon R W and White E E and Associates (eds), *Serving personal and community needs through adult education*, Jossey-Bass.

Swingewood (1984) *A short history of sociological thought*, St Martins.

Tennant M (1988) *Psychology and Adult Learning*, Routledge.

Tesch R (1984) 'Phenomenological studies: A critical analysis of their nature and procedures', paper given at AERA Annual Meeting.

Thomas J E (1982) *Radical adult education: Theory and practice*, University of Nottingham.

Thompson J (ed) (1980) *Adult education for a change*, Hutchinson.

Thompson J (1983) *Learning liberation: Women's response to men's education*, Croom Helm.

Tisdell E J (1993) 'Interlocking systems of power, privilege and oppression in adult higher education classes', *Adult education quarterly*, Vol 3 No 4, pp 203–26.

Titmus C (1989) *Lifelong education for adults: an international handbook*, Pergamon Press.

Torbert W (1981) 'Why educational research has been so un-educational: The case for a new model of social science based on collaborative enquiry', in Reason P and Rowan J (eds), *Human inquiry, a sourcebook of new paradigm research*, Wiley.

Usher R (1993) 'From process to practice research, reflexivity and writing in adult education', *Studies in continuing education*, Vol 15 No 2, pp 98–117.

Usher R (1993) 'Experiential learning and learning from experience: Does it make a difference?', in Boud D, Cohen R and Walker D (eds), *Using experience for learning*, Society for Research into Higher Education and Open University Press.

Usher R and Bryant I (1989) *Adult education as theory, practice and research the captive triangle*, Routledge.

Valle R S and King M (1978) 'An introduction to existential-phenomenological thought in psychology', in Valle R S and King M (eds), *Existential-phenomenological alternatives for psychology*, Oxford University Press, pp 3–17.

Valle R S and Halling S (1989) 'An introduction to existential-phenomenological thought in psychology', in Valle R S, King M and Halling S (eds), *Existential-phenomenological alternatives for psychology*, Plenum Press, pp 3–16.

Vandenberg J H (1966) *The psychology of the sickbed*, Duquesne University Press.

van Doren M (1967) *Selected poems of Thomas Merton*, New Directions Books.

van Kaam A (1969) *Existential foundations for psychology*, Appleton-Century-Crofts.

van Manen M (1977) 'Linking ways of knowing with ways of being practical', *Curriculum enquiry*, Vol 6 No 3, pp 205–228.

van Manen M (1982) 'Phenomenological pedagogy', *Curriculum inquiry*, Vol 12 No 3, pp 283–99.

van Manen M (1984) '"Doing" phenomenological research and writing: An introduction', *Phenomenology and pedagogy*, Vol 2 No 1.

van Manen M (1990) *Researching lived experience: Human science for an action centred pedagogy*, The Althouse Press.

van Manen M (1991) 'Reflectivity and the pedagogical moment: The normativity of pedagogical thinking and acting', *Journal of curriculum studies*, Vol 21 No 6, pp 507–36.

van Manen M (1994) 'Pedagogy, virtue and narrative identity in teaching', *Curriculum inquiry*, Vol 24 No 2, pp 135–170.

van Manen M (1995a) 'Pedagogic politics? Political pedagogy?', in Miedema S, Biesta G, Boog B, Smaling A, Wardekker W and Levering B (eds), *The politics of human science*, VUBPRESS.

van Manen M (1995b) *Phenomenological research*, workshop notes, Monash University, East Gippsland Campus, 23–25 January.

Vandenberg D (1971) *Being and education*, Prentice Hall.

Vandenberg D (1987) 'Interpretive, normative theory of education', *Educational philosophy and theory*, Vol 19 No 1, pp 1–11.

Vella J (1994) *Learning to listen: Learning to teach*, Jossey Bass.

Warner-Weil S and McGill I (eds) (1989) *Making sense of experiential learning: Diversity in theory and practice*, The Society for Research into Higher Education/Open University Press.

Wertz F J (1985) 'Method and findings in a phenomenological psychological study of a complex life-event: Being criminally victimised', in Giorgi A (ed), *Phenomenology and psychological research*, Duquesne University Press, pp 155–216.

White M (1995) *Re-authoring lives: Interviews and essays*, Dulwich Centre Publications.

Willis G (1991) 'Phenomenological enquiry: Life world perceptions', in Short E C (ed), *Forms of curriculum enquiry*, State University of New York Press.

Willis G (1995) *Curriculum: Alternative approaches, ongoing issues*, Marsh J C and Willis G (eds), Novell.

Willis P (1980) 'Patrons and riders: Conflicting roles and hidden objectives in an Aboriginal development programme in Kununurra' (unpublished MA thesis ANU).

Willis P (1986) 'The flight of the pelican: Training Aboriginal adult educators in Australia', *Convergence*, Vol XIX No 1, pp 32–38.

Willis P (1987) *Riders in the chariot: Aboriginal conversion to Christianity in remote Australia*, Charles Strong Memorial Trust.

Willis P (1991a) 'Community education in Australia: Reflections on an expanding field of practice', *Australian journal for adult and community education*, Vol 31 No 2, July, pp 71–87.

Willis P (1991b) 'Education for Life Transition: Recollections of practice', *Studies in continuing education*, Vol 13 No 2, pp 101–14.

Willis P (1994) 'Researching practice in adult education for human development: Questions of method', in Neville B, Willis P and Edwards M (eds), *Qualitative research in adult education*, Centre for Research in Education and Work, University of South Australia.

Willlis P and Neville B (1996) *Qualitative research practice in adult education research*, David Lovell Publishing.

Willis P (1998) 'Enriching the learning community: Leadership and informal education at school', in Ehrich L C and Knight J (eds), *Leadership in crisis: Restructuring principled practice*, Central Queensland University Press.

Wirth J (1979) *John Dewey as educator*, Robert Krieger.

Wittgenstein L (1953) *Philosophical investigations*, Blackwell.

Wolcott H (1992) 'Posturing in qualitative research', in Le Compte M, Milroy W and Preissle J (eds), *The handbook of qualitative research in education*, Academic Press.

Wolff K H (1984) 'Surrender-and-catch and phenomenology', *Human Studies*, Vol 7 No 2, pp 191–210.

Wolff K H (1989) 'From nothing to sociology', *Philosophy of the social sciences*, Vol 19 No 3, pp 321–39.

Yeatman A (1991) 'Corporate managerialism: An overview', paper presented to Conference of the NSW Teachers Federation Conference, *The management of public education: A question of balance*, 8–9 March, Sydney.

Young M F D (ed) (1971) *Knowledge and control: New directions in the sociology of education*, Collier-Macmillan.

Zaner R M (1970) *The way of phenomenology: Criticism as a philosophical discipline*, Pegasus.

INDEX BY SUBJECT